International
Trade and
Economic Growth

International Trade and Economic Growth

Hendrik Van den Berg and Joshua J. Lewer

M.E.Sharpe
Armonk, New York
London, England

Copyright © 2007 by M.E. Sharpe, Inc.

Library of Congress Cataloging-in-Publication Data

Van den Berg, Hendrik, 1949–
    International trade and economic growth / Henrik Van den Berg, Joshua J. Lewer.
        p. cm.
    Includes bibliographical references and index.
ISBN-13: 978-0-7656-1802-3 (alk. paper)
ISBN-10: 0-7656-1802-8 (alk. paper)
    1. International trade. 2. Economic development. I. Lewer, Joshua J., 1972– II. Title.

HF1379.V363 2007   2006044369
338.9—dc22

Printed in the United States of America

The paper used in this publication meets the minimum requirements of
American National Standard for Information Sciences
Permanence of Paper for Printed Library Materials,
ANSI Z 39.48-1984.

∞

BM (c)   10   9   8   7   6   5   4   3   2   1

To our families:
Barbara, Paulo, Matthew, and Thomas Van den Berg
and
Melissa, Stephanie, and Jacob Lewer

Contents

List of Tables

List of Figures

Preface

The writing of this book on economic growth and international trade has been a most satisfying project. We certainly learned a lot, as is always the case when writing a book. We also received strong encouragement from colleagues and students. In fact, we were most encouraged by our students enthusiasm for our focus on economic growth and our extensions of trade theory beyond the traditional static models. We must admit, however, that more than one colleague characterized our quest to shift the focus of international trade theory toward a dynamic growth perspective as something akin to tilting at windmills. No doubt, the traditional static models of international trade are among the most firmly entrenched models in economics, but the publication of this book makes it clear that we have chosen to ignore those warnings. How dangerous can windmills be, after all? We leave it up to you, the reader, to judge how well we succeed in pushing the analysis of international trade beyond the conventional static models and toward the much more interesting and, potentially, more important realm of economic growth.

Be assured that we approach the relationship between international trade and economic growth objectively and pragmatically, not quixotically. Our motive is simple; we examine whether a growth-oriented analysis reveals the benefits of international trade more effectively than the traditional static arguments for free trade do. Static analysis of trade is logically sound, but it often fails to convince. Years of discussing international trade with policy makers, colleagues, students, businessmen, special interest groups, and the general public have convinced us that we can better support free trade policies by linking trade to economic growth, which is usually viewed much more favorably. While critics of free trade are seldom moved by stories about comparative advantage, they are more inclined to rethink their positions when challenged to explain how an economy can grow if it is closed to trade and, therefore, isolated from the world's knowledge and technology?

This book details the many intricate and complex interactions among economic growth, technology, competition, and international trade. Complexity often leads to ambiguous outcomes, and the chapters that follow show that there is still much work to be done. We do not yet fully understand how international trade and economic growth influence each other in all circumstances. Fortunately, many economists have already clarified many of links between international trade and economic growth. Many have carried out empirical tests of the hypothesized relationships. It is fair to say that the case for a growth oriented analysis of trade has already been well prepared. It is our hope that this survey of the "trade and growth" literature, augmented with some new insights and suggestions, helps to convince trade economists to focus more on economic growth. We also hope this book stimulates further research to tighten up the many lose ends that still remain in building a dynamic case for free trade. Most of all, we hope that you, the reader, will appreciate and enjoy our growth perspective on international trade.

Acknowledgments

There are many people to thank for the planning, content, and completion of this book. We are especially grateful to Les Oxley and Joy Mazumdar, who provided very substantial comments on Chapter 2. Craig R. MacPhee provided continued comments and insights. Among our many graduate students, Hans Czap, David Kaiser, Kanybek Nur-Teggin, Mariana Sáenz, and Marwan Touman contributed substantially to this book. Individually, each of us acknowledge the assistance and encouragement of many people.

Joshua Lewer:

First of all, I thank my parents, James and Joan Lewer, who instilled in me the values of education and hard work. At Augustana College, Brian Eggleston and Kenneth Bouge exponentially expanded my understanding of economics. The graduate faculty at the University of Nebraska-Lincoln transformed me into the economist that I am today. Key to my education there were Hendrik Van den Berg, Criag R. MacPhee, James R. Schmidt, Matthew J. Cushing, and Lilyan Fulginiti.

Hendrik Van den Berg:

As Joshua noted just above, a book of this nature reflects the influence of our teachers. At the State University of New York at Albany, Fred Dickey convinced me to major in economics, Helen Horowitz inspired me to become a teacher of economics, and Pong Lee introduced me to the highest levels of economic theory. At the University of Wisconsin–Madison, Gary Chamberlain, Arthur Goldberger, Tom Holmes, Nobu Kiyotaki, Charles Manski, Kenneth West, and Randall Wright greatly advanced my economic skills. This book most directly reflects the teaching and inspiration of my professors in international economics and development economics, Franklin Walker and Marvin Sternberg at Albany and Robert Baldwin, J. David Richardson, Rachel McCulloch, and Kenneth Rogoff at Wisconsin. Finally, this book owes much to my wife Barbara, who, aside from making my life so wonderful, provided the most comprehensive and critical editing throughout the project.

International
Trade and
Economic Growth

Introduction

*The specializations of the nineteenth century were not simply a device for using to the greatest effect the labours of a given number of human beings; they were above all an **engine of growth**.*
(D. H. Robertson)[1]

Contrary to the popular notion that economists cannot agree on anything, they really do agree that international trade improves human welfare. Beginning with Adam Smith's explanation of absolute advantage in the late 18th century and David Ricardo's comparative advantage shortly thereafter, economists have over the past two hundred years developed strong logical arguments to justify free trade policies. Early in the 20th century, Eli Heckscher and Bertil Ohlin developed the general equilibrium model that is still the centerpiece of trade theory. Economists routinely use the Heckscher-Ohlin model to show that free trade takes an economy to a higher level of real national income than can be attained when trade is restricted. Later in the 20th century, Paul Samuelson and others derived additional theoretical implications of the Heckscher-Ohlin model, such as the Rybczinski theorem that describes how international trade reacts to increases in factors such as capital and labor and the Stolper-Samuelson theorem that details how the gains from trade are distributed among the owners of the factors of production. A couple of decades ago, when the Heckscher-Ohlin model was criticized for assuming that markets operate under perfect competition, James Brander, Gene Grossman, Elhanan Helpman, Paul Krugman and others strengthened the arguments for free trade by showing that there are gains from trade even when production occurs in imperfectly competitive industries that exhibit increasing returns to scale.

---

[1] Robertson (1938), p. 5; bold print added by the authors.

There have been repeated attacks on the doctrine of free trade. In his elegant history of economists' thinking on international trade, Douglas Irwin (1996a) recounts the many challenges to free trade and how economists developed logical arguments to counter the challenges. Irwin describes economists' defense of free trade against protectionists as an intellectual victory:

> the free trade doctrine has been subjected to close and searching scrutiny, and has sometimes come under serious doubt. Yet the idea of free trade, the conceptual case for free trade, has survived largely intact against the tide of repeated critical inquiry. This examination has, of course, shed light on the strengths and weaknesses of the free trade doctrine, and has sometimes resulted in valid theoretical qualifications to the doctrine. The case for free trade has endured, however, because the fundamental proposition that substantial benefits arise from the free exchange of goods between countries has not been overshadowed by the limited scope of various qualifications and exceptions. Free trade thus remains as sound as any proposition in economic theory which purports to have implications for economic policy is ever likely to be.[2]

To the casual observer, Irwin's optimistic declaration of victory for economists in the free trade debate probably comes across as little more than wishful thinking. Outside the economics profession, free trade is not viewed nearly so favorably. In fact, surveys and policy decisions suggest that the general public and policy makers in most countries remain stubbornly suspicious of international trade.

The Fragility of Economists' Case for Free Trade

A survey by Blendon et al. (1997) confirmed that, indeed, an overwhelming majority of economists favored trade liberalization, but only about half of the general public in the United States agreed that further agreements to liberalize trade would be "good for the economy." Scheve and Slaughter (2001) reviewed opinion surveys from the past several decades, and these show that people have consistently been doubtful about the benefits of free trade. Especially notable is a 2000 survey reported in a *Wall Street Journal* article appropriately entitled "Trade Can't Get Any Respect, Even Amid Boom"; in a year when the U.S. economy reached record-low unemployment and record-high rates of economic growth, 48 percent of

---

[2] Irwin (1996a), p. 8.

U.S. residents still felt that trade had been "bad for the economy" and only 34 percent said it had been "good for the economy."[3]

The public's skepticism about the benefits of international trade is reflected in trade policies. The history of trade policies in the 20th century shows that policy makers have never hesitated to ignore economists' arguments for free trade when faced with conflicting political and economic issues. The period between the world wars reminds us how quickly policy makers will close their countries' borders to trade when domestic political pressures for protection rise. Even today, after fifty years of negotiations to reduce trade barriers, governments throughout the world still actively apply tariffs, quotas, "voluntary" export restraints, anti-dumping measures, safeguards against import surges, arbitrary health and safety regulations, artificially burdensome customs procedures, and many other barriers to trade. Political leaders repeatedly violate the terms of free trade agreements that they themselves promoted and signed. Recall U.S. President Bush's imposition of new tariffs on foreign steel and Canadian lumber in 2002 only months after he had, amid great pomp and ceremony, supported the resumption of the Doha round of multilateral trade negotiations and had campaigned for prompt action by all leaders in the Western Hemisphere nations to negotiate a *Free Trade Area of the Americas*. Clearly, economists have not yet won over the general public and the leaders who set and carry out their countries' trade policies. It is therefore a bit premature to speak of an intellectual victory.

Much of the resistance to free trade no doubt comes from special interests who actually gain from protectionism, and they will never be convinced of free trade's welfare gains. Nevertheless, special interests often get away with using faulty economic arguments to justify their requests for protection. They can succeed because the public is not much interested in learning about the economics of international trade.[4] To economists, the solution to this perversion of trade theory is obvious: the public needs to learn more economics. But, what would it take to get people and policy makers to listen more attentively to economists arguments for free trade?

---

[3] Gerald F. Seib (2000), "Trade Can't Get Any Respect, Even Amid Boom," *The Wall Street Journal*, May 10.

[4] Blinder and Krueger (2004) discuss the public's poor understanding of economics.

Part of the blame for the practical failures of economists' case for free trade may lie with economists themselves. Economists have not made their case as convincing and compelling as they could. Economists have done the equivalent of tying one hand behind their back in their intellectual battle with protectionists by framing most of their arguments in the very restrictive theoretical structure called comparative statics. Static models of trade, such as the popular Heckscher-Ohlin model, take the economy's resources and technology as given and then illustrate how total output or welfare increase as an economy shifts from restricted trade to free trade. Such static analysis concludes that, *all other things equal*, an open economy provides its citizens with a higher level of welfare than does an economy that restricts its citizens' ability to exchange goods and services with the rest of the world. This argument is logically sound, but the comparative static models explain only a small portion of trade's long-run effects on human welfare. Frankly, the short-run gains from trade described by the traditional static models have been estimated to be rather small. Furthermore, the static models also show that the expansion of international trade changes the distribution of real income and welfare within an economy. The *net* welfare gains from trade are positive, but not every sector and household gains from international trade in the all-other-things-equal world of static analysis. In short, a possible reason for still incomplete intellectual victory of free trade may be due to economists' use of static models that show positive but small net gains from free trade that are unevenly distributed across populations in such a way that some people will suffer real declines in welfare. That economists' arguments for free trade often fall on deaf ears should not be surprising.

Economists' case for free trade is not as hopeless as suggested here, however. Static analysis does not explain the full welfare effects of international trade. Unlike what static analysis always assumes, all other things never remain the same in real economies. There is no such thing as an isolated one-time change in a real economy. Any change in economic activity inevitably triggers many further changes. Static models of trade, therefore, ignore the long-term dynamic effects of international trade on economic growth. Recall D. H. Robertson's quote at the start of this chapter describing 19th century globalization: "The specializations of the nineteenth century were not simply a device for using to the greatest effect the labours of a given number of human beings; they were above all an engine of growth."[5] There is, in fact, mounting statistical evidence that international trade contributes significantly to economic growth. Economic

---

[5] D. H. Robertson (1938), p. 5.

growth has large long-run welfare effects because it is a very powerful *compound process*. Small differences in countries' rates of economic growth translate into very large differences in standards of living within just a generation or two. For example, the very large difference in living standards between the United States and Mexico is the result of the U.S. per capita real GDP growing just one percentage point per year faster than Mexico over the past two centuries. In this light, the recent evidence suggesting that economies with few trade restrictions grow on average one or two percentage points faster than economies that severely restrict foreign trade suggests that traditional static models of international trade are missing much of the real action.

A Dynamic Case for Free Trade?

Economists can make a much more accurate, and potentially much stronger, case for free trade if they are willing to venture beyond the safety and convenience of their familiar *static* models into the *dynamic* realm of economic growth. By dynamic we mean the economic analysis that looks at changes over time. Dynamic models contain variables dated in more than one time period. Dynamic analysis is difficult, however, and dynamic models are inevitably more complicated than the "all other things equal" comparative static models. Economists have been studying economic growth off and on since the time of Adam Smith. But only recently has a consensus developed about how to model the process of economic growth. And, as difficult as it is to accurately model economic growth, it is even more difficult to distinguish international trade's role in that complex process of economic growth and change. Therefore, venturing beyond the traditional static realm of traditional trade theory is not an easy task for international economists. As a result, the statistical evidence of a positive correlation between economic growth and international trade does not yet have a consistent, proven, and well-understood theoretical framework to accompany it. The dynamic growth case for free trade is not yet as elegantly developed as the static case for free trade. In the meantime, economists continue to frame their arguments in terms of their familiar and simpler static models of international trade when called on to analyze the economic effects of international trade on human welfare.

The dynamic analysis of international trade requires that economists combine the fields of international trade and economic growth. Even though the past two centuries stand out in human history for their unprecedented rates of economic growth and technological progress, economists have not always devoted much attention to analyzing economic development. As a result, the field of economic growth and development is today still not nearly as familiar to economists and students of economics as the traditional fields of microeconomics, macroeconomics, monetary theory, public finance, labor economics, and static international economics, for example. Fortunately, there has been a flurry of research in recent decades, and a solid body of growth theory is now available. Therefore, the time is ripe for the development of a set of practical and accurate dynamic models of international trade. The power of compounding adds a touch of urgency to the development of a dynamic theory of international trade. If trade indeed stimulates economic growth, then the continued wavering on trade policy by current world leaders may be much more damaging to human welfare than traditional static models imply. Just as trade's growth effects potentially compound into very large long-run welfare gains, the postponement of those long-run welfare effects compounds into very large potential welfare losses.

The purpose of this book is to stimulate the development of a more understandable and practical set of models with which to analyze the long-run growth effects of international trade. While much work has already been done and is available for us to draw on, this book distinguishes many areas where further research will be needed to gain a useful understanding of how international trade affects long-run human welfare. Fortunately for the reader, the dynamic analysis of international trade leads through some of the most exciting fields of economics, including economic growth, technological progress, entrepreneurship, and political economy.

Outline of the Book

This book will take you places that traditional trade theory does not reach. Instead of production possibilities frontiers and indifference curves in static models of output and welfare, international trade will be analyzed in terms of the Solow growth model and the process of creative destruction. In place of supply and demand curves that reflect given levels of technology and factor endowments, we will analyze how trade influences technological progress and the growth of physical and human capital stocks.

The first chapter begins your new journey with a review of the traditional static models of international trade and the estimates of the gains from trade derived from these static models. The chapter also illustrates the power of compounding and shows how much larger the gains from trade would be in the long run if trade raises the rate of economic growth. Chapter 2 surveys the vast empirical literature on the relationship between international trade and economic growth. The evidence is fairly consistent and supportive of a positive, and economically very meaningful, trade-growth nexus. The statistical results from the many studies are even consistent enough to venture an estimate of the long-run growth effects of international trade. However, there are some inevitable weaknesses in the econometric methodology that leaves us with some doubts about trade's true influence on economic growth. Chapter 3 details early growth models by Adam Smith and the classical economists in the late 18th and early 19th centuries, then jumps into the 20th century with the Harrod-Domar growth model, and concludes with a detailed development of the Solow growth model. This latter model is the centerpiece of current growth theory. Chapter 4 begins the discussion of the more recent growth models that explicitly seek to explain technological progress, Chapter 5 highlights the recent models of technological progress based on the ideas of Joseph Schumpeter, and Chapter 6 incorporates international trade into Schumpeter's creative destruction model. These latter three chapters effectively present where we currently stand in terms of our understanding of how international trade influences economic growth.

There are some complications with the dynamic analysis developed through Chapter 6, and there are several extensions worth emphasizing. Chapter 7 examines the so-called sectoral models of growth, which explicitly look at how international trade affects overall economic growth when its effects are not the same across all sectors of an economy. Sectoral models permit a wide variety of outcomes, and this greatly complicates our quest for a clear theoretical framework that can explain the statistical results summarized in Chapter 2. Conclusions about how international trade influences a country's rate of economic growth are shown to be dependent on how knowledge and technology move between countries, industries, and economic sectors. Chapter 8, therefore, focuses on international technology transfers. The research on technology transfers is still in its infancy, in large part because it is so difficult to measure knowledge and technology. There is enough evidence to venture some preliminary conclusions, however, and international trade does appear to play a significant role in facilitating the spread of knowledge. Chapter 9 concludes with a realistic evaluation of the importance of international trade for economic growth and the potential for developing a more compelling dynamic case for free trade.

The dynamic analysis of international trade is not yet as well established as the static theories of comparative advantage and increasing returns. Nevertheless, this book will show how economists are gradually piecing together a dynamic case for free trade that is potentially much more powerful and accurate than the traditional static case. Recent empirical results suggest that the long-run gains in human welfare from trade's positive influence on countries' rates of growth are much larger than the estimated static gain from trade. But, since few people are convinced by statistics, economists must learn to communicate the complex concepts and ideas about economic growth and the dynamic effects of trade to the general public and policy makers. Their success will depend on how well they can translate these concepts and well-supported hypotheses into intuitive and understandable models. This book is an attempt, first of all, to convince our fellow economists that we can use growth theory and existing analysis to build a stronger and more realistic case for international trade. Hopefully, by taking stock of what we know and suggesting many directions for further research, this book will also contribute to the continued development of a coherent set of ideas and models with which to better convince a skeptical public and their political leaders of the substantial long-run benefits of free trade and the large long-term losses from continued protectionism.

Chapter One

The Welfare Gains from Trade

The proposition that freedom of trade is on the whole economically more beneficial than protection is one of the most fundamental propositions economic theory has to offer for the guidance of economic policy.
(Harry Johnson)[6]

Economists have made their case for free trade in two ways. First, they have developed logical models to prove international trade increases human welfare. These models have also provided useful insights into why international trade increases human welfare. Second, economists have used their models to estimate the welfare gains from reducing or eliminating barriers to trade. Since theoretical models are not easy to summarize into a short sound bite, the news media have often presented economists' numerical estimates of the gains from trade as economists' main contribution to the debate about trade. Economists themselves often use estimates of the gains from trade to support their more abstract arguments for free trade.

When it comes to the estimates of the gains from trade, economists are actually quite vulnerable. For one thing, in going from the basic logic of comparative advantage to specific estimates of the gains from free trade, economists are forced to make specific assumptions about the shapes of the curves, the elasticities of demand and supply, and the distribution of the gains and losses across economic sectors. Different economists make different assumptions and thus come up with different estimates. The differences between the estimates often undermine the credibility of economists. More damaging to their case for free trade, however, is the fact that economists' estimates of the gains from trade are usually very small.

---

[6] Johnson (1971), p. 187.

Objective observers cannot help but ask whether the inevitable controversy surrounding shifts in trade policy are worth all the fuss.

This chapter examines how economists have estimated the gains from trade. Since most of the popular estimates of the gains from trade have been based on the strict logic of the equally popular static models of international trade, the chapter begins by reviewing these models and how estimates are derived from them. A careful examination of the estimates makes it clear that many potential gains from trade have been missed by the most popular estimates of the gains from trade. It becomes obvious that the estimated gains from trade have been small because the models used to guide the estimates do not capture all of the gains from trade. The next section begins our reexamination of economists' models of international trade and how those models are used to estimate the welfare effects of international trade.

1.1 Static Models and the Gains from Trade

The welfare effects of international trade have usually been analyzed using either static *general equilibrium* models of trade or static *partial equilibrium* models. General equilibrium models capture the effects of an economic event, such as a change in international trade, throughout the entire economy. Partial equilibrium models, on the other hand, show the welfare effects of a shift in international trade in just one market or sector of the economy. By applying the familiar "all other things equal" assumption, partial equilibrium models effectively ignore the effects of trade elsewhere in the economy as well as the feedback from those economy-wide effects on the particular market or sector the partial equilibrium model focuses on. In principle, general equilibrium models of trade are preferable because they more accurately capture all the effects of international trade throughout the economy. Economists fundamentally think in general equilibrium terms, recognizing that an economy is effectively a large system of simultaneous relationships. "Everything depends on everything else," economists are noted for saying. Recently, the growing power of computers has permitted economists to apply elaborate mathematical models that capture the full general equilibrium effects of trade, but these are still somewhat experimental. Economists continue to use partial equilibrium models of trade to estimate the effects of trade, however, because they offer a simple and practical method for calculating the welfare gains and losses from international trade.

1.1.1 The General Equilibrium Gains from Trade

The most popular general equilibrium model of international trade is the Heckscher-Ohlin, or *neoclassical*, model of trade. The simplest version of this model assumes a "small" economy producing two products. For illustrative purposes, suppose the two products are Ricardo's well-known wine and cloth.[7] The model consists of a concave production-possibilities frontier (PPF) and a set of convex indifference curves, as in Figure 1-1. That is, production of wine and cloth are subject to increasing marginal opportunity costs, and consumer behavior reflects diminishing marginal utility. In the absence of international trade, the highest level of national welfare that a "closed" economy can achieve is represented by the indifference curve I_2, which is tangent to the PPF at the production/consumption point A. Under the assumption of perfect competition, the slope of the line p, which is equal to the slope of the PPF and the indifference curve I_2

at the tangency point A, reflects the relative prices, the relative marginal utilities, and the relative marginal opportunity costs of wine and cloth. An implication of this model is that a closed economy must produce everything it consumes, and the standard of living enjoyed by the people living in a closed economy is determined exclusively by the resources and the technology available within the border. The economy can allocate inefficiently by producing at point B, but it

Figure 1-1
Equilibrium in the Closed Economy

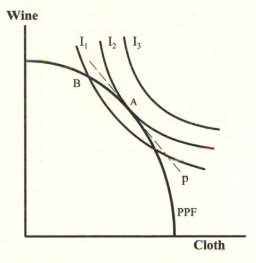

---

[7] The "H-O" model is presented in most international economics textbooks, such as Dennis R. Appleyard and Alfred J. Field, Jr. (2001), *International Economics*, 4th ed., New York: McGraw-Hill; Beth V. Yarbrough and Robert M. Yarbrough (2000), *The World Economy*, 5th ed., Fort Worth, TX: Harcourt; Hendrik Van den Berg (2004), *International Economics*, New York: McGraw-Hill; or Jagdish N. Bhagwati, Arvind Panagariya, and T.N. Srinivasan (1998), *Lectures on International Trade*, Cambridge, MA: MIT Press.

can do no better than the point A on I_2. Consumption points on I_3 are beyond the economy's reach.

International trade brings points outside the PPF within reach. Suppose the relative prices of cloth and wine in the rest of the world are not the same as in the self-sufficient small economy shown in Figure 1-1. Specifically, suppose that in the rest of the world the relative price of cloth is lower relative to the price of wine in the small economy, so that the international price line p* is less steep than the small economy's price line p. This case is illustrated in Figure 1-2. The different relative prices of cloth and wine imply different opportunity costs of production at home and abroad. These differences in opportunity costs determine a country's comparative advantage and its trade pattern.

The economy exploits its comparative advantage by shifting productive factors from the production of cloth and into the production of wine. Wine's opportunity cost is relatively higher in the rest of the world while cloth's opportunity cost is lower abroad. By specializing and shifting production to the combination of wine and cloth at point B in Figure 1-2, the economy's real income rises. In this case, consumers maximize their welfare by allocating their real income to the combination of wine and cloth represented by C on the higher indifference curve I_3. International

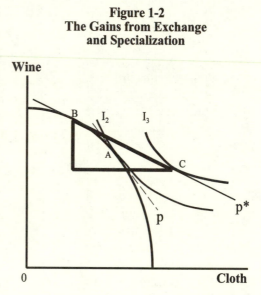

Figure 1-2
The Gains from Exchange
and Specialization

trade can be represented by the bold *trade triangle* that has as its corners the production point B and the consumption point C. The welfare gain from trade is represented by the shift in consumption from a point on I_2 to a point on I_3. The gains from trade illustrated in Figure 1-2 are difficult to quantify, however. It is well known that the logic behind indifference curves warns us of the dangers in going beyond the qualitative conclusion that the combination of wine and cloth at C provides more total welfare than the combination at A.

It is possible to quantify the gains from trade from a general equilibrium perspective by following the logic of the simple small country Heckscher-Ohlin model above. Computer simulations have been used to find the equilibrium values for production and consumption in large multi-industry mathematical versions of the simple two-product model above. These mathematical models require many specific assumptions about the production functions in the various sectors included, however. Also, a specific welfare function must be assumed in order to precisely determine the welfare gains from a change in relative product prices caused by a change in international trade. That is, specific utility levels must be assigned to the mathematical equivalent of the indifference curves in Figure 1-2, which is something the basic logic of indifference curves does not justify. Because of the many assumptions that must be made in building mathematical general equilibrium models, the accuracy of their welfare estimates are inevitably subject to challenge. It remains an open question whether the conceptual advantage of the general equilibrium approach over the partial equilibrium approach overcomes the practical difficulties of applying the general equilibrium approach for estimating the welfare gains from trade. As the next section shows, the partial equilibrium method has some distinct practical advantages.

1.1.2 The Partial Equilibrium Gains from Trade

Partial equilibrium models of trade provide a simpler method for estimating the gains from trade, and that is the method economists have most often used in published studies. Partial equilibrium models focus on one market at a time, effectively assuming that nothing changes elsewhere in the economy even as curves, prices, and quantities change in the sector of the economy illustrated in the model.

A standard two-country, two-product partial equilibrium model of trade is presented in Figure 1-3. Specifically, this model illustrates the effects of a tariff on the markets for cloth in Homeland and Abroad. The center diagram in Figure 1-3 summarizes the effects of a tariff or equivalent quota that restricts imports to the quantity 0e and raises the Homeland price from its free-trade level p_W to its tariff-induced level p_T. The tariff lowers the price in Abroad to p_A.

Students of international economics know that in the case of a tariff the Homeland economy loses the *deadweight loss* areas B+D. These areas are also known as the "Harberger triangles" in honor of Arnold Harberger who first used them to measure the welfare effects of economic policies.

The areas A and C in Figure 1-3 are transfers from consumers to producers and from consumers to the government, respectively. A large country will gain part of its tariff revenue at the expense of foreign producers; Abroad's producers in effect transfer the area C to the Homeland government when prices decline in response to the reduction in international demand caused by Homeland's tariff. In the case of a quota, the areas C and c represent quota rent. This rent can accrue to either Homeland importers or Abroad's suppliers. If the quota is a voluntary export restriction that is enforced by the foreign government, the rent will accrue to Abroad's exporters, and Homeland's losses are the sum B+C+D. If the elasticities of the demand and supply curves can be estimated, it is possible to calculate the sizes of the triangles and rectangles. If enough markets are included in the study, the total net welfare gains from international trade can be estimated.

Figure 1-3: The Cost of Protection

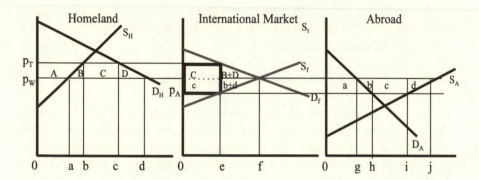

1.2 Estimates of the Static Gains from Trade

Many studies have estimated the gains from trade by following the logic of the static general equilibrium and partial equilibrium models of trade. The studies have used available estimates of the elasticities of industry supply and demand and calculated the various rectangles and triangles that make up the transfers, gains, and losses in welfare as detailed in the previous section. The surprising thing about these estimates is that they uncover only small gains from trade, even in the case of major shifts in trade policy. Some of the most often cited examples are presented below.

1.2.1 Measuring the Harberger Triangles

One of the earliest studies that measured the gains from international trade was by Basevi (1966). He set the tone for later studies when he estimated that trade restrictions cost the United States one-tenth of one percent of the value of U.S. GDP. Many subsequent estimates of the cost of trade restrictions to the United States have seldom been much larger. Feenstra (1992) surveyed the pre-1990s studies that estimated the costs of protection for the U.S. economy using the logic of the partial equilibrium model of trade illustrated in Figure 1-3. Feenstra concluded that, based on the available estimates on the various geometric areas from the "Homeland" side of Figure 1-3 for a great number of different U.S. industries, the total losses to the United States of its protection across all industries was about $30 billion at 1986 prices, or about three quarters of one percent of GDP. Of course, U.S. protectionism also caused deadweight losses to other countries, such as the deadweight triangles b+d. Foreign countries also lost tariff revenue or quota rent to U.S. customs agents or importers equal to the area c in Figure 1-3. Feenstra concluded that these foreign losses were about equal to the United States' losses, which implied that the total cost of U.S. trade restrictions to the world were about $60 billion. This is by no means a small number, but it is a very small percentage of total world income.

Some of the most quoted studies of the costs of protection are those sponsored by the Institute of International Economics, including Hufbauer and Elliott's (1994) estimates of the costs of U.S. trade protection, Sazanami, Urata, and Kawai's (1995) study of Japanese protection, Zhang, Zhang, and Wan's (1998) study of China, and Messerlin's study of European protection (2001). After estimating consumer surplus, quota rent, tariff revenue, producer surplus, and the remaining deadweight losses, Hufbauer and Elliott found that for 21 of the most protected sectors of the U.S. economy, trade restrictions caused a net welfare loss to the U.S. of about $10 billion. They then assumed that these 21 sectors caused about half of the total loss of welfare from trade restrictions, and they concluded that the total net welfare costs from protection in the United States were $20 billion, or about 0.5 percent of 1990 U.S. GDP. Total consumer surplus loss was estimated at $70 billion, 1.3 percent of U.S. GDP, which suggests that protection had a much greater effect on the distribution of welfare than it had on total welfare. Sazanami, Urata, and Kawai found higher consumer and producer surplus effects from protectionism in Japan, although *net* losses were still estimated to be well under 1 percent of Japan's total GDP. In China, the losses to consumers were estimated to exceed 10 percent of

GDP because China's import barriers were so much higher, but the *net* welfare losses after accounting for producer surplus, quota rents, and tariff revenue were not much more than one percent of Chinese GDP. Messerlin estimated that European protectionism caused consumer surplus losses in excess of 1 percent of GDP, but after accounting for producer surplus and tariff revenues, the *net* costs of protection were only about 0.5 percent of European GDP.

Wall (2000) offered an interesting extension of Hufbauer and Elliott's results. Wall used a *gravity model* of international trade to estimate what total U.S. exports and imports would be in the absence of protectionist measures.[8] The gravity model effectively explains the volume of trade between pairs of countries as a positive function of the size of the two economies and a negative function of the distance between them. The model is popular for empirical research because it explains a very large portion of actual trade flows observed in the world. Wall uses Hufbauer and Elliott's findings that for every $1 decrease in imports due to import protection, there is a $2 loss in consumer surplus, a $0.49 gain in producer surplus, and an $0.11 deadweight loss to estimate the total gains from increasing U.S. trade from its actual level to the hypothetical level of free trade predicted by the gravity model of trade. He calculates that the net welfare loss from protectionism in the United States in 1996 was nearly $100 billion, or 1.45 percent of U.S. GDP.

The gains from international trade suggested by the static models of trade, in the range of 0.5 to 2 percent of GDP, add up to hundreds of billions of dollars per year throughout the world. Extended indefinitely into the future, a 1 percent increase in GDP has a present value equal to 20 percent of GDP assuming a discount rate of 5 percent.[9] This is clearly a very large number. But, given the opposition of vested interests and many other people's fears that the opening of the economy to free trade will cause them difficulties, a 1 percent increase in the annual value of world

---

[8] The gravity model of trade was pioneered by Tinbergen (1962), Linneman (1966), and Anderson (1979); recent applications include McCallum (1995), Deardorff (1998), and Feenstra, Markusen, and Rose (2001).

[9] The 5 percent discount rate is purely hypothetical; according to Frederick, Lowenstein, and O'Donoghue (2002), economists do not have a very clear idea about what the correct discount rate should be for this specific case. The very-long-run discount rate is likely to be smaller than 5 percent, perhaps close to zero, which would make the present value of a 1 percent of GDP gain extended indefinitely into the future even greater.

output does not translate into an overwhelming case for free trade. Economic growth routinely adds more than 1 percent to most economies every year. Clearly, the estimated gains from trade are not as large as most people would expect given economists' enthusiastic and persistent support of free trade.

1.2.2 Beyond the Harberger Triangles

An article in *The Economist* once referred to researchers' tendency to limit quantitative estimates of the losses from protectionism to the Harberger triangles in Figure 1-3 as the "tyranny of triangles."[10] Realistically, the Harberger triangles from the static models of trade must be seen as lower bounds for the costs of protectionism because there are many other consequences of protection not captured by the partial equilibrium model of trade.

For one thing, international trade mostly involves manufactured goods, which are often produced in industries characterized by increasing returns to scale. This implies that much of the world's production occurs in an economic environment that is less than perfectly competitive. Perfect competition is not sustainable when costs decline with firm size; a small number of large firms will tend to dominate the economy, and these firms will enjoy some degree of market power. Under imperfect competition, international trade generates some welfare effects not captured in the partial equilibrium model shown in Figure 1-3. For example, Krugman (1979) reminds us that increasing returns to scale tend to reduce product variety. If consumers prefer *more* variety to less variety, then the presence of increasing returns to scale in production creates a trade-off between lower unit costs and more variety. Should the economy's resources be concentrated in a small number of large industries that produce large volumes of a few products very inexpensively or spread among a larger variety of smaller-scale, higher-cost industries? Krugman shows that international trade enhances welfare because it gives an economy whose firms operate under increasing returns to scale a much more favorable set of trade-offs between unit costs and product variety. When an economy is open to trade, some of its firms can expand and produce for the global economy rather than only the domestic economy. They can, therefore, greatly reduce their unit costs. However, increased export production by some firms necessarily reduces the number of domestic producers. Consumers do not suffer a loss of variety, however, in an open economy;

---

[10] *The Economist* (1994), "The Tyranny of Triangles," July 16.

to the contrary, international trade permits consumers to purchase products from an increased number of producers in the rest of the world, each of whom are global exporters and thus have lower unit costs than the domestic firms that they replace. Consumers thus gain both lower prices and increased variety, which constitutes an unambiguous improvement in welfare.

Supporting Krugman's (1979) analysis, Broda and Weinstein (2004) estimated that in the U.S., the increase in variety from imports has been worth about 2.8 percent of GDP. Harris (1984) estimated that international trade's estimated welfare effect is about four times as great when industries are not perfectly competitive than when they are assumed to be competitive. Harris attributes his larger estimate to the fact that when closed markets are characterized by monopolistic firms, international trade increases competition in addition to exploiting comparative advantage. Also of interest is Whalley and Hamilton's (1996) survey of a set of studies that estimated the likely benefits of reducing trade barriers after the Uruguay Round. They found that the various studies surveyed estimated that the planned trade liberalization would raise welfare between .5 and 2 percent of world gross product. Of these gains, however, the static gains associated with the Harberger triangles account for much less than 1 percent of world GDP. One of the studies reviewed estimated that only .35 percent of the estimated gain of 1.3 percent of GDP came from the recovery of deadweight losses; the greatest part of the estimated gains were predicted to come from the future exploitation of increasing returns.

The gains from variety are exclusively related to increasing returns to scale. Romer (1994a) criticized the standard partial equilibrium model of trade by pointing out that the model only captures the gains from liberalizing trade in existing markets. Free trade in fact expands the range of products available to consumers, and hence estimates of the gains from free trade must also include the consumer surplus areas for all of the goods that are not available with current levels of protectionism but would become available with free trade. Feenstra (1994) reached the same conclusion when he argued that international prices are biased when free trade makes available new and better products. Hence, that the areas in Figure 1-3 determined by pre-trade data on prices and quantities are likely to underestimate the potential gains from free trade.

Another possible source of additional gains from free trade was suggested by Leibenstein (1966):

for a variety of reasons people and organizations normally work neither as hard nor as effectively as they could. In situations where competitive pressure is light, many people will trade the disutility of greater effort, of search, and the control of other peoples' activities for the utility of feeling less pressure and of better interpersonal relations. But in situations where competitive pressures are high, and hence the costs of such trades are also high, they will exchange less of the disutility of effort for the utility of freedom from pressures, etc.[11]

According to Leibenstein, the "x" in the production function $x = f(y, z)$ is a variable even when the inputs y and z are fixed because effort and efficiency varies according to competitive market conditions. This idea that the level of competition determines an economy's level of efficiency suggests that international trade, by increasing competition, will raise a country's managerial and productive effort and, hence, its output, all other things equal. Bergsman (1974) provides some estimates of potential improvements in efficiency due to international trade's competitive effect on x-efficiency in a number of protectionist developing economies. Bergsman's method cannot distinguish between x-inefficiency and monopoly profits, so he only reports the potential combined costs of the two sources of welfare loss. For example, he estimated that the combined losses due to x-inefficiency and monopoly deadweight losses were 6.8 percent of GDP in Brazil, 2.2 percent of GDP in Mexico, and 5.4 percent of GDP in Pakistan, among others. These percentages point to potentially much larger gains from trade liberalization than suggested by the traditional Harberger triangles.

The traditional models of trade also ignore the costs of *rent-seeking* behavior by special interests seeking to influence trade policy. In a well-known paper, Krueger (1974) estimated that in the protectionist economies of India and Turkey during the early 1970s, rent-seeking activity to influence the awarding of import permits may have cost as much as 14 percent of GDP.[12] Schap (1985) has pointed out, however, that care must be taken to avoid double counting of protectionism's effects on rent seeking, x-efficiency, and monopoly profits. These three categories of potential welfare costs are represented by overlapping areas in the typical supply and demand diagram.

---

[11] Leibenstein (1966), p. 393.

[12] Tullock (1967, 1993) first used the term "rent-seeking activity."

1.2.3 The Gains from Trade and Economic Growth

Bernhofen and Brown (2005) argue that estimates of the gains from comparative advantage have been hampered by the fact that the cases analyzed usually involved modest trade liberalizations, not the shifts from complete autarky to complete free trade hypothesized by static models of trade such as in Figures 1-1 and 1-2. Bernhofen and Brown therefore focus on Japan's shift from near-complete autarky to open international trade after 1853: "Since the Japanese economy fits the assumptions of the neoclassical trade model and its trading pattern is in accord with the theory of comparative advantage, we are able to estimate the gains from trade resulting from comparative advantage."[13] They estimated that the static gains from comparative advantage after Japan opened its economy were on the order to 8 to 9 percent of GDP. They also warn that their study:

> suggests caution in justifying free trade on the grounds of welfare gains based on static comparative advantage. Since the dynamic aspects of international trade probably have a much larger impact on national income, future empirical research on the nature and magnitude of these dynamic gains is indispensable.[14]

Huber (1971) used data on real wage rates available for several professions to estimate increases in real welfare in Japan as a result of the shift from complete self-sufficiency before 1854 to open trade in the 1870s. He found that between 1858 and 1870, real wages rose by 65 percent, which he suggests as the upper bound of the real gains from trade for Japan. Unlike Bernhofen and Brown's estimates, Huber's less precise estimates captured the gains from economic growth as well as the static gains from comparative advantage. An increase of welfare of anything close to 65 percent in just two decades is quite large indeed.

The need to estimate the dynamic gains from international trade is especially urgent given economists' arguments that free trade is one of the policies that developing countries should embrace in order to close the income gap between rich and poor countries. Figure 1-4 shows clearly that even a static gain of 8 or 9 percent of GDP, as Bernhofen and Brown found for Japan's exceptional shift in trade policy in the mid-1800s, cannot contribute much to closing the 1,000 or 2,000 percent differences in per

---

[13] Bernhofen and Brown (2005), p. 222.

[14] Ibid.

capita incomes between developed and less developed economies. For most people living in the less developed economies of Africa, Latin America, and Asia, the issue is not about moving from I_1 to I_2 in the low-income economy in the bottom left corner of Figure 1-4. Rather, what is needed are the welfare gains associated with moving from I_1 to I_{20} in Figure 1-4. That requires the outward shift of the PPF, not the one-time gain from trade of at most a few percent of GDP at the bottom left corner of Figure 1-4. Such an outward shift of the PPF requires many years of economic growth.

Figure 1-4
Comparing the Gains from Trade and Economic Growth

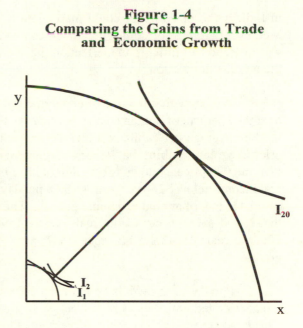

1.3 Economic Growth and International Trade

The relationship between international trade and economic growth is complicated by the fact that specialization and exchange have occurred for much of human history, albeit on a small scale, but economic growth is a very recent phenomenon. Hence, trade's hypothesized positive influence on economic growth must also be a recent phenomenon. When we appropriately define economic growth as an improvement in individual welfare, that is, an increase in average per capita real income, it is clear that the rapid rates of economic growth that many countries routinely experience today did not occur before 1800. For most of human history, people lived relatively short lives as hunters and gatherers at a subsistence level of output. Subsistence is the term economists use to describe the level of income that provides just enough consumption to maintain the species and, perhaps, permit some very slow growth in numbers. For nearly all of human history, changes in standards of living, if they occurred at all, were so slow that they were imperceptible to most people. People expected to die in the same conditions that they were born into. A few lucky people were able to move up in the ranks of society; a Roman slave could gain freedom, in India a son or daughter could marry into a higher caste family, or in Medieval Europe a son could enter the priesthood. But such social mobility was rare and had little, if any, effect on the average level of well-being of the world's population.

We know that the rate of economic growth was virtually zero for over 99.9 percent of human history because we have reliable estimates that in 1800 average per capita real income was not more than $600 in 1990 prices. We can combine that figure with the observation by Pritchett (1997) that, in 1990 prices, human life could not have been sustained at a level of real income below $250 per year, or $.68 per day, per person to arrive at an estimated rate of annual economic growth. The compound rate of growth that raised average per capita real income from $250 to $600 over the 200,000 years of human existence is effectively zero, or 0.0000001 to be precise.

Population growth is a somewhat earlier phenomenon, although it too accelerated noticeably only recently. In the year 10,000 B.C. humans had already existed for well over 95 percent of their total existence on earth in their present form, but the human population was probably still less than five million.[15] Population growth accelerated with the transition from hunting and gathering to farming, a shift in technology that occurred throughout the world between 10,000 and 2000 B.C. However, even at the height of the Roman Empire, just 2,000 years ago, there were still less than 200 million people on earth, nearly all living at or near subsistence levels.

1.3.1 The History of Economic Growth

It was not until the 19th century that rapid economic growth began to increase the welfare of entire populations at a rate fast enough for most people to be aware of their improving conditions. Since 1800, economic growth has raised per capita incomes many times over to unprecedented levels in nearly all countries of the world. Table 1-1 presents Angus Maddison's (1995, 2001, 2003) estimates of real per capita world income, and Figure 1-5 graphically depicts the extraordinary acceleration of economic growth over the past 200 years. In most countries, we have come to expect that we will die in a more prosperous world than the one we arrived in as babies, and we expect that our children and grandchildren will enjoy even higher standards of living.

---

[15] Kremer (1993).

Figure 1-5
World Economic Growth: 0-2000

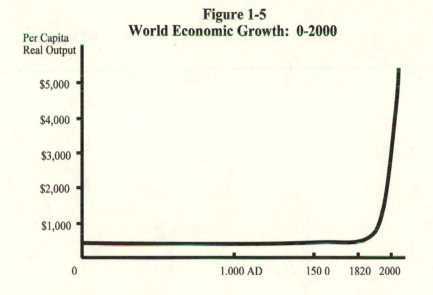

To compile his estimates of past standards of living and rates of economic growth, Maddison used a great variety of sources of information on output, consumption, prices, population, international trade, government tax revenues, etc., many from official government publications, others from independent studies.[16]   The well-known Penn Tables often used by macroeconomists researching the post World War II period closely resemble Maddison's methodology and data. The advantage of Maddison's data series is that they extend back for centuries. We must certainly assume a sizeable margin of error when we use Maddison's estimates of economic growth for the pre World War II period, but the increase in per capita output over the past two-hundred years is so enormous that there is little doubt about the general trend in world economic growth. We are indeed very lucky to be living in this very unique time.

Table 1-1 shows that population growth began to slow during the period 1973-2001 after a gradual but persistent acceleration of population growth up to 1973. The growth of real per capita GDP also slowed after the unprecedented growth during the period 1950-1973. It has been a challenge for economists to explain the stunning changes in growth rates over time. What caused the sudden surge in growth after 1800? And, what caused the variations in growth across countries and during the 20th century? Fortunately, the field of economic growth and development provides many insights to help us answer these questions.

---

[16] See Maddison (1995) for a detailed description of his methodology.

Table 1-1
Real per Capita Gross Domestic Product: 0 - 2001

Year	World Population (millions)	World GDP (billions $1990)	Per Capita GDP ($1990)
Annual Levels:			
0	231	103	444
1000	268	117	435
1500	438	247	565
1820	1,041	694	667
1870	1,270	1,101	867
1913	1,791	2,705	1,510
1950	2,524	5,336	2,114
1973	3,913	16,059	4,104
2001	6,149	37,194	6,049
Annual Compound Growth Rates (% per year):			
0 - 1000	0.02	0.01	0.00
1000-1500	0.10	0.15	0.05
1500-1820	0.27	0.32	0.05
1820-1870	0.40	0.93	0.53
1870-1913	0.80	2.11	1.30
1913-1950	0.95	1.85	0.91
1950-1973	1.92	4.91	2.93
1973-2001	1.62	3.05	1.41
1820-2001	*0.98*	*2.21*	*1.22*

Source: Angus Maddison (2001), *The World Economy: A Millennial Perspective*, Paris: OECD, Tables 1-1, 1-2, 1-3 on p. 28, and Appendix Tables B-10, B-11, B-18, B-19, B-21, B-22. Angus Maddison (2003), *The World Economy: Historical Statistics*, Paris: OECD, Tables 8a, 8b, and 8c on pp. 256-263.

The aggregate worldwide growth rates shown in Table 1-1 hide the fact that economic growth has not been uniform across all countries. Some economies have grown much faster than others. Nor have growth rates been consistent over time for individual countries even as aggregate worldwide economic growth accelerated throughout the period. The growth experiences of individual countries have often diverged from the worldwide average growth path. The different growth experiences over the past 200 years are what in fact caused today's very large differences in per capita incomes across countries. Per capita income in what Maddison calls the

"Western offshoots," that is, Australia, Canada, New Zealand, and the United States, is today about twenty times larger than that of the average African economy. Differences between individual economies are, of course, even greater than the regional differences shown in Figure 1-6. Maddison estimates that in 2001 per capita incomes in Sierra Leone and the United States were $386 and $27,948, respectively, in 1990 prices. That is a ratio of 1 to 72.4.

The differences in incomes across countries are also a phenomenon of the past 200 years. Before 1800, people were poor everywhere. Today, many people have become very rich compared to their compatriots 200 years earlier. But, where growth has lagged large numbers of people still live in poverty not much different from that faced by most people 200 years ago. The different growth experiences challenge economists to explain why some economies have grown so much faster than others. At the same time, the variation in growth rates across countries and time periods provides economists with many different growth experiences to study and helps them distinguish the determinants of economic growth.

Figure 1-6
Economic Growth: 1820-2001

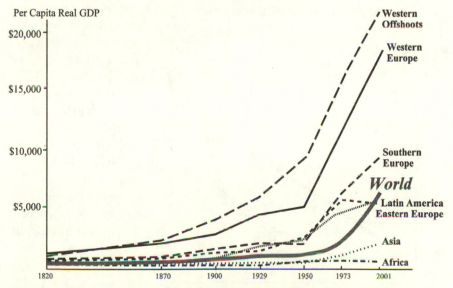

Based on data from: Angus Maddison (2003), *The World Economy: Historical Statistics*, Paris: OECD, Table 8c, p. 262.

1.3.2 Trade and Per Capita Output Follow Similar Paths

Trade has been referred to as an "engine of growth" in the field of development economics. Recently, economists have accumulated statistical evidence showing that economic growth and international trade are positively correlated. Even a casual view of the paths of growth and trade over the past 200 years, shown in Figure 1-7, suggests a positive correlation between trade and growth. Table 1-2 details the last 200 years' growth of trade and per capita real output. International trade involved less than 1 percent of the world's production in 1800. By 1870, the percentage had risen to 5 percent. The building of railroads and the development of large steel-hulled steamships had reduced the costs of transporting bulk goods overland. The reduction of tariffs and other trade barriers also contributed to the explosion in international trade. By 1929, the year before the Great Depression, exports reached 9 percent of world GDP. After the sharp increase in protectionist trade policies during the Great Depression of the 1930s and a second devastating world war in the first half of the 1940s, exports had declined to just 5.5 percent of world GDP by 1950.

Since 1950, however, world trade has grown much faster than world output. Even as average per capita income grew at unprecedented rates after 1950, international trade also grew faster than it had ever grown before. Between 1950 and 1998, worldwide GDP increased about six-fold while total worldwide exports increased nearly twenty-fold. Exports were equal to 17 percent of world GDP in 1998, they reached 20 percent of GDP in 2000, and they exceeded 25 percent of world GDP by 2005.

Figure 1-7
World Economic Growth and Trade

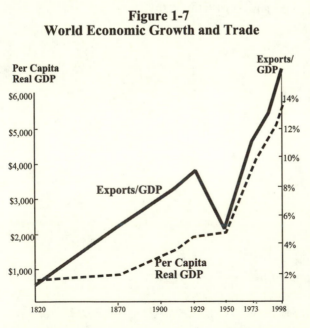

Table 1-2
World Exports and Per Capita GDP: 1820-2004

Year	World Exports (millions 1990$)	World GDP (millions 1990$)	Exports as % of World GDP	Per Capita $1990 GDP
Maddison's Real Per Capita Estimates:				
1820	7,255	694,442	1.0	667
1870	50,345	1,101,369	4.6	867
1913	212,425	2,704,782	7.9	1,510
1929	334,408	3,696,156	9.0	1,806
1950	295,621	5,336,101	5.5	2,114
1973	1,690,648	16,059,180	10.5	4,104
1998	5,817,080	33,725,635	17.2	5,709
2001		37,194,000		
International Monetary Fund's Nominal Figures:				
2004	11,069,000	40,671,000	27.2	-

Source: The figures for 1820 and 1929 are from Angus Maddison (1995), *Monitoring the World Economy 1820-1992*, Paris: OECD, Tables E-2, p. 211, and I-4, p. 239. The years 1870, 1913, 1950, and 1998 are from Angus Maddison (2001), *The World Economy: A Millennial Perspective*, Paris: OECD, Tables F-3 and F-5, and Table C5-b. The 2004 nominal figures are from the International Monetary Fund (2005), *World Economic Outlook*, April 2005, Washington, DC: IMF, Table 1, p. 201, and Table 20, p. 230.

    The past half-century's growth of trade has been driven, in part, by air freight, containerization, and improvements in transportation logistics that further improved the efficiency with which we could move products between countries. Very recently, improved communications and the Internet have encouraged the outsourcing to distant countries of services that had always been considered to be "nontradables." Governments also actively worked to reduce trade barriers through international agreements such as the General Agreement on Tariffs and Trade (GATT) and the World Trade Organization (WTO). Equally important for the recent surge in international trade has been the internationalization of business. Firms have increasingly spread production and marketing across borders as competition increased and incomes rose. By breaking production down into separable activities, firms have been able to reduce overall production costs by locating each activity in accordance with national comparative advantages.

About four-fifths of international trade today involves a multinational firm as exporter and/or importer. For these and many other reasons, trade continues to grow faster than total output, which is itself growing at a very rapid rate. The question, of course, is whether the rapid economic growth is "caused" by the growing trade.

1.4 The Power of Compounding

The previous section showed that both per capita incomes and international trade have grown rapidly. This apparent correlation does not prove causality, of course. It is urgent that we figure out whether there is indeed a causal relationship between trade and growth. This urgency is due to the fact that even the slightest increase in an economy's rate of growth eventually has a very large impact on human welfare. Economic growth is a compound process, and compound processes are very powerful.

Some simple examples can illustrate the power of compounding. In general, if per capita real GDP grows at an annual rate of R, then after T years the level of per capita real GDP will be

$$(1\text{-}1) \qquad\qquad PCGDP_T = PCGDP_{t=0}(1 + R)^T$$

For example, suppose a country with a per capita real GDP of $2,000, about equal to that of Honduras or Uzbekistan in 2000, grows for ten years at an annual growth rate of 2.5 percent, the average growth rate for low-income countries in 2000.[17] At 2.5 percent per year, after 10 years per capita real GDP will rise from $2,000 to

$$(1\text{-}2) \qquad\qquad PCGDP_{t=10} = \$2000(1 + .025)^{10} = \$2,560$$

Honduras and Uzbekistan have indeed been growing at rates close to 2.5 percent in recent years, and they have, therefore, been able to increase their per capita real incomes by more than 25 percent in a decade. If Honduras and Uzbekistan continue to grow 2.5 percent for an entire century, then shortly after 2100 they will end up with a real per capita income of

$$(1\text{-}3) \qquad\qquad PCGDP_{t=100} = \$2000(1 + .025)^{100} = \$23,627$$

---

[17] World Bank (2001), *World Development Report 2000/2001*, Oxford, U.K.: Oxford University Press, Table 1, pp. 274-275.

Thus, if these currently poor countries can continue to grow at their current rates of growth for 100 years, which is not a very long period in the course of human history, they will be able to achieve standards of living that exceed those of most developed economies today.

If Honduras and Uzbekistan increase their annual growth rates by one percentage point to 3.5 percent per year, which is still only half of China's growth rate over the past 20 years, then in 100 years real per capita income will grow to

$$(1\text{-}4) \qquad PCGDP_{t=100} = \$2000(1 + .035)^{100} = \$62,383$$

That is, an annual growth rate just one percentage point higher, 3.5 percent instead of 2.5 percent, takes a very poor country to a standard of living more than twice as high as the citizens of the most prosperous country enjoy today. The \$62,383 is also nearly three times higher than the real per capita income achieved by the country that grows at 2.5 percent for one century. A small change in a growth rate has a very large absolute effect within a surprisingly short time. This *power of compounding* gives international trade potentially a much more potent role in increasing human welfare than its traditional static role in taking the economy beyond its production possibilities frontier. Of course, whether international trade can play such a dynamic role powered by compounding depends on whether trade does indeed raise a country's rate of economic growth.

1.5 Does Trade Cause Growth?

The positive correlation between international trade and economic growth is a statistical regularity in need of an explanation. Such an explanation is not so easy to piece together, however. For example, the concurrent improvements in transportation and growth of international trade described earlier in Section 1.3 suggest that the relationship between trade and economic growth may be driven by bi-directional causality. Not only does trade stimulate economic growth, as Adam Smith and many other economists since Smith have suggested, but improved technology and economic growth in turn are likely to create more trade. The relationship between trade and economic growth is probably even more complex than that. Both growth and trade depend on many other economic, social, and political factors. Clearly, the building of a dynamic case for free trade, which requires an accurate model of the complex relationship between trade and growth, is not a simple project.

It is not entirely clear that trade always has a positive influence on a country's rate of economic growth. In fact, there are more than a few economists and critics of free trade policies who have alleged that international trade can actually retard long-run economic growth. Perhaps the most influential of the trade critics was the one-time head of the United Nations Economic Commission for Latin America, Raúl Prebisch (1950, 1959). Prebisch strongly advocated the protectionist trade policies that were in fact put in place by many developing countries in the 1940s, 1950s, and 1960s. There is not much convincing statistical evidence of a negative relationship between trade and growth, however. Prebisch's favored import substitution policies have a very mixed record of success, and have now been largely abandoned by most countries that adopted them. Proponents of free trade can point to a very large body of statistical evidence supporting the hypothesis that trade exerts a positive influence on economic growth. But, as in the case of trade theory, many have questioned the statistical evidence.

Before we begin the complex task of building a theoretical framework that links international trade and economic growth, a careful examination of what the statistical evidence tells us about the relationship between trade and growth is in order. The next chapter surveys the vast empirical evidence that, according to many, confirms a positive relationship between trade and growth. However, the many econometric problems that plague these empirical studies have left some doubt about exactly what the statistical evidence tells us. These doubts add to the importance of the remaining chapters of the book; if the econometric evidence cannot unequivocally decide whether trade enhances growth, then we had better be able to justify our conclusions with logically sound models linking trade and growth. At the same time, the great variety of statistical studies surveyed in the next chapter also helps us build the necessary theoretical framework by providing very useful insights into how international trade may influence economic growth.

Chapter Two

Trade and Growth:
The Empirical Evidence

No nation was ever ruined by trade.
    (Benjamin Franklin)

Over the past four decades, economists have produced a large amount of statistical evidence on the relationship between international trade and economic growth.[18] Economists have estimated correlation coefficients and regression coefficients, tested for cointegration, and performed a variety of other statistical tests to prove or disprove the existence of a relationship between international trade and economic growth. They have used data sets covering a wide variety of countries, time periods, and economic variables. The results of this research largely support the hypothesis that, all other things equal, countries open to international trade provide their residents with higher incomes and higher rates of economic growth. The research is even more definitive in its rejection of the alternative hypothesis that trade slows economic growth. There is no convincing statistical evidence suggesting that trade and economic growth are negatively correlated. To paraphrase Benjamin Franklin, quoted above, no nation appears to have been ruined by trade.

---

[18] This chapter draws, in part, on Joshua J. Lewer and Hendrik Van den Berg (2003b), "How Large is International Trade's Effect on Economic Growth?" *Journal of Economic Surveys*, Vol. 17(3), pp. 363-396 and Joshua J. Lewer and Hendrik Van den Berg (2003), "How Large Is International Trade's Effect on Economic Growth?" in Donald A.R. George, Les Oxley, and Kenneth I. Carlaw, eds., *Surveys in Economic Growth*, Oxford, U.K.: Blackwell Publishing.

Not everyone agrees that the many statistical studies provide definitive proof that international trade causes a country's economy to grow faster, however. Each of the studies can be, and often has been, criticized for shortcomings related to the data or the statistical methods used. It is difficult to accurately measure the economic variables that must be included in the empirical models that relate international trade and economic growth, especially in developing economies. Most economic data inaccurately represents the true economic variables in the models. Also, the practical application of statistical methods inevitably requires simplifying assumptions about the true underlying models, the distributions of the observations, and the nature of the data. Technically accurate and well-supported accusations of omitted variables, simultaneity, spurious regressions, incomplete samples, biased estimators, errors in variables, or any number of other econometric problems have been directed at most of the empirical studies.

Despite the justified criticism, the consistency of the statistical results across the many different studies has made it increasingly difficult to deny that there is a positive relationship between international trade and economic growth. It seems to matter little which sample of countries is used, what time period is covered, which model is specified, or what statistical methods are used; the studies usually support the hypothesis that international trade is positively related to the growth of real per capita output. Support of the hypothesis seems to be "robust" to the particulars of the statistical tests. This robustness of the statistical evidence has been embraced by many economists as proof of free trade's positive role in the growth process.

Even if one accepts that the statistical results robustly show that economic growth is correlated with the growth of international trade, however, statistical significance does not automatically imply that international trade *causes* economic growth. And, even if there is causality, that does not necessarily imply that the relationship between international trade and economic growth is an *economically important* relationship. Recall that the previous chapter brought up the results of studies showing that the gains from international trade suggested by the traditional static models are very small. Therefore, before the statistical evidence on the relationship between trade and growth can be accepted as proof of the hypothesis that free trade is a major determinant of economic growth, economists must show that there is a statistically significant relationship that is both positive and quantitatively meaningful. The power of compounding implies that the growth effects of trade do not have to be very large for them to be very important for human welfare in the long term. Nevertheless, this chapter examines the available empirical evidence on the relationship between trade and growth not only to distinguish the statistical significance of the trade-growth relationship but also to judge the economic significance of the statistical findings.

Several more complex and subtle statistical issues are also addressed in this chapter. Especially troublesome is the issue that Rodriguez and Rodrik (1999, 2001) and Rodrik, Subramanian, and Trebbi (2002) recently brought up. These authors argue that, because international trade policy is closely correlated with many other economic policies, statistical methods cannot accurately distinguish between trade's effects on economic growth and the effects of other variables and policies on growth. Omitted variable bias and simultaneity bias plague much of the empirical literature on economic growth, of course. These biases are probably the major reason why empirical analysis has not yet been able to settle so many of the disagreements about the causes of economic growth. Also troubling about the empirical literature is the fact that not all statistical studies find significantly positive correlations between trade and growth. Therefore, claims of robustness remain somewhat suspicious despite the overwhelming majority of studies that do find significant results.

Econometrics has not precisely defined what constitutes a *robust* result. This chapter examines the robustness of the evidence on the trade-growth relationship in several ways. For one thing, it examines whether the relatively few exceptions to the evidence that mostly confirms the hypothesis of a positive trade-growth correlation are due to methodological improvements that uncovered information not found by the majority of empirical studies. In other words, are the small number of negative results methodologically superior to the very large number of positive results? This chapter therefore orders statistical studies over time in order to examine whether the results of more recent studies, which presumably use more sophisticated methods and better data sets, generate statistical results that differ systematically from the average results from earlier studies. Special attention is given to recent studies that explicitly attempt to generate more robust results by running repeated regressions with alternative data sets and regression models. This chapter also details several innovative statistical studies that effectively move beyond the simple tests for correlation that characterize most statistical studies and seek to uncover exactly *how* trade influences economic growth.

2.1 The Statistical Relationship between Trade and Growth

The early empirical studies of international trade and growth were stimulated by the divergent trends in economic growth throughout the world. Most of the countries that had adopted protectionist import substitution policies after World War II were experiencing declining growth rates by the 1970s. However, a small number of East Asian economies made the growth of international trade a central part of their overall economic policies, and they experienced unprecedented rates of economic growth.[19] The question on most development economists' minds was why these open economies were doing so much better than most other developing economies in Asia, Africa, and Latin America. Many of the studies that addressed this question were detailed studies that examined policies and economic performances in individual economies or groups of countries. Beginning in the 1950s, the field of econometrics provided economists with increasingly powerful statistical tools that could be applied to analyze the relationship between economic variables such as trade and growth. As computing power became cheaper, these more sophisticated methods became easier to apply and empirical analysis came to dominate the literature on the trade-growth relationship. The earliest empirical studies used correlation and simple regression methods that could be performed on mechanical calculators, but by the 1980s multiple regression analysis had became the standard tool of analysis. Much of the research on the relationship between trade and growth over the past two decades used increasingly sophisticated statistical methods to seek more accurate estimates of the relationship between trade and growth.

2.1.1 The Early Statistical Studies

Typical of the early studies were Michaely (1977) and Balassa (1978). Michaely used simple correlation analysis to test whether the average rate of economic growth was positively related to the change in the ratio of international trade to GDP. For a sample of 41 developing economies for the period 1950-1973, he found a strong positive correlation and concluded that the protectionist import substitution policies applied in many developing countries were ill advised. Balassa applied simple regression analysis to a sample of 10 countries between 1956 and 1974 and found that trade export volume were positively related to a country's rate of economic

---

[19] For discussions of the 1970s studies of trade and growth sponsored by the National Bureau of Economic Research (NBER), see Krueger (1978, 1983, 1997).

growth. More importantly, regression analysis permitted him to estimate the size of the quantitative relationship. Ever since, regression analysis has become the preferred statistical method.

Empirical studies of the relationship between foreign trade and economic growth most often specified linear econometric models of the form

$$(2\text{-}1) \qquad G_{GDP} = a_0 + a_1 G_K + a_2 G_L + a_3 TRADE + a_4 Z + u$$

where G_{GDP}, G_K, and G_L are the growth rates of real gross domestic product, capital stock, and labor force, respectively, TRADE represents the growth of trade, Z is a set of other variables thought to explain economic growth, and u is the standard error term. This specification is convenient because data to proxy the model's variables are readily available from national accounts and large data bases such as the *Penn World Tables* and Angus Maddison's (1995, 2001, 2003) historical time series.[20]

The regression model (2-1) has a solid theoretical foundation because it can be derived directly from the neoclassical production function. Suppose that output, Y, is a function of the stock of capital, K, and the labor force, L, and the level of technology A. Suppose further that output follows the Cobb-Douglas production function, $Y = AK^\alpha L^{1-\alpha}$, in which $0<\alpha<1$. The Cobb-Douglas function is a convenient version of a neoclassical production function: it is subject to constant returns to scale, individual factors are subject to diminishing returns, and α and $(1-\alpha)$ turn out to be the income shares of capital and labor. Suppose, finally, that technology grows at the rate p. In this case, the level of technology depends on the time period t and is equal to $A = e^{pt}$, and the Cobb-Douglas production function is $Y = e^{pt}K^\alpha L^{1-\alpha}$. Converting this function to logarithms and differentiating with respect to time yields

$$(2\text{-}2) \qquad G_Y = p + \alpha G_K + (1-\alpha)G_L + u$$

The variable p in the Cobb-Douglas production function is the growth rate

---

[20] For a description of the *Penn World Table*, see Summers and Heston (1991). Most researchers use the ratio of investment to GDP, or I/Y, in place of the growth of the capital stock because capital stock data are not available for most countries. Many researchers also substitute the total population growth for labor force growth when labor force data omits large numbers of informal and self-employed persons.

of technology or *total factor productivity*. The regression equation (2-1) is called the *sources of growth equation* because it shows output growth as the sum of factor growth and productivity growth as in equation (2-2).

Strictly speaking, equation (2-1) is an "augmented" sources of growth equation because it also includes the variables TRADE and Z. These additional explanatory variables help to explain the variation in output that would otherwise be captured by the constant, which equation (2-2) shows is total factor productivity growth. The regression model (2-1) is in accordance with authors such as Feder (1982), Rivera-Batiz and Romer (1991), MacDonald (1994), Edwards (1998), Clerides, Lach, and Tybout (1998), Bernard and Jensen (1999b), and a great many others who claim that open economies achieve more rapid productivity growth.

2.1.2 The Shortcomings of Linear Regression Analysis

There are many reasons why linear regressions fail to provide accurate estimates of how the independent variables influence the dependent variable. The data are often inaccurate, and the dependent variable is influenced by many variables not included in the regression model. These are the familiar econometric problems of *measurement error* and *omitted variable bias*. Furthermore, since in an economic system everything is related to everything else, the inherent interdependence of all economic variables creates the so-called *simultaneity* problem. More recently, the availability of ever longer time-series has inspired economists to use more time-series analysis, but time-series analysis requires *cointegration* tests to detect spurious regression results caused by the likelihood that time-series variables grow together over time even though there is no direct causal relationship causal between them. The studies reviewed below represent a progression of attempts to overcome econometric problems such as these so that the "true" relationship between international trade and economic growth will be revealed.

2.2 Regressing Economic Growth on International Trade

Regression studies can be said to provide *robust* evidence on the relationship between trade and growth if estimates of the coefficient for the TRADE variable are similar for a large variety of data sets, time periods, or samples. The degree of robustness of the statistical results becomes difficult to judge when the econometric models differ. However, the task of comparing results is made easier by the fact that most of the regressions used to test the relationship between international trade and economic growth fall into one of five general categories: (1) cross-section and time-series regressions using the basic sources of growth equation, (2) cross-section and time-series regressions using a per capita version of the sources of growth equation, (3) cross-section and time-series regressions using Feder's (1982) two-sector model, (4) cross-section and time-series regressions using simultaneous equations models, and (5) regressions using instrumental variables. Fortunately, with some adjustments it will still be possible to compare average coefficient estimates for the different categories of statistical results. This section and the sections that follow summarize the many empirical estimates found in the literature over the period 1970-2003. These studies appeared in a wide range of economic journals covering the fields of international economics and economic growth and development.

2.2.1 Cross-Section Sources of Growth Regressions

Table 2-1 summarizes the results of cross-section regressions using models like the sources of growth equation (2-1) with TRADE represented by the growth rate of real exports. To reduce the "noise" of cyclical disturbances, observations were often constructed as five- or ten-year averages. There are 34 cross-section studies that include a total of 196 separate regressions. The average value of the coefficient of the growth of real exports variable is 0.22. With the variables all in terms of growth rates, this coefficient value implies that for each 1 percentage point increase in the growth rate of trade, the economy's rate of growth increased by just over one-fifth of one percentage point. On average, the statistical significance of the coefficient estimates exceeds the 99 percent level, and the average *t*-value is 3.46. Fifty-seven percent (111 of the 196) coefficients fall between 0.15 and 0.45.

Figure 2-1 supplements the averages reported in Table 2-1. The left diagram shows the estimated regression coefficients for the growth of exports from each of the 196 cross-section regressions, listed from left to right in order of publication date. The diagram on the right shows the 95 percent confidence intervals of the 196 point estimates. Over 90 percent of the coefficient values covered by the confidence intervals are positive. Note that the distributions differ across the various studies. While we group similar regressions, they are, of course, not exactly the same in terms of data sets, sample size, other variables included in the equations, etc.

Table 2-1
Cross-Section Regressions:[1] The Growth of Real
Exports and the Growth of Real Per Capita GDP

Statistic	*Average Value*
Average Coefficient Value	0.220
Median Coefficient Value	0.189
Average t-Statistic	3.460**
Maximum Coefficient Value	1.851
Minimum Coefficient Value	−1.433
Average Standard Error	0.021
Average 95% Confidence Interval	±0.042

**Significant at the 95% level.

[1] Lubitz (1973), Michalopoulos and Jay (1973), Balassa (1978), Krueger (1978), Tyler (1981), Feder (1982), Kavoussi (1984), Ram (1985), Rana (1986), Goncalves and Richtering (1987), Ram (1987), Rana (1988), Kohli and Singh (1989), Mbaku (1989), Moschos (1989), Fosu (1990), Sheehey (1990), Alam (1991), Esfahani (1991), Moore (1992), Sheehey (1992), Sprout and Weaver (1993), Coppin (1994), Hotchkiss et al. (1994), Van den Berg and Schmidt (1994), Yaghmaian (1994), Amirkhalkhali and Dar (1995), Song and Chen (1995), Yaghmaian and Ghorashi (1995), Balasubramanyam et al. (1996), Burney (1996), Fosu (1996), Park and Prime (1997), Sun and Parikh (2001).

Figure 2-1
The Scatters and 95% Confidence Distributions of Coefficient
Estimates for *Cross-Section* Regressions from Table 2-1

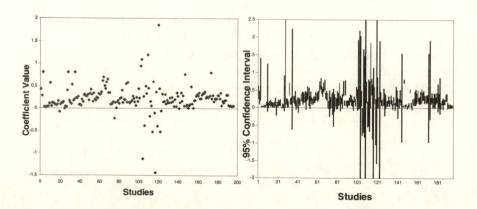

Notice that in Figure 2-1 neither the coefficient estimates or the confidence intervals change noticeably over time. This suggests that the more sophisticated econometric methods of the more recent studies have not uncovered patterns in the data that were not revealed by earlier studies. It does not appear that there were systematic biases in the early studies, which, unlike later, studies, did not directly address issues of omitted variables, simultaneity, and the quality of data.

2.2.2 Time-Series Sources of Growth Regressions

Time-series analysis became popular in the 1990s after statisticians developed ways to reduce the likelihood that standard OLS estimates will report "spurious" relationships in cases when variables are nonstationary. Variables are nonstationary if they persistently increase or decrease over time.[21] Time-series regressions offer some advantages over cross-section analysis. Cross-section regressions effectively assume that the underlying production functions and regression parameters are constant across countries, and they generate results that do not clearly apply to any individual country. Hence, the results may not translate into country-specific conclusions. Time-series analysis, on the other hand, permits researchers to analyze the importance of growth factors for individual countries. Also, because institutions and production functions may vary less over time than they do across countries, time-series analysis may be less vulnerable to Rodriguez and Rodrik's (2001) critique that the trade variable mistakenly captures the effects of other institutional and structural factors that vary across countries. Time-series analysis for individual countries has the added benefit of permitting researchers to compare country results and to explicitly analyze the potential causes of the country-by-country differences. Cross-section estimates do not reflect conditions in any one country in the sample.

Table 2-2 summarizes the coefficient values for the 402 time-series regressions from 19 different studies that specified regression equations similar to the sources of growth equation (2-1) with trade specified as the growth of real exports. The average value of the 402 coefficients for the growth of real exports variable is 0.22, surprisingly similar to the average cross-section results. Thus, the time-series studies suggest that, on average and all other things equal, for every one percentage point increase in the rate of growth of international trade, the rate of growth of the economy

---

[21] See Granger and Newbold (1974) or most econometrics textbooks for a discussion of the spurious regression problem.

increases by a little over one-fifth of one percentage point. The power of compounding turns and 0.22 percent higher growth rate into a 10 percent higher level of output in about a generation.

Table 2-2
Time-Series Regressions: The Growth of Real
Exports and the Growth of Real Per Capita GDP

	All Regressions (n=402)	Simple Regression (n=100)	Multiple Regression (n=302)
Average Coefficient	0.215	0.200	0.219
Median Coefficient	0.119	0.138	0.113
Average t-Statistic	3.641**	3.277**	3.771**
Maximum Coefficient	1.386	1.386	1.301
Minimum Coefficient	-0.652	-0.590	-0.652
Average Standard Error	0.014	0.029	0.016
Average 95% Interval[3]	± 0.028	± 0.058	± 0.032

	No Unit Root Test (n=299)	Unit Root Test (n=103)	Open Economies[1] (n=91)	Closed Economies (n=311)
Average Coefficient	0.261	0.081	0.309	0.187
Median Coefficient	0.167	0.059	0.230	0.096
Average t-Statistic	4.172**	2.126**	4.533**	3.389**
Maximum Coefficient	1.386	0.463	1.386	1.301
Minimum Coefficient	-0.652	-0.417	-0.652	-0.590
Average Standard Error	0.018	0.012	0.035	0.015
Average 95% Interval[3]	± 0.035	± 0.023	± 0.070	± 0.029

	Low Income[2] (n=147)	Lower Middle (n=141)	Upper Middle (n=85)	High Income (n=29)
Average Coefficient	0.206	0.217	0.154	0.429
Median Coefficient	0.113	0.123	0.073	0.365
Average t-Statistic	3.212**	4.178**	2.350**	7.085**
Maximum Coefficient	1.301	1.285	1.301	1.386
Minimum Coefficient	-0.138	-0.417	-0.590	-0.652
Average Standard Error	0.022	0.022	0.027	0.081
Average 95% Interval[3]	± 0.044	± 0.043	± 0.054	± 0.166

**Significant at the 95% level.

Time-series regressions of growth of real exports on growth of real GDP are from: Darrat (1987), Ram (1987), Grabowsky (1988), Serletis (1992), Dodaro (1993), Khan, Ashfaque, and Saqib (1993), Atesoglu (1994), Sengupta and Espana (1994), Van den Berg and Schmidt (1994), Yaghmaian (1994), Amirkhalkhali and Dar (1995), Kwan et al. (1996), Van den Berg (1996a, 1996b), Al-Yousif (1997), Dhananjayan and Devi (1997), Van den Berg (1997), Amin Gutierrez de Pineres and Ferrantino (1999), Vohra (2001).

[1] We follow the Sachs and Warner (1995) criterion to classify trade regimes.

[2] Income groups are based on World Bank classification, see *World Development Reports.*

[3] The mean of all of the 95 percent confidence intervals in the set of regressions included in the column.

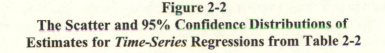

Figure 2-2
The Scatter and 95% Confidence Distributions of
Estimates for *Time-Series* Regressions from Table 2-2

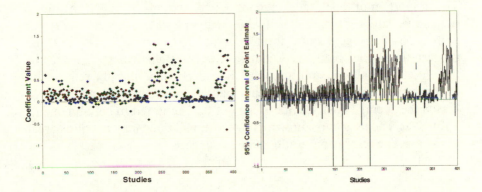

Figure 2-2 presents the scatter of estimated coefficients and the 95 percent confidence intervals of the time-series regressions listed from left to right in chronological order by date of publication. 84 percent of the confidence intervals for the 402 regressions cover positive values, which is slightly lower than the 91 percent of the confidence intervals that exceeded zero for the cross-section regressions using the same model. The scatter of point estimates and the intervals in Figure 2-2 do not appear to show any clear trends over time, suggesting that earlier time-series results were not less accurate than those of more recent and econometrically-superior studies. Table 2-2 also breaks up the results of the 402 regressions according to whether (1) regressions used simple or multiple regression models, (2) unit root tests were or were not applied, (3) trade policy is open or closed, and (4) data were for developed or developing economies. The average of the 100 simple regression time-series estimates have a mean of 0.20, which is slightly smaller than the 0.22 average for the 302 multiple regression estimates. The proportion of the confidence intervals covering positive coefficient values is 82 percent for simple regression estimates and 85 percent for multiple regression estimates. There is not much difference between simple and multiple regression results.

There is a very large difference between the results of the regressions that did not apply unit root tests for stationarity and those that did. The average value of the 299 coefficients from time-series regressions for which no unit root tests were performed is 0.26, which is over three times as large as the average 0.08 value for the trade coefficients from 103 time-series regressions for which time-series estimation procedures were adjusted in accordance with unit root test results. The diagrams in Figure 2-3 present the scatters of coefficient estimates and the 95 percent confidence intervals of time-series regressions that were not adjusted for potential unit roots and those that were adjusted for unit root test results. The proportion of the 95 percent confidence intervals falling in the range of positive values is almost exactly the same for both subsets of time-series regressions, 85 percent for the former versus 82 percent for the latter. Thus, modern time-series methods do not weaken the statistical significance of trade's effect on economic growth. However, they sharply reduce the estimated size of the effect. It appears that spurious regression results have biased the average coefficient estimate of 0.22 reported in column one of Table 2-2. The long-run gains from international trade may not be as great as the average regression results seem to suggest.

Figure 2-3
The Scatter and 95% Confidence Distributions of Coefficient
Estimates for Time-Series Regressions Without (top)
and With (bottom) *Unit Root Tests* **from Table 2-2**

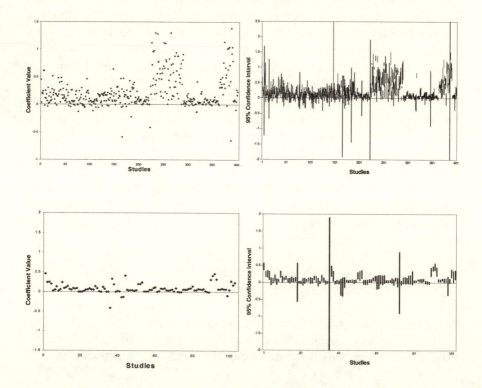

Table 2-2 also splits the time-series regression results according to whether countries were "open" or "closed" using Sachs and Warner's (1995) classification of countries' trade policies. The influence of international trade on growth is much greater in economies that had few restrictions on trade than in highly protected economies. The coefficient estimates for open economies is 0.31 compared to 0.19 for the closed economies. Moreover, the percentage of the confidence intervals that cover positive values is greater for economies classified as open, 92 percent, than those classified as closed, 81 percent. Since Sachs and Warner implicitly used institutional and policy variables to classify countries as open or closed, these differences in regression results for open and closed countries effectively support Rodriguez and Rodrik's (2001) concern that empirical analyses of trade and growth have indeed been biased by omitting institutional variables correlated with international trade. Much more complex models may be necessary to correctly separate the various contributions of, and interrelationships between, international trade and the other institutional variables.

Finally, Table 2-2 splits the sample according to the World Bank's (2002) classification of high, upper-middle, lower-middle, or low income countries. As for the cross-section results, time-series estimates suggest that trade stimulates growth more in countries with higher incomes. The average coefficient on export growth for high income countries is 0.43, 0.15 for upper-middle, 0.22 for lower-middle, and 0.21 for low income. The fraction of the 95 percent confidence intervals covering the range of positive coefficient values is 93, 83, 88, and 80 percent for high, upper-middle, lower-middle, and low income low countries, respectively. Other researchers, including Tyler (1981), Kavoussi (1984), Moschos (1989), and Burney (1996) among the studies reviewed in this chapter, have found similar differences in coefficient values between high income and low income countries. The different growth rates may be due to developing countries' lower capacity to apply the foreign technology that accompanies trade, as suggested by Evenson and Singh (1997) and Coe, Helpman, and Hoffmaister (1997). The low coefficient values that we find for upper-middle income countries suggest that the relationship between income and the potential growth effects of international trade is not monotonic.

2.2.3 The Per Capita Income Version of the Model

Not all researchers have specified regression models exactly like equation (2-1). Some researchers sought to explain per capita real income rather than total output, which makes sense when we recognize that the real goal of economic growth is to raise the welfare of individual people, not just some collective measure of national output. A per capita growth equation can be derived from the Cobb-Douglas production function if we assume that the labor force grows at the same rate as the overall population. This is a reasonable assumption only in the very long run, but since economic growth is a long-run concept, economists often accept this assumption. Dividing the production function $Y = e^{pt}K^{\alpha}L^{1-\alpha}$ by the stock of labor L gives us per worker output $Y/L = e^{pt}(K/L)^{\alpha}$. Putting this equation in logarithms and differentiating with respect to time yields the *per capita growth equation:*

(2-3) $G_{Y/L} = p + \alpha G_K - \alpha G_L + a_3 TRADE + a_4 Z + u$

All variables are the same as in equation (2-1), except, of course, for the growth of per capita output, $G_{Y/L}$.

Table 2-3
Regressions of the Growth of Real GDP
Per Capita on the Growth of Real Exports

Statistic	*Cross-Section Data[1]* (37 regressions)	*Times-Series Data[2]* (57 regressions)
Average Coefficient	0.199	0.211
Median Coefficient	0.140	0.101
Average t-Statistic	4.045**	2.118**
Maximum Coefficient	0.450	2.373
Minimum Coefficient	-0.122	-0.170
Average Standard Error	0.027	0.056
Average 95% Interval	± 0.054	± 0.113

**Significant at the 95% level.
[1] The cross-section 37 regressions are from: Emery (1967), Syron and Walsh (1968), Salvatore (1983), Otani and Villaneuva (1990), Salvatore and Hatcher (1991), Greenaway and Sapsford (1994b).
[2] The 57 time-series regressions are from: Salvatore and Hatcher (1991), Greenaway and Sapsford (1994a), Rashid (1995), Greenaway, Morgan, and Wright (1997), Lin (2000).

In general, the estimated coefficient for the TRADE variable in equation (2-3) should be the same as the estimated coefficient for TRADE in a regression equation like (2-1), all other things equal. For a given rate of population growth, the marginal effect of TRADE on total and per capita output will be the same. Indeed, Table 2-3 shows that for the cross-section regressions, when per capita income is the dependent variable in the regression, the average coefficient value is 0.20, very similar to the 0.22 average value for the earlier cross-section results. The average per capita time-series coefficient of 0.21 is nearly identical to the earlier time-series average of 0.22.

Figure 2-4

The Scatter of Coefficient Estimates and 95% Confidence Intervals of the Per Capita Income *Cross-Section* Regressions from Table 2-3

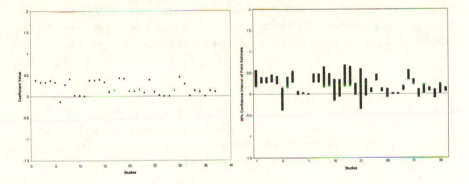

Figure 2-5

The Scatter of Coefficient Estimates and 95% Confidence Intervals of the Per Capita Income *Time-Series* Regressions from Table 2-3

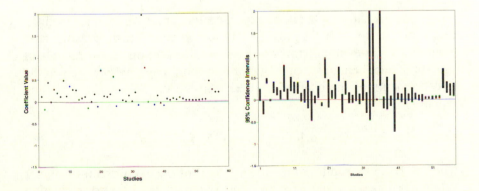

Figure 2-4 presents the coefficient scatters and the 95 percent confidence intervals for the cross-section per capita income regressions. Figure 2-5 shows the coefficient scatters and the 95 percent confidence intervals for the time-series per capita income regressions. On average, 92 percent of the cross-section intervals lie above zero, and 80 percent of the time-series intervals lie above zero, proportions that are similar to the results for the average cross-section and time-series results reported earlier above.

2.3 The Feder Model

An interesting variant on the growth regressions reported earlier is the popular regression specification pioneered by Gershon Feder (1982). Feder divided the economy into an export sector and a non-export sector. He specified the production function of the export sector as

$$(2\text{-}4) \qquad\qquad X = g(K,L)$$

X stands for output in the export sector, K is the capital stock, and L is the labor force in the export sector. Feder assumed that the export sector generates positive externalities for the rest of the economy, and he therefore specified the non-export sector production function as

$$(2\text{-}5) \qquad\qquad N = f(K,L,X)$$

In equation (2-5) output in the non-export sector of the economy, N, is determined by the externalities generated from production X in the export sector as well as by the capital stock and the labor force.

Feder showed that if the export sector is more productive than the non-export sector, then the growth of the export increases the growth of the economy's non-export sector and, therefore, the economy's overall rate of growth. Under certain strong assumptions about marginal products in the two segments of the economy, Feder derived the following regression equation:

$$(2\text{-}6) \qquad\qquad G_Y = \alpha(I/Y) + \beta G_L + \delta(X/Y)G_X + \theta G_X$$

The coefficient δ captures the growth effect of the export sector's higher relative productivity and θ captures the externalities of export production on the rest of the economy.

Table 2-4
Results of Regressions Based on Feder's (1982) Model

Statistic	Cross-Section Data[1] (99 regressions)	Times-Series Data[2] (116 regressions)
Average Coefficient	0.520	0.421
Median Coefficient	0.466	0.419
Average t-Statistic	2.844**	1.953**
Maximum Coefficient	1.747	1.899
Minimum Coefficient	-0.880	-0.049
Average Standard Error	0.041	0.049
Average 95% Interval	± 0.082	± 0.098

**Significant at the 95% level.

[1] The 99 cross-section regressions are from: Feder (1982), Balassa (1985), Rana (1986), Rana (1988), Kohli and Singh (1989), Sheehey (1990), Moore (1992), Hotchkiss et al. (1994), Song and Chen (1995), Park and Prime (1997), McNab and Moore (1998), Sun and Parikh (2001).

[2] The 116 time-series regressions are from: Ram (1987), Grabowsky (1988), Sengupta (1993), Hansen (1994), Al-Yousif (1997), Ibrahim and MacPhee (1997), Vohra (2001).

The average coefficients from the 99 cross-section and 116 time-series regressions using the Feder regression model are reported in Table 2-4. Notice that they are about twice as large as the coefficient estimates using either the total income or per capita income *sources of growth* models. The average coefficient values of over 0.40 are close to those found by Feder in his own study. He argued that his higher coefficient estimates were evidence that trade's positive effect on economic growth has two causes: (1) the export sector of the economy is more productive, and (2) trade generates externalities that increase growth in other parts of the economy.

The diagrams in Figure 2-6 show the coefficient scatters and the 95 percent confidence intervals for the cross-section (top) and time-series (bottom) regressions of the Feder model, respectively. The confidence intervals fall predominantly in the positive region; on average, 91 percent of the confidence intervals for the cross-section regressions of Feder's model lie above zero, and 79 percent of the confidence intervals for the time-series regressions lie above zero. The higher average coefficient value from estimating Feder's model suggests that perhaps the average coefficient values of 0.22 reported for the sources of growth regressions are too low because they fail to capture the positive externalities that exporting provides to the rest of the economy.

Figure 2-6
The Scatter of Coefficient Estimates and 95% Confidence Intervals:
Cross-Section and Time-Series Feder Regressions from Table 2-4

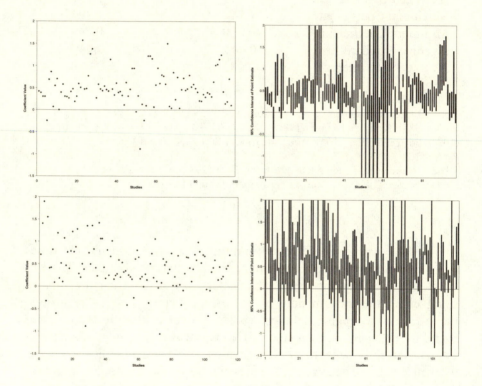

2.4 Dealing with Simultaneity

In the case of international trade and economic growth, it is highly likely that trade affects, and is affected by, the economy's rate of economic growth. That is, the relationship between trade and growth is likely to be *bi-directional*. The presence of interrelationships among the dependent and independent variables in a regression model can cause *simultaneity bias*. Researchers have dealt with this problem in several ways. One method has been to carry out *causality analysis* to determine the direction of influence between two variables. Another approach is to build *simultaneous equations models* that explicitly capture the bi-directional influences that cause simultaneity bias in single-equation models. Efficient estimation methods for systems of simultaneous equations in effect create instrumental variables from the model's exogenous variables. The most popular method for dealing with potential simultaneity bias has been to use single equation regression models but to replace variables likely to cause biased estimates with *instrumental variables* that are free of simultaneous influences.

2.4.1. Causality Analysis

Most of the early time-series studies of the relationship between trade and growth applied *Granger causality* tests instead of the standard growth regressions discussed in the previous section. The Granger tests claim to determine the direction of causality between two variables by regressing the present value of one variable on the lagged value of the other and then the present value of the latter variable on the lagged value of the former variable. The finding of a significant relationship is taken to imply causality because the lagged value occurred before the current value and hence must therefore have *caused* the subsequent value of the other variable. When causality is confirmed for only one direction it is called *uni-directional causality*; coefficients that are significant for both regressions is taken as evidence of *bi-directional causality*.

Causality studies have provided at best very weak support for the hypothesis that trade causes economic growth. Jung and Marshall (1985), Hsiao (1987), Ahmad and Kwan (1991), and Dodaro (1993) found little or no evidence of causality. Chow (1987), on the other hand, confirmed causality between exports and output growth for the small number of countries covered in his study. Causality studies have all used time-series data because of their inherent need to have earlier values of some variables explain later values of other variables, but few of the studies applied modern time-series methods to verify whether variables were stationary. Bahmani-Oskooee and Alse (1993) and Ahmad and Harnhirun (1995) performed unit root tests and corrected for nonstationary variables; they were able to confirm bi-directional Granger causality between export growth and GDP growth for five Asian countries.

The overall validity of causality tests has been widely disputed. First of all, the simple Granger causality regressions lack an obvious theoretical foundation. Also relevant is Leamer's (1985a) point that *precedence* describes the Granger methodology more accurately than *causality*, and precedence no more implies causality than does correlation among contemporaneous variables. Furthermore, because the standard causality regressions examine the relationship between trade and growth in isolation, causality regressions are likely to suffer omitted variable bias. Omitted variable bias may be reduced by using vector autoregressions (VARs), which are multi-equation causality models in which each of a large number of variables are regressed on the lagged values of all the other variables. Van den Berg (1996a, 1997) found little evidence of causality from trade to growth using a VAR model for Asian and Latin American economies, respectively.

Causality studies often report only the statistical significance levels of the overall Granger regressions or VARs, not individual regression coefficients, allegedly because the models lack a firm theoretical structure that systematically relates the individual variables. Granger causality regressions that did report coefficients from regressing current economic growth on past trade growth revealed an average coefficient value of 0.17 for lagged trade variables in equations where economic growth was the dependent variable.[22] This estimated value is similar to the coefficient estimates from the sources of growth regressions surveyed earlier.

2.4.2 Simultaneous Equations Models

A theoretically more attractive approach to dealing with simultaneity is to specify a simultaneous equations model that explicitly accounts for the hypothesized simultaneous relationships among the variables in the model. If the various channels of influence can be accurately specified, the coefficients of variables that simultaneously influence and are influenced by other variables in the model can be efficiently estimated.

Esfahani (1991) used cross-section data in a three-equation model whose first equation is equation (2-1) with trade represented by both the growth of exports and the growth of imports. The model's second and third equations explain exports and imports, respectively. The growth of output serves as an explanatory variable in the second and third equations to capture the reverse influences of growth on trade. Sprout and Weaver (1993) used cross-section data for 72 less developed economies for the period 1970-1984 in a three-equation model. Sprout and Weaver's first

---

[22] Hsiao (1987), Sung-Shen, Biswas, and Tribedy (1990), Supo Alege (1993), Holman and Graves (1995), Shan and Sun (1998), and Amin Gutierrez de Pineres and Ferrantino (1999)

equation is identical to the standard regression equation (2-1), and they use the growth of exports as their TRADE variable. Their other two equations capture the reverse effects of growth on investment and trade.

Sprout and Weaver split their large sample of 72 developing economies into three smaller samples of (1) small non-primary product exporters, (2) small primary product exporters, and (3) large developing economies. They confirmed a significantly positive coefficient for the growth of trade in the first equation for the samples of small non-primary product exporters and large developing countries, but not for small primary product exporters. Sprout and Weaver also found significant relationships in the other equations, thus confirming that there are indeed simultaneous relationships between economic growth and export growth and between growth and other variables in the basic regression equation (2-1). Their finding that primary product exports do not affect economic growth confirmed the suspicions of many development economists who have often advised countries to diversify away from traditional agricultural and mining exports.

Van den Berg (1996a, 1996b) expanded on Esfahani and Sprout and Weaver and applied time-series data to a simultaneous-equations model consisting of a sources of growth equation and three other equations that explicitly explained exports, imports, and investment. Interestingly, Van den Berg compared single-equation and simultaneous-equations estimates for Asia and Latin America and found the estimated coefficients for the growth of exports in the simultaneous equations models were nearly all larger and more significant than when the data was used to regress the first equation alone. This suggests that the positive coefficients in single equation models may not have been exaggerated by simultaneity bias.

The results for cross-section and time-series studies that use a standard growth equation (2-1) *and* adjust for potential simultaneity by using a simultaneous-equations regression model are summarized in Table 2-5. The average coefficient value for the 14 cross-section regressions is 0.29. The average coefficient value for the 21 time-series regressions is 0.19. The 95 percent confidence intervals fall predominantly in the positive region, as before, and the pattern of the point estimates and intervals is similar to earlier results. Most important, average coefficient estimates are similar to the average coefficient values of the regressions reported earlier, which suggests that simultaneity did not bias the single equation regressions.

Table 2-5
Coefficients from Simultaneous-Equations Models:
Regressing the Growth of Real GDP on the Growth of Real Exports

Statistic	*Cross-Section Data[1]* (14 regressions)	*Times-Series Data[2]* (21 regressions)
Average Coefficient	0.286	0.185
Median Coefficient	0.246	0.093
Average t-Statistic	1.261	2.613**
Maximum Coefficient	1.851	0.904
Minimum Coefficient	-0.518	-0.006
Average Standard Error	0.153	0.046
Average 95% Interval	± 0.329	± 0.097

**Significant at the 95% level.

[1] The selected cross-section articles that use a simultaneous equations model to correct for potential measurement errors include: Esfahani (1991) and Sprout and Weaver (1993). We have not included the 1960-1973 negative outlier from Esfahani in the summary.

[2] The time-series studies included: Grabowsky (1988), Khan , Ashfaque, and Saqib (1993), Atesoglu (1994), Van den Berg (1996a, 1996b), Van den Berg (1997), Amin Gutierrez de Pineres and Ferrantino (1999).

2.4.3 Instrumental Variables

The estimation of a simultaneous equations model effectively creates *instrumental variables* to replace the growth of trade variable in a single equation regression model. An instrumental variable is an alternative variable that is closely correlated with the desired independent variable but independent of the other explanatory variables in the model. Researchers suspicious of simultaneity bias have most often simply found an appropriate instrumental variable and inserted it into their single equation model after duly testing the instrumental variable for correlations with the other variables in the model. Sheehey (1990, 1992) was one of the first to use instrumental variables in place of direct measures of trade.

In a very popular recent study, Frankel and Romer (1999) used four geographic variables to construct an instrumental variable to replace their trade variable. Frankel and Romer reasoned that geographic constants like distance and location would make good instrumental variables, since they are closely correlated with trade but clearly cannot be influenced by any variables in the model. Frankel and Romer also diverged from most previous empirical studies on international trade and economic growth by using variables stated in terms of levels rather than growth rates. Of course, such a specification cannot be directly derived from a general neoclassical production function and is based on the less plausible assumption that factors enter the production function in a linear form. They argued that they could get better statistical results because levels vary more than growth rates across countries, which gives statistical method greater power to distinguish what causes some countries to be wealthier than others. Frankel and Romer estimated that a one percentage point increase in the trade share raised income per person by 2.0 percent.

Because Frankel and Romer's results are derived from regressing variables in levels, they are not comparable to the large number of cross-section and time-series regressions reported above, in which a country's economic growth rate was regressed on the growth rate of trade. However, some quick calculations suggest that their results are in the ballpark. Specifically, taking into consideration Maddison's (2001) data showing that international trade accounted for about 12 percent of world GDP during the 1980s, the period covered by most of the cross-section and time-series studies of trade and growth, it is straightforward to reason that a 1 percentage point increase in the growth rate of trade would be equivalent to an absolute annual increase in trade equal to about 0.12 percent of GDP. Frankel and Romer's estimate "that a one percentage point increase in the trade share raised income per person by 2.0 percent" thus suggests that such an increase in trade's share of 0.12 percent of GDP caused by a 1 percentage point increase in the growth of trade would increase per capita GDP by about 0.24 percent of per capita GDP. Such an increase falls neatly within the range of values suggested by the cross-section and time-series regressions examined earlier.

2.5 Trade's Growth Effects Using Qualitative Measures

Some statistical studies of the relationship between international trade and economic growth eschewed direct measures of the growth of trade as the independent variable in a regression equation such as (2-1) and replaced them with indicators of an economy's openness to international trade. The results of these studies are not comparable to the results of regressions that relate measures of actual trade and economic growth. These studies simply test whether there is a statistically significant relationship between some qualitative measure of an economy's openness to trade and economic growth. This category of studies includes World Bank (1987), Dollar (1992), and Sachs and Warner (1995), reportedly the three most-often cited empirical studies on trade and growth.[23]

2.5.1 Three Popular Studies of Trade and Growth

The World Bank's study was reported in the widely-read *World Development Report 1987*. World Bank economists first subjectively classified countries' trade policies as either "strongly outward-oriented," "moderately outward-oriented," "moderately inward-oriented," or "strongly inward-oriented" on the basis of information on tariff levels, non-tariff barriers, black market premiums, etc. A comparison of the average growth rates of each of the groups of economies in Table 2-6 shows that the "strongly outward-oriented" economies grew the fastest, and growth rates were successively lower across the remaining three groups. Per capita real output actually declined in the "strongly inward-oriented" group of countries over the period 1973-1985.

Table 2-6
World Bank Results: Growth of Real GDP per Capita

	Strongly Outward Oriented	Moderately Outward Oriented	Moderately Inward Oriented	Strongly Inward Oriented
1963-73	6.9%	5.0%	3.9%	1.6%
1974-85	5.9%	1.8%	1.9%	-0.1%
Average	6.4%	3.4%	2.9%	0.8%

Source: World Bank (1987) *World Development Report 1987*, Figure 5.2, p. 84.

Dollar (1992) sought to improve on the World Bank study by creating a more objective measure of openness. He used an exchange rate model to estimate the exchange rate that would exist under free trade, and then took the difference between that estimated exchange rate and the actual

---

[23] According to Rodriguez and Rodrik (1999, 2001).

exchange rate as an indicator "of the extent to which incentives are geared to the domestic or international market."[24] Dollar's regression results suggested that, on average, economies could increase their per capita GDP growth by more than 2.1 percentage points, by fully opening their economies to free trade.

Sachs and Warner (1995) followed the procedures used by the World Bank and subjectively classified countries according to their openness to trade. They used a larger sample and covered a broader time period than previous studies, however. They found:

> a strong association between openness and growth, both within the group of developing and the group of developed countries. Within the group of developing countries, the open economies grew at 4.49 percent per year, and the closed economies grew at 0.69 percent per year. Within the group of developed countries, the open economies grew at 2.29 percent per year, and the closed economies grew at 0.74 percent per year.[25]

To put these growth rates into perspective, note that the differences in growth rates imply annual compounding would take approximately 16 years to double output in the average developing open economy, but would require 101 years to double output in the average closed economy.

2.5.2 Evaluating the Results of Qualitative Studies

Many others have tested the openness-growth relationship using a variety of measures to proxy an economy's openness to trade. Table 2-7 summarizes the regression results from these of studies. Some of the studies use an index of openness to trade, others use proxies that represent the restrictiveness of trade policies. In the case of qualitative variables that measure the degree of openness of an economy and its trade policies, a significantly positive coefficient supports the hypothesis of a positive relationship between trade and growth. For variables that measure the *restrictiveness* of trade policies, the estimated coefficient must be negative to support the hypothesis.

---

[24] Dollar (1992), p. 525.

[25] Sachs and Warner (1995), p. 524.

Table 2-7
Average Coefficient Estimates in Qualitative Studies

Statistic	Trade Openness[1] (30 regressions)	Trade Intervention[2] (114 regressions)
Percent of Coefficients:	78%	6%
Average t-Statistic:	2.801**	-2.235**

**Significant at the 95% level.

[1] The selected articles that contain openness indicators or liberalization indicators on economic growth include: Edwards (1992), Levine and Renelt (1992), Rashid (1995), Sachs and Warner (1995), Sala-i-Martin (1997), Greenaway, Morgan, and Wright (1997), Hall and Jones (1999), Rodriguez and Rodrik (2001).

[2] The selected articles that contain trade restrictions or trade intervention indicators on economic growth include: Heitger (1987), Dollar (1992), Edwards (1992), Levine and Renelt (1992), Easterly (1993), Lee, J-W (1993), Sala-i-Martin (1997), Harrison and Hanson (1999), Rodriguez and Rodrik (2001).

Table 2-7 shows that the average results of the entire group of qualitative regressions support the hypothesis that open economies grow faster than closed ones. In fact, the regressions suggest that economies classified as being "open" have grown between 2 and 3 percent faster than economies classified as "closed." This result is compatible with the other empirical studies reviewed above. According to average coefficient values estimated in the cross-section and time-series regressions reported in Tables 2-1 and 2-2, for example, an economy grows 2.5 percentage points faster than another economy if, all other things equal, its trade grows about 10-15 percentage points faster. During the 1980s, the East Asian economies, most of whose trade policies were fairly "open," increased exports by 11.1 percent per year, while Sub-Saharan Africa and its more "closed" economies increased its exports by just 2.4 percent per year, a difference of nearly 10 percentage points. During the 1990s, the difference was 12.6 percent versus 4.4 percent.[26] Some of the fast-growing export-oriented developing economies, such as Taiwan, South Korea, Singapore, Hong Kong, and more recently China, did actually expand their exports at annual rates that were 10 percentage points faster than most economies in South

---

[26] World Bank (2001), *World Development Report 2000/2001*, New York: Oxford University Press, Table 11, pp. 294-295.

Asia, Africa, and Latin America.[27] These quantitative effects of trade liberalization are similar to those reported for the other studies above.

A weakness of most of the "openness" studies is that the classifications of openness were often constructed using subjective selection methods. Edwards (1998) tested a number of alternative variables found in the literature. He found that it does not make much difference for the statistical results how the qualitative openness variables were constructed, which he interpreted as supporting the existing openness studies. However, Edwards did not address another serious problem that undermines the reliability of the "openness" studies results, which is their use of fixed country classifications even though trade policy often changed over the time period covered by the data. Wacziarg and Horn Welch (2003) recently estimated the effects of shifts in trade policy over the period 1950-1998, taking into account changes in countries' trade policies during the long period. They found that their results are very sensitive to the time periods covered; results for data from the 1970s and 1980s do not closely match results for the 1990s. This suggests that results reported by studies such as Sachs and Warner's are not necessarily *robust* across all time periods and policy regimes.

2.6 Robust Studies

Rodriguez and Rodrik (2001) argued that the frequent finding of significant relationships between trade and growth may be a reflection of international trade's close correlation with other important variables that determine economic growth. That is, trade-growth regressions are likely to suffer *omitted variable bias* because they do not include many other important determinants of economic growth. Studies on the East Asian "tigers" have pointed to education, stable macroeconomic policies, the rule of law, and the lack of social conflict, among many other things, as major factors in their rapid growth.[28] If only a TRADE variable is added to the basic sources of growth regression, and other causal variables are omitted, then some of the improvement in total factor productivity actually due to omitted variables will be wrongly attributed to trade by the standard statistical estimation methods. For example, if TRADE grows and the country's

---

[27] See Maddison (2001), Tables F-2, F-4, and F-5.

[28] See for example the description of East Asian economic development by the World Bank (1993).

institutions improve and become more growth-friendly over the same period of time, but no institutional variables are included in the regression, then the TRADE variable will likely be given more credit for the economy's growth than is actually warranted. Skeptics of trade and growth regressions have also noted that the inclusion in growth regressions of a few countries like Taiwan, Korea, Singapore, and Hong Kong, open economies that grew very rapidly during the post World War II period, guaranteed that the TRADE coefficient would turn out positive even though for the rest of the sample the relationship between trade and growth was weak or nonexistent. This is a well-known econometric problem, namely that outliers have a disproportionate influence on regression results.

2.6.1 Levine and Renelt's Sensitivity Analysis

The obvious solution to omitted variable bias is to include all relevant variables in the regression. This is not usually possible, however. First of all, no one knows with certainty what all the relevant variables are. However, even if we knew exactly what variables influence economic growth, we seldom have accurate data with which to represent the variables, nor do we ever have enough observations, or degrees of freedom, to estimate regression equations with very large numbers of variables. Edward Leamer (1983, 1985b) has proposed *sensitivity analysis* to address these problems. Leamer's method is to run a very large number of regressions, with each regression combining the *focus variable*, trade in our case, with different subsets of all other possible explanatory variables. Leamer claims that if the coefficient of the focus variable remains significant and of the same sign as it is repeatedly combined with different combinations of other variables, then that variable can be assumed to be an unbiased explanatory variable.

Levine and Renelt (1992) reviewed the vast literature on the determinants of economic growth and found more than 50 variables that were statistically significant in at least one study. They apply Leamer's sensitivity analysis using data for over fifty variables for 119 countries over 1960-1989 and estimated repeated versions of the regression equation

$$(2\text{-}7) \qquad Y = \beta_I I + \beta_M M + \beta_Z Z + \mu$$

in which Y is the average annual growth rate of per capita GDP, I is a set of variables always included in the regression, M is the focus variable being tested for consistency across the many combinations of other expanatory variables, and Z includes other variables that past studies suggest as potentially important variables for explaining economic growth. For the **I** variables, Levine and Renelt included the investment share of GDP, the initial level of real GDP per capita in 1960, the secondary school enrollment rate, and the rate of population growth. Levine and Renelt found that these **I** variables explained about one-half of the cross-country variance in growth, which is not surprising given that three of the four variables in **I** are from the basic sources of growth equation. For each focus variable M, Levine and Renelt then introduced the remaining **Z** variables three at a time and ran repeated regressions.

Of the many focus variables tested, only the variable measuring the share of investment in GDP stood up to Leamer's stringent test that the regression coefficient remain of the same sign across all regressions. Levine and Renelt did "not find a robust independent relationship between any trade or international price-distortion indicator and growth."[29] However, they did find a robust relationship between the share of international trade and the share of investment in other regressions they ran, which led Levine and Renelt to conclude that the positive relationship between trade and growth found in so many other studies may be more driven by trade's positive effect on resource *accumulation* than on its effect on resource *allocation*. But they admitted this was pure speculation in their part.

2.6.2 Sala-i-Martin's Less Zealous Sensitivity Analysis

Sala-i-Martin (1997) argued that Levine and Renelt's requirement that variables be significant and of the same sign in all regressions was too strong. Random disturbances and omitted variables will inevitably prevent virtually every variable from passing this test, no matter how important the variable actually is for economic growth. He suggested an alternative test based on a confidence interval estimated from the variability of the variables themselves. Sala-i-Martin required only that 95% of a variable's coefficients have the same sign. He used the same equation (2-7) as Levine and Renelt. In his article, appropriately entitled "I Just Ran Two Million Regressions," Sala-i-Martin tested 62 variables that he found to be significantly correlated with growth in at least one regression in the vast empirical growth literature. He found 22 variables that fit his relaxed criteria for significance. These results were later replicated by Doppelhofer, Miller, and Sala-i-Martin (2000).

---

[29] Levine and Renelt (1992), p. 954.

Among Sala-i-Martin's (1997) 22 "robust" determinants of growth, there are four variables related to international trade: (1) years that the economy is open to trade, (2) the foreign exchange black market premium, (3) primary exports, and (4) exchange rate distortions. The first, second, and fourth variables are similar to the qualitative classifications of countries as being open or closed to trade. The latter two are similar to Dollar's approach described above. Sala-i-Martin also finds that primary product exports are negatively correlated with economic growth.

Table 2-8
Significant Variables from Sala-i-Martin's Two Million Regressions

Independent Variables	Coefficient Value	Standard Deviation	Percentage + or - Zero
Equipment Investment	0.2175	0.0408	100.0
Years of Open Economy	0.0195	0.0042	100.0
Fraction Confucian	0.0676	0.0149	100.0
Rule of Law	0.0190	0.0049	100.0
Fraction Muslim	0.0142	0.0035	100.0
Political Rights	-0.0026	0.0009	99.8
Latin America Dummy	-0.0115	0.0029	99.8
Sub-Saharan Africa Dummy	-0.0121	0.0032	99.7
Civil Liberties	-0.0029	0.0010	99.7
Revolutions and Coups	-0.0118	0.0045	99.5
Fraction of GDP in Mining	0.0353	0.0138	99.4
Black Market Premium	-0.0290	0.0118	99.3
Primary Exports	-0.0140	0.0053	99.0
Degree of Capitalism	0.0018	0.0008	98.7
War Dummy	-0.0056	0.0023	98.4
Non-equipment Invest.	0.0562	0.0242	98.2
Absolute Latitude	0.0002	0.0001	98.0
Exchange Rate Distortions	-0.0590	0.0302	96.8
Fraction Protestant	-0.0129	0.0053	96.6
Fraction Buddhist	0.0148	0.0076	96.4
Fraction Catholic	-0.0089	0.0034	96.3
Spanish Colony	-0.0065	0.0032	93.8

Source: Table I, Xavier Sala-i-Martin (1997), "I Just Ran Two Million Regressions," *American Economic Review*, Vol. 87(2), pp. 178-183.

As shown in Table 2-8, Sala-i-Martin found many other variables to have a robust influence on economic growth, several of which are institutional variables that are not normally included in growth equations. These results therefore support Rodriguez and Rodrik's (2001) point that a regression equation specified as a sources of growth equation augmented only by a TRADE variable and excluding any institutional variables are likely to generate biased estimates of trade's influence on economic growth. Rodrigues and Rodrik argue that many of the missing institutional variables are correlated with trade, which means that in a single equation model such as equation (2-1) omitted variable bias causes the estimated coefficient of the TRADE variable to overstate trade's influence on growth.

2.7 Testing *How* Trade Affects Growth

The empirical studies that so often find a positive correlation between trade and growth provide little insight into *how* international trade liberalization affects economic growth. When the relationship fails to materialize, as in the case of the poor economic growth in Latin America after the widespread opening to trade in the 1980s and 1990s, the models provide few insights into the reasons for the failure. There have been several innovative studies that do give us some insight into exactly *how* international trade influences economic growth, however. These empirical studies are worth reviewing here.

2.7.1 Distinguishing the Channels of Trade's Influence

Section 2.3 above described Feder's (1982) regression model that explicitly estimated the export sector's externalities to the rest of the economy. Feder found that marginal productivity was substantially higher in the export sector, and he therefore concluded that resources should be reallocated to the highly productive export sector. Frankel and Romer (1999), mentioned above as an example of instrumental variables estimation, specified a model that distinguished three *channels* through which trade has been hypothesized to influence real income. Frankel and Romer followed Hall and Jones (1999) and built a model derived from a Cobb-Douglas production function with labor-augmenting technological progress

$$(2\text{-}8) \qquad\qquad Y = K^\alpha \, (Ae^{\varphi E} \, L)^{1-\alpha}$$

where A is the level of technology and φ is a function that augments the labor force L by education E. Education is included as a proxy for human capital. With some manipulation, this equation is transformed into

(2-9) $\ln(Y_i/L_i) = \{\alpha/(1-\alpha)\}\ln(K_i/Y_i) + \varphi(E_i) + \ln A_i$

which expresses the log of the output per worker as the weighted sum of the log of capital relative to output, the level of education, and the level of technology in each sector i of the economy. In effect, this model specifies that per worker output grows as a result of (1) capital deepening, (2) human capital investment, and (3) the improvement in labor productivity.

Frankel and Romer then regress each of the three determinants of per worker output on an instrumental variable for international trade. Their results suggest that international trade has much less impact on capital depth and human capital accumulation than it has on technology: "a one-percentage point increase in the trade share raises the contributions of both physical capital depth and schooling by about one-half of a percentage point, and the contribution of technology to per capita output by about two percentage points."[30]

2.7.2 A Simultaneous-Equations "Channels" Model

Arguably the most ambitious attempt to model the channels through which international trade influences economic growth is Wacziarg (2001). He constructed an openness index for a large sample of countries, which he then used to test six potential channels through which international trade could affect economic growth. Specifically, Wacziarg hypothesized that trade affects economic growth through (1) macroeconomic policy quality, (2) government size, (3) price distortions or black market premium, (4) investment share of GDP, (5) technology, and (6) foreign direct investment.

Wacziarg set up a simultaneous equations model in which the first equation is a sources of growth equation augmented by a set of "channel variables" representing the channels through which trade influences economic growth. Specifically, Wacziarg's first equation is

(2-10) $PCY = a_0 + a_1 PCY_{1960} + a_2 FH + a_3 MH + a_4 MACRO + a_5 G$
    $+ a_6 BMP + a_7 INV + a_8 MFGEX + a_9 FDI,$

in which PCY is real per capita income, PCY_{1960} is *initial* per capita income, FH is female human capital, MH is male human capital, MACRO

---

[30] Frankel and Romer (1999), p. 390.

is macro policy quality, G is government consumption, BMP is black market premium, INV is the investment rate, MFGEX is manufactured exports (technology proxy), and FDI is foreign direct investment. The first three explanatory variables are the convergence and production variables found in many growth regressions, such as Barro (1997), Barro and Lee (1993), and Barro and Sala-i-Martin (2004). The last six explanatory variables represent the six channels through which trade is hypothesized to influence economic growth. The remaining six equations in the model explain each of the channel variables, and an index of an economy's openness to trade is among the explanatory variables in each of the "channel equations." The coefficient of the openness variable in each of the six channel equations measures the effect of trade on economic growth through each of the hypothesized channels. The full effect of trade on economic growth through each of the six channels is the product of (1) the coefficient of the channel in the growth equation and (2) the coefficient of the openness variable in the corresponding channel equation.

Table 2-9
Summary of Wacziarg's Channel Effects

Channel	Effect of Channel on Growth	Effect of Trade on Channel	Total Effect Trade on Growth
Black Market Premium	-0.007	-0.334	0.002
	(-9.08)**	(-0.63)	(0.63)
Government Consumption	-0.042	0.154	-0.007
	(-1.57)	(3.73)**	(-1.52)
Manufactured Exports	0.004	0.635	0.002
	(0.45)	(4.59)**	(0.45)
Investment Rate	0.143	0.317	0.045
	(6.86)**	(6.72)**	(5.12)**
FDI	0.320	0.045	0.014
	(4.68)**	(4.01)**	(3.79)**
Macro Policy Quality	0.489	0.027	0.013
	(4.22)**	(2.19)**	(1.90)**
Total Effect			0.071
			(5.94)**

Figures in parentheses are *t*-statistics. ** Indicates significance at the 95% level.
Source: Roman Wacziarg (2001), "Mesuring the Dynamic Gains from Trade," *World Bank Economic Review*, Vol. 15(3), p. 408.

Table 2-9 summarizes Wacziarg's results. Openness raises growth through five of the six channels. The only negative channel is government consumption. After accounting for all six channels, a 10 percent increase in the trade openness measure is associated with a 0.71 percent increase in annual growth rates. The most important channels are investment, which accounts for 63 percent of trade's total growth effect, technology transmission (22.5 percent of trade's total growth effect), and stabilizing macroeconomic policy (18 percent of trade's total growth effect).

Wacziarg's results are compatible with Levine and Renelt's (1992) findings that international trade acts through investment to influence economic growth, as well as others' findings that trade influences the rate of technological progress. Wacziarg's finding that trade enhances the quality of macroeconomic policy provides some insight into why it has proven difficult to separate the growth effect of international trade from the growth effects of other economic institutions. Trade may influence growth through other institutions. Many researchers have noted that trade policy is closely correlated with other macroeconomic policies.

2.8 Summary and Assessment of the Empirical Results

Most of the empirical studies testing the hypothesis that international trade raises the rate of economic growth have used linear regression models to test the effect of international trade on economic growth. A few studies have introduced innovative statistical methods to extract useful information from the data that the standard regression studies ignored. The results of these many statistical studies suggest that trade liberalization not only has a statistically significant effect on human welfare, but the effect is also *economically significant*. On average, the cross-section and time-series studies suggest that the rate of growth of real GDP rises by about 0.20 percentage points for every 1 percentage point increase in the growth rate of international trade. The importance of such a modest increase in the rate of economic growth is derived from the power of compounding. For example, an economy that puts in place free trade policies that cause its international trade to grow 5 percentage points faster than trade grows in its more protectionist neighbor will grow about one percentage point faster than its neighbor, all other things equal. After one century, a one percent faster growth rate translates into a per capita GDP that is 2.7 times as large as its neighbor's. That is the difference between a highly developed economy's per capita income of $27,000 per capita and a middle-income developing economy's per capita income of $10,000.

Many economists accept the statistical studies as proof of trade's positive role in the growth process. Srinivasan (1997) examined many of the weaknesses of the empirical studies of trade and growth and concludes that:

> Nonetheless, the fact that a number of studies using different data sets, countries and methodologies happened to arrive at similar conclusions...that are also consistent with a priori reasoning, suggests that they deserve serious consideration, with due allowances being made for their conceptual and statistical deficiencies.[31]

That is, the huge set of statistical studies together form a very large robust study whose results consistently show trade to be positively correlated with economic growth. Individual studies that sought robustness by simultaneously testing many different regression models in a broad variety of specifications have also found trade and openness to be significant. The studies by Levine and Renelt (1992), Sala-i-Martin (1997), and Edwards (1998) stand out in this respect. Also strengthening the results of the many statistical studies is our finding that the conclusions of statistical studies have not changed much even as more sophisticated estimation methods were employed to deal with the many statistical shortcomings of the earlier studies.

The numerous consistent statistical results have not yet definitively decided the matter of how international trade and economic growth are related, however. Not all of the econometric concerns have been convincingly overcome yet, and new concerns continue to appear. For example, Florax, de Groot, and Heijungs (2002) have found a very large number of potential models that could explain any observed economic behavior, and therefore studies that just examine a small number of alternatives cannot be said to robustly *prove* a specific model's validity. Equally disturbing is Rodriguez and Rodrik's (1999, 2001) argument that international trade policy is so closely correlated with many other economic policies that it is impossible to differentiate between the trade's effect on growth and the growth effects of those other policies. They strongly suggest that economic growth probably depends more on "those other policies" than trade policy. Rodrik, Subramanian, and Trebbi (2002) recently showed that trade actually becomes an insignificant variable in a growth equation that includes explicit variables representing a number of institutional factors. Things like the rule of law, property rights, human

---

[31] Srinivasan (1997), p. 36.

rights, patents and copyrights, a consistent legal system, and many other institutions seem to be more important for growth than opening the borders to trade. Rigobon and Rodrik (2004) employed a new econometric method to compensate for simultaneous effects of many variables, which is called identification through heteroskedasticity. They found that in the presence of other institutional variables, their openness variable actually has a *negative* impact on income levels. Lee, Ricci, and Rigobon (2005) used the same method with a different model and found that trade's influence on growth is reduced well below most earlier estimates, although it is still positive.

Many critics of the empirical studies surveyed in this chapter have argued that the statistical analysis has given us few insights into precisely *why* trade is positively correlated with economic growth. A few innovative empirical studies have tried to distinguish the channels of influence through which trade enhances economic growth, but the results so far are little more than suggestive. Feder (1982) found that there are externalities to exporting. Levine and Renelt (1992), Wacziarg (2001), and Hall and Jones (1999) argued that trade is likely to stimulate investment. Wacziarg (2001), Edwards (1998), and Frankel and Romer (1999) presented evidence suggesting that trade raises the rate of economic growth by generating technology transfers. Wacziarg (2001) also presented evidence showing that trade promoted trade-enhancing foreign direct investment and it may encourage more economically friendly macroeconomic policies. Empirical tests of specific channels of influence have been few in number, however. Studies such as Wacziarg's are at this point little more than suggestions for continued research.

It is not clear to what degree these latter studies undermine the many studies that have found trade and growth to be significantly and substantially related. What is clear from the recent empirical work, however, is that international trade's effect on economic growth is intertwined with many other influences on growth. At the end of his survey of individual country case studies and recent empirical studies dealing with the relationship between international trade and growth, Baldwin (2003) sums up the situation well:

> It is true developing countries are often given the advice that decreasing trade barriers is a more effective way of achieving higher sustainable rates of growth than tightening trade restrictions. But...those giving such advice also emphasize the need, as a minimum, for a stable and non-discriminatory exchange-rate system

and usually also the need for prudent monetary and fiscal policies and corruption-free administration of economic policies for trade liberalization to be effective in the long-run. It seems to me that the various country studies do support this type of policy advice and the cross-country statistical studies do not overturn this conclusion. But the recent critiques of the latter studies demonstrate that we must be careful in attributing any single economic policy, such as the lowering of trade barriers, as being a sufficient government action for accelerating the rate of economic growth.[32]

It is also important to note that, despite their critical view of the recent statistical research, Rodriguez and Rodrik state that they "know of no credible evidence–at least for the post-1945 period–that suggests that trade restrictions are systematically associated with higher growth rates."[33] Or, as Benjamin Franklin stated at the head of this chapter, "No nation was ever ruined by trade." Thus, we are left with the conclusion that international trade is most likely good for growth and unlikely to be the cause of economic stagnation, but by itself trade does not guarantee that an economy will experience a rising standard of living.

These tentative conclusions are reminiscent of the conflict between D. H. Robertson's (1931) claim that trade was "the engine of growth," and Irving Kravis' (1970) later qualification that trade is more likely to be just a "handmaiden of growth." That is, the empirical evidence does not clearly establish whether international trade itself drives economic growth or whether it merely accompanies economic growth. Policy makers are, therefore, faced with the difficult choice between actively promoting free trade or focusing on other policies and institutions that may be more important for achieving rapid economic growth.

After so many regressions, the challenge for economists is now to build better models and to put forward more precise and probing hypotheses to test. Merely adding more variables and new data sets to the same basic regression models will probably not get us much closer to a fundamental understanding of exactly how trade influences economic growth. One obvious route for economists at this point is to develop more detailed dynamic models of trade and growth that can give us more insight and help us formulate more precise hypotheses to test. More accurate models could

---

[32] Baldwin (2003).

[33] Rodriguez and Rodrik (1999), p. 37.

also permit us to estimate the magnitudes, and thus economic importance, of the many variables that are part of the growth process. The remaining chapters of this book examine what economists already know about the process of economic growth and the role of international trade in that process. You will be pleasantly surprised by how much we already know.

Chapter Three

International Trade
and
Factor Accumulation

Knowledge is the only instrument of production not subject to diminishing returns.
        (J.M. Clark)[34]

The search for logically sound and convincing explanations of why economic growth is closely correlated with international trade necessarily takes us into the field of economic growth. This field of economics has been very active in the last two decades, and with the help of two centuries of accumulated economic thought economists now have a good understanding of the process of economic growth. Most important, we have insightful models of the process of technological change. This chapter makes it clear why these latter models are so important: technological progress is the fundamental driving force of long-run economic growth.

The fundamental concepts embodied in the growth models we use today date from earlier economists. The first section of this chapter discusses the ideas of Adam Smith, who had quite a bit to say about growth and trade in his great work, *The Wealth of Nations*. Very important for the development of growth models is the concept of diminishing returns, and we use it to examine the economic growth in the presence of fixed factors of production. In the second section of this chapter there is a brief

---

[34] J.M. Clark is an early 20th century American institutional economist whose work contributed to the development of modern macroeconomics.

description of the Harrod-Domar growth model that was popular when interest in economic growth revived after World War II. The chapter concludes with a rigorous development of the neoclassical model of economic growth developed by Robert Solow in the 1950s.

Over 200 years ago, Adam Smith described economic growth as a welfare-enhancing process that was driven by both investment in capital and innovation. That is, the growth in real per capita output is the result of either (1) an increase in the amount of productive resources or (2) an improvement in the technology that defines the economy's efficiency with which it can transform its resources into welfare-enhancing goods and services. Subsequently, models have varied in their emphasis on factor accumulation and technological progress. Robert Solow's well-known growth model shows clearly that factor accumulation alone cannot explain the spectacular growth experienced by many countries over the past two centuries.

Recently, economists have made progress in explaining the process of technological innovation. The two following chapters describe recent models of technological progress. Together with the basic Solow growth model presented in this chapter, these models together form a logically sound analytical framework for analyzing economic growth. The conclusion that technological progress is fundamental to the long-run process of economic growth implies that if international trade does indeed have a positive effect on long-run economic growth it must in some way facilitate the creation and adoption of new knowledge and technology. But now we are getting way ahead of our story. We begin by reviewing the historical ideas on economic growth that influenced the development of today's most popular growth models. We will, of course, fit international trade into the discussion whenever possible.

3.1 The Early Growth Models

Adam Smith is best known for his 1776 work entitled *An Inquiry into the Nature and Causes of the Wealth of Nations*, usually referred to simply as *The Wealth of Nations*. In his *Wealth of Nations*, Smith sought to explain how a nation's economy could increase the wealth of its citizens. Living at the start of the Industrial Revolution, he was fascinated by the economic changes that he was witnessing. He was keenly aware of what was driving those changes.

3.1.1 Adam Smith on Specialization and Exchange

Adam Smith combined his keen observation of his contemporary Europe, especially England and Scotland, with his vast knowledge of economic history to conclude that one of the fundamental characteristics of growing economies was the increasing specialization of individual economic activities:

> The greatest improvements in the productive powers of labour, and the greater part of the skill, dexterity, and judgement with which it is any where directed, or applied, seem to have been the effects of the division of labour.[35]

Smith's appreciation for the gains from specialization, or what he refers to as the *division of labor*, led him logically to the concept of absolute advantage, a close cousin to the important principle of *comparative advantage* attributed to David Ricardo several decades later. Smith's explanation of how specialization and international exchange raised human welfare was not just related to his interest in international trade. More fundamentally, Smith was interested in international trade because he saw it as part of the process of economic growth. The division of labor required that people exchange goods and services. The more people could trade, the more specialization (division of labor) would occur, and hence the greater would be economic growth. Why cut this welfare-enhancing trade and specialization short by stopping at the border?

In his analysis of the Industrial Revolution that was beginning to transform the societies and economies of Scotland and England, Adam Smith used his famous story of the pin maker to explain another important dynamic phenomenon that we now call *economies of scale*. Smith noted the large differences in productivity between the traditional cottage system of production and the *factory system* that characterized the Industrial Revolution. He explained that these differences in productivity required large-scale factories; they could not be generated by simply multiplying the number of cottage industries. Large-scale production and the specialization, or division of labor, that goes along with the factory system, was nothing other than a form of technological change, which we now know is the fundamental source of economic growth.

---

[35] Smith (1776[1976]), Volume 1, p. 7.

3.1.2 Specialization and Technological Progress

Smith's writings optimistically suggested that economic growth could continue indefinitely into the future so long as there were no obstacles to ever greater division of labor. His optimism was also influenced by his view of specialization not only as a source of one time gains in efficiency, but also as an incentive for continued technological progress:

> the invention of all those machines by which labour is so much facilitated and abridged, seems to have been originally owing to the division of labour. Men are much more likely to discover easier and readier methods of attaining any object, when the whole attention of their minds is directed towards the single object, than when it is dissipated among a great variety of things.[36]

Specialization makes it more likely that people will develop new tools and technologies to assist them in performing their specialized tasks. And Smith's suggestion that people "are much more likely to discover easier and readier methods of attaining any object, when the whole attention of their minds is directed towards the single object" is closely related to a concept that we now refer to as *learning-by-doing*. This idea has been incorporated into several recent growth models, and it enables the economy to permanently generate technological progress and economic growth.

Smith also recognized that technological improvements were often the result of intentional efforts to invent, innovate, and explore. Smith pointed out that with specialization, some people may come to specialize in innovation:

> All the improvements in machinery, however, have by no means been the invention of those who had occasion to use the machines. Many improvements have been made by the ingenuity of the makers of machines, when to make them became the business of a peculiar trade; and some by that of those who are called philosophers or men of speculation, whose trade is not to do any thing, but to observe every thing; and who, upon that account, are often capable of combining together the powers of the most distant and dissimilar objects. In the progress of society, philosophy or speculation becomes, like every other employment, the principal or sole trade and occupation of a particular class of citizens.... Each citizen

---

[36] Smith (1776[1976]), Volume 1, p. 13.

becomes more expert in his own peculiar branch, more work is done upon the whole, and the quantity of science is considerably increased by it.[37]

These "philosophers and speculators" are now usually referred to as *entrepreneurs,* those energetic and risk-loving individuals who play a central role in the process of economic growth in a popular model developed by the twentieth century economist Joseph Schumpeter. Smith also seems to be suggesting in the above quote that the new technologies developed by the entrepreneurs are made available to the rest of the economy "embodied" in the machines provided by the capital goods sector of the economy. Some other recent growth models are based on this insight and describe technological progress as a function of investment in new equipment that embodies new techniques.

3.1.3 The Importance of Institutions

Smith is often criticized for suggesting *laissez faire* is the best policy in all circumstances. However, those who have actually read *The Wealth of Nations* know that Smith was quite modern in his recognition of the need to establish a variety of *institutions* if markets are to work properly. By institutions we mean such things as laws, rules, regulations, customs, justice systems, traditions, religions, and many other assorted social pressures that encourage or constrain people in their quest to maximize their welfare. Smith was convinced that for specialization to continue expanding and for it to generate further technology improvements, a limited government was necessary. For innovation and specialization to flourish, it was necessary for government to protect person and property, maintain law and order, and operate a fair and predictable legal system. Also useful was the role of government in establishing copyright and patent protection, building commercial institutions such as contract law and uniform weights and measures, and regulating the supply of "coin and currency." Smith's recognition of the importance of managing the supply of coin and currency reflected his knowledge of the Dutch economy, which had achieved rapid economic growth by developing its commercial activities well before Britain achieved its growth acceleration with its Industrial Revolution.[38]

---

[37] Smith (1776[1976]), Volume 1, pp. 13-14.

[38] The Dutch economic historians de Vries and van der Woude (1997) mention the "monetization" of the Dutch economy back in the early 1500s as one of the critical contributors to Holland's subsequent economic growth.

The exchanges necessary for specialization are much easier when money replaces barter. In short, while Smith was certainly no champion of expansive government interference in the economy, he fully appreciated the government's role in maintaining and managing many of the complex institutions necessary in a capitalist economy.

3.1.4 Transportation and Communications

Smith saw reductions in transport costs that made it easier to move goods between buyers and sellers located in different regions as conducive to specialization and economic growth. To emphasize the universal importance of transportation for specialization, Smith wrote:

> The sovereigns of China, those of Bengal..., and those of Egypt, are said accordingly to have been extremely attentive to the making and maintaining of good roads and navigable canals, in order to increase, as much as possible, both the quantity and value of every part of the produce of the land, by procuring to every part of it the most extensive market which their own dominions could afford.[39]

In the case of China, Smith was undoubtedly referring to China during the Sung dynasty between the 8th and 12th centuries, when the Chinese government constructed a 30,000 mile long national network of canals to unify the country. As Kelly (1997) details, the Chinese economy grew rapidly with the construction of the waterways because trade expanded, money came into general usage, and specialization allowed levels of industrial productivity not seen again in the world until the Industrial Revolution took hold in Europe in the 1800s. Kelly refers to Chinese growth at that time as *Smithian growth*, spurred by increased specialization.

3.1.5 National Welfare

Yet another of Adam Smith's contributions to growth theory is his clear explanation of what constitutes the economic welfare of a nation. Prior to the writings of Smith and others influenced by the Enlightenment, a nation's welfare was usually viewed in terms of the strength of a nation's military, the health of particular sectors of the economy, or the size of a nation's population and territory. Smith saw national welfare "according to which its produce is naturally distributed among the different ranks and

---

[39] Smith (1776[1976]), Volume 2, p. 364.

conditions of men in the society."[40]   This concern with the "general welfare" of the population was radical in Smith's day, but it is fundamental to welfare analysis today.

3.1.6 A Graphic Smithian Growth Model

Smith never presented a formal model of economic growth, but if we put together his various ideas on economic growth it is possible to construct a model of economic growth with two distinct sources of economic growth, one directly linked to specific *increases* in specialization, the other related to how the *level* of specialization encourages the creation of new ideas. In the first case, every time specialization increases, there are new gains from exchange as individuals, firms, and entire countries exploit the gains from comparative advantage and increasing returns to scale. These gains in specialization may be due to sudden changes in institutions, transportation improvements, or sudden breakthroughs in human knowledge. Secondly, as the *level* of specialization increases, individuals and firms are more likely to "discover easier and readier methods of attaining any object, when the whole attention of their minds is directed towards the single object, than when it is dissipated among a great variety of things."[41] That is, the amount of learning-by-doing from concentrating on specialized tasks increases with the level of specialization. Also, the specialization of people in the tasks associated with invention and innovation, entrepreneurship, becomes possible the more specialized society becomes. Therefore, the rate of technological progress increases as specialization increases.

The Smithian growth model is depicted graphically in Figure 3-1. Suppose the level of per capita income at time t=0 is equal to A, the result of past factor accumulation and innovation. As time passes, from t=0 to t=1, innovation, research, discovery, and learning by doing are continually taking place. Between t=0 and t=1 per capita income grows to B as the economy traces out the *growth path* Ab, whose slope depends on the amount of innovation that the degree of specialization and society's institutions stimulate. At t=1, suppose that the introduction of money permits a sudden increase in specialization, which raises per capita income to C. Then, innovation, research, discovery, and learning-by-doing continue at a higher rate because specialization is greater allowing an even greater "direction of the minds towards single objects." Note that the

---

[40] Smith (1776[1976]), Volume 1, p. 2.

[41] Smith (1776[1976]), Volume 1, p. 13.

segment cd of the economy's growth path rises at a more rapid rate than it did before the increase in specialization.

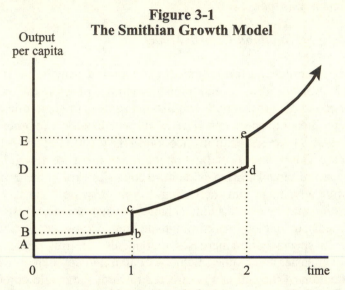

Figure 3-1
The Smithian Growth Model

Suppose a second institutional change, say a switch to free trade, occurs at t=2. There will be another sudden jump in specialization, causing per capita income to rise from D to E. With the greater specialization permitted by free trade, the economy's growth path rises more steeply after t=2 as the rate of technological progress accelerates through learning-by-doing and specialized entrepreneurial efforts. Smithian economic growth thus consists of both discrete jumps caused by institutional changes, advances in transportation, the invention of money, etc., and continuous technological progress between the sudden discrete jumps that depends on the level of specialization. Increases in specialization drive innovation, the resulting technology growth in turn drives further specialization, which then stimulates further innovation. In the Smithian model, international trade has a very positive effect on economic growth. A sudden shift in trade policy that opens up new trade provides an immediate gain in real per capita income, which, in turn, accelerates technological progress and increases the rate of economic growth permanently.

Smith also recognized that new technologies were often embodied in equipment, so that international trade of the equipment enhances the spread of technology. In sum, the Smithian model links trade to both a one-time gain in per capita output, as prescribed by traditional models of international trade, and the permanent increase in the rate of economic growth found by the many econometric studies.

3.2 The Classical Economists and Diminishing Returns

The foundation of modern growth theory was built by many economists since the time of Adam Smith. Modern growth theorists have borrowed from the entire history of economic thought in order to build a logical set of models that have proven useful to modern policy makers. One of the concepts that has become central to modern growth models is *diminishing returns*. This concept was applied to the process of economic growth by Thomas Malthus, David Ricardo, John Stuart Mill, and other early 19th century economists.

3.2.1 An Example of Diminishing Returns

To illustrate diminishing returns, suppose that output, Y, is a function of labor, L, and land, N. Suppose, furthermore, that the *production function* is of the general form

(3-1) $$Y = f(L,N)$$

Finally, suppose that the stock of land is in fixed supply. In the absence of technological progress, the only way to increase output is therefore to increase the amount of labor. But, because labor is combined with a fixed stock of land, labor is subject to diminishing returns. That is, as more and more labor is added to the production process, output rises but by smaller and smaller increments.

Production functions subject to diminishing returns to labor are illustrated in Figure 3-2. For a quantity of labor of 2 and a fixed quantity of 100 units of land for the labor to work with, output is equal to 15 units, a rise of 15 units compared to when no labor is employed. When another 2 units of labor are employed, output rises to 20, a

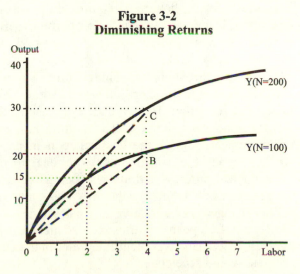

Figure 3-2
Diminishing Returns

marginal increase of only 5 units. Because the quantity of other factors like land is fixed, labor is subject to diminishing returns. Diminishing returns causes the average product of labor to fall from $15/2 = 7.5$ to $20/4 = 5$. This fall in average product is also evidenced by the difference in the slopes of the lines connecting the origin with points A and B.

Figure 3-2 can be used to show that diminishing returns to labor can be avoided if the quantity of land is expanded proportionately along with labor. Suppose the increase in land from 100 to 200 units raises the entire production function for labor from $Y(N=100)$ to $Y(N=200)$. Therefore, if the increase in labor from 2 to 4 units is accompanied by an increase in land from 100 to 200 units, the economy moves from the combination A to C and output increases from 15 to 30 units. Now there is no diminishing returns to labor as inputs and output all increase by the same proportion. This example illustrates *constant returns to scale*, the situation in which, when all inputs are increased by the same proportion, the marginal and average products of all factors remain unchanged.

This example provides an important insight about economic growth. Because economic growth is defined as an improvement in human welfare, as Adam Smith advocated, economic growth must be quantified in terms of per capita real income, not total income. Thus, our example of constant returns to scale in which output increases from 15 to 30 while the labor force grows from 2 to 4 illustrates a case of economic stagnation, not economic growth. Granted, stagnation is better than decline, which is what happens when diminishing returns reduced labor's average product. Economic growth, however, requires output to increase faster than the quantity of labor, namely that the economy experience *increasing returns to scale*.

The concept of diminishing returns is important because the world is likely, at least in the short run, to face diminishing returns to individual factors of production. There are always reasons why the quantity of some factors cannot easily be expanded. Diminishing returns may have seemed especially worrisome to the classical economists of the early 19th century. At that time, the world was experiencing population growth and technological progress had always been a very slow and erratic process. Therefore, it was natural for the early economists to focus on the problem of increasing workers relative to what seemed to be a fixed quantity of fertile land. European countries avoided income declines by sending people overseas where land was plentiful. Later in the 19th century, technological progress would accelerate.

3.2.2 Diminishing Returns and Technology

Figure 3-2 can be used to analyze the relationship between diminishing returns and technological progress. Suppose that the two production functions represent two different levels of technology rather than two different amounts of "other factors" like land. It should be obvious that an improvement in technology can enable the economy to overcome diminishing returns. If technology puts the economy on the higher production function in Figure 3-2 at the same time that the labor force doubles from 2 to 4, per worker output remains unchanged. It is because of diminishing returns, therefore, that technology plays a critical role in the process of economic growth. Had there been no technological progress, diminishing returns to labor implies that the increase in the labor force from 2 to 4 units would have caused a decline in per capita output. In fact, it should be clear that technology must raise the production function faster than the labor force increases in order for the economy to experience true economic growth in the form of continually rising per capita incomes.

3.2.3 Diminishing Returns and Population Growth

The evidence available to the classical economists in 1800 shows that population growth had consistently caused standards of living to revert back to subsistence levels. As Table 3-1 shows, per capita real income remained nearly constant for the 1,800 years between 0 and 1820. Population growth gradually accelerated over that period, but average output per person hardly changed at all despite advances in technology and the increased "division of labor" brought about by urbanization, improved transportation, and the introduction of coin and currency. In effect, gradual rises in the production function were almost entirely offset by increases in the labor force, and diminishing returns kept per capita output nearly constant despite occasional technological progress. The evidence suggests that in a world where production is subject to diminishing returns and technological progress is very slow, population growth is detrimental to economic growth.

The stagnation of per capita real income actually extends back to the emergence of humans a few hundred thousand years ago, and to the ancestors of modern humans before that. For nearly all of their history, humans lived as hunters and gatherers at a *subsistence* level of output, which is the level that provides just enough consumption to maintain the species and, perhaps, permit some very slow growth in numbers. According to Pritchett (1997), the subsistence level of output at Maddison's 1990 U.S. dollar prices cannot be lower than about $250 per year, or $.68 per day, per person. It is difficult to imagine anyone sustaining life with food, clothing, and shelter worth less than that, no matter how benign the climate and how basic the food and shelter. By the year 10,000 B.C. the human race had already existed for 99 percent of its total existence on earth, but the total human population was probably still less than five million.[42] Population growth accelerated with the transition from hunting and gathering to farming, a major shift in technology that occurred in much of the world between 10,000 and 5000 B.C. However, even at the height of the Roman Empire there were still less than 200 million people on earth, nearly all living at or near subsistence levels.

Table 3-1
Annual Percentage Economic Growth Rates: 0 - 2001

Years	World Population (millions)	World GDP (billions $1990)	Per Capita GDP ($1990)
0-1000	0.01	0.01	0.00
1000-1500	0.10	0.15	0.05
1500-1820	0.27	0.32	0.05
1820-2001	0.98	2.21	1.22

Source: Angus Maddison (2001), *The World Economy: A Millennial Perspective*, Paris: OECD, Tables 1-1, 1-2, 1-3 on p. 28, and Appendix Tables B-10, B-11, B-18, B-19, B-21, B-22. Angus Maddison (2003), *The World Economy: Historical Statistics*, Paris: OECD, Tables 8a, 8b, and 8c on pp. 256-263.

Some classical economists, most notably Malthus (1798), argued that there was a direct relationship between improvements in per capita real income and population growth. They claimed that higher income improved nutrition and living conditions, which reduced death rates and increased birth rates, thereby accelerating population growth. Diminishing returns, on the other hand, translated the higher population growth back into falling per capita real incomes, thus creating a vicious cycle from economic growth to population growth to economic contraction. The writings of Malthus and other classical economists went well beyond such a dismal

---

[42] These population figures are from Kremer (1993).

scenario, and they were aware of the potential role for technology in avoiding eternal poverty. Recall that Adam Smith was well aware of the role of entrepreneurs in producing invention and spurring technological progress. Nevertheless, the idea that population growth reduces human welfare remains popular today even though our experience over the past 200 years shows that society can overcome both diminishing returns and population growth to greatly increase average per capita real incomes. The estimates for the years after 1820 in Table 3-1 make that very clear. Nevertheless, it should also be clear from both the pre-1820 data and the theoretical analysis above that continued economic growth can only occur so long as the production function shifts up fast enough to overcome diminishing returns. This is the reason why modern growth theory devotes so much time to explaining technological progress.

3.2.4 International Trade's Role in the Growth Process

The role of international trade in the classical or "Malthusian" model of diminishing returns is obvious. Standard models of international trade show that trade effectively increases the efficiency with which an economy's resources are transformed into welfare-enhancing goods and services. The expansion of international trade therefore represents a spurt of technological progress. Prior to 1800, positive productivity shocks occurred, as with the gradual expansion of trade or improvements in machines, but they were apparently not frequent enough to overcome diminishing returns to the gradually rising population. Hence, since trade grew slowly but people's standards of living barely changed, there was no apparent correlation between trade and growth.

After 1820, however, the growth of international trade coincided with humanity's escape from poverty toward ever-higher real per capita incomes, a process that continues today. Note in Table 3-1 how the rate of economic growth surges during the period 1820-2001. How was this great escape from eternal poverty possible? You might expect that economists would have focused on the unprecedented acceleration of economic growth in the 1800s, but most did not. After the early 19th century classical economists examined the growth process, mainstream economics directed its attention elsewhere. In fact, one of the great mysteries of economic thought is why, precisely when unprecedented rates of economic growth and technological progress were being achieved, economists seemed to devote so little effort to explaining it. Marx, of course, developed an all-encompassing model of economic and political change in the mid-19th century, but in the latter half of the 1800s economists were more focused on developing much of the static theory that is now called microeconomics. This may explain why international trade theory came to be largely based on the traditional static microeconomic concepts such as supply and demand, consumer surplus, general equilibrium, the production possibilities frontier, and indifference curves rather than growth theory. In the 1930s, in response to the Great Depression, John Maynard Keynes developed his well-known macroeconomic model that provided the standard framework for determining macroeconomic policy for several decades after World War II. The Keynesian model was designed to address the pressing problem of unemployment, however, not to explain long-run economic growth.

3.3 The Harrod-Domar Growth Model

Interest in economic growth resumed after World War II when the Cold War featured two rival economic systems vying for the world's favor. The independence of many former colonies, which were relatively poor compared to the world's major economies, created a battleground for the competing ideologies. There was a clear need for economic models to explain growth or, in the case of some countries, the lack thereof. A growth model that was very popular after World War II was the Harrod-Domar model, presented independently in separate articles by Harrod (1939) and Domar (1946). The Harrod-Domar model is quite simple, which no doubt helps to explain its popularity. Unfortunately, as Easterly (1999) emphasized, it was also inaccurate and often quite damaging when used to guide economic policy. The Harrod-Domar model was based on the Keynesian macroeconomic model, which made it a short-run model appropriate only for analyzing short-run economic changes and not for analyzing long-run economic change. A brief discussion of the Harrod-Domar model is in order, if for no other reason than to force us to question how such an inaccurate model could gain such prominence.

3.3.1 The Basic Harrod-Domar Model

Assume that the economy's output, Y, consists of two categories of commodities, consumption goods, C, and investment goods, I:

(3-2) $$Y = C + I$$

Investment is defined as the change in the stock of capital, K. Using the symbol "Δ" for "change in," we can substitute ΔK for I in equation (3-2) to derive

(3-3) $$Y = C + \Delta K$$

Note that the assumption that the change in the capital stock is equal to investment implies that the capital stock never wears out or becomes obsolete, that there is no depreciation. This is clearly a weakness in the Harrod-Domar model; in the long run, capital most definitely depreciates. Finally, Harrod and Domar assumed a constant capital-output ratio $K/Y = \gamma$, which effectively makes output proportional to the stock of capital. Hence, the production function can be written as

(3-4) $$Y = (1/\gamma)K = AK$$

where $A = (1/\gamma)$. There clearly are no diminishing returns to capital in this model.

The Harrod-Domar model effectively assumes that there is an unlimited stock of other factors available to combine with capital so that there are constant returns to scale. If we remember that both Harrod and Domar based their growth model on the Keynesian macroeconomic model, it is obvious where their assumption comes from. The Keynesian model was designed to explain the persistence of the depression during the 1930s, and it also assumed unlimited factor availability. An important implication of a constant capital-output ratio is that the *change* in output is proportional to the *change* in the stock of capital, or

(3-5) $$\Delta Y = (1/\gamma)\Delta K = A\Delta K$$

For the economy to invest in capital, there must be saving. If people save a constant fraction σ, where $0 < \sigma < 1$, of their income, then the change in the capital stock is

(3-6) $$\Delta K = I = S = \sigma Y$$

Combining equations (3-5) and (3-6), it follows that

(3-7) $$\Delta Y = A\sigma Y$$

Dividing both sides of equation (3-7) by Y and recalling that the ratio of the *change* over the *level* represents the rate of growth of Y, G_Y, we find that

(3-8) $$\Delta Y/Y = G_Y = \sigma A = \sigma/\gamma$$

The model thus shows that the growth rate of the economy is a constant, determined by the economy's rate of savings, σ, and the technical capital-output ratio, γ. Hence, as long as investment increases the stock of capital, growth will continue indefinitely. The Harrod-Domar model is, therefore, an example of a model that attributes economic growth exclusively to factor accumulation.

The simplicity of Harrod-Domar model no doubt contributed to its popularity. Anyone could become a development planner. Just set a goal for growth, say 10 percent per year, estimate the capital-output ratio, and you can calculate exactly how much society must save in order to achieve the target growth rate. If the capital-output ratio is 2, for example, then the country needs a saving rate of 20 percent for it to grow 10 percent per year. Such a saving rate could be achieved by providing incentives for people to save, forcing people to save through regulation and taxation, or borrowing savings abroad. Unfortunately, in the real world things seldom work out as planned.

3.3.2 The Experience of the Harrod-Domar Model

The Harrod-Domar model says nothing about how savings are channeled to investment projects. It suggested that all that mattered for growth was *how much* was invested, and that *how* savings were invested mattered little at all. The Harrod-Domar model's assumptions of a constant capital-output ratio and the elastic supply of labor were inappropriate assumptions for a growth model. Economic growth is a long-run phenomenon, and in the long run, the supply of labor is not infinite. With limited supplies of labor, the capital-labor ratio in production is not a constant, and thus the marginal product of capital is not a constant either. Indeed, the capital-output ratio varies widely over time and from country to country.

In regard to our purpose in this book, the Harrod-Domar model seems to offer no obvious role for international trade in the process of economic growth. What matters for growth is the rate of saving and investment. Many development economists and policy makers in the 1940s, 1950s, and 1960s, in fact, argued that the rate of saving could be raised whether the economy was open or closed to trade. Some even argued that it is easier to raise the rate of saving, and hence the rate of growth, when domestic consumers were not tempted to consume attractive foreign products, implying that trade had a negative influence on growth.

There are subtle ways in which trade does enter the Harrod-Domar model, however. Most important, trade can serve as an influence on how savings are invested. Note that the model implicitly assumes that all savings are somehow productively invested. In reality, the allocation of savings is seldom fully efficient. Meier (1988) argued that the East Asian economies were successful because their policies of promoting exports created a strong link between a country's comparative advantage and domestic investment. The large studies on trade and development sponsored by the National Bureau of Economic Research (NBER) and the World Bank emphasized that trade restrictions in developing countries seriously distorted domestic prices, thus causing savings to be misallocated. These studies are detailed by Bhagwati (1978), Krueger (1978), and Papageorgiou, Michaely, and Choski (1991). In terms of the logic of the Harrod-Domar model, what these studies concluded was that in an open economy prices more accurately reflect true opportunity costs. More accurate prices improve the allocation of resources, which effectively implies a lower capital output ratio and, hence, a higher rate of economic growth.

While the Harrod-Domar growth model provides some potentially useful insights, its overall view of the growth process is potentially misleading. Recently, Easterly (2001) lamented the continued application of the model by World Bank economists and elsewhere. Most economists have abandoned the model, however. Most telling are Evsey Domar's (1957) sentiments a decade after his paper was published, when he claimed he had an "ever-guilty conscience" about his model. He explained that he no longer saw his model as an appropriate one for analyzing long-run economic growth, and that in fact he had never intended it to be used for that purpose. In withdrawing his own model from discussions about economic growth, Domar instead endorsed the model developed in the 1950s by Robert Solow.

3.4 Robert Solow and His Neoclassical Growth Model

Robert Solow won the Nobel Prize in economics for his contributions to growth theory. His growth model has come to be known simply as the *Solow model*. Solow's (1956, 1957) model was a response to the Harrod-Domar model and some of its obvious weaknesses, especially its assumption of a constant capital-output ratio. Because Solow incorporated the "marginalist" thinking of the nineteenth century classical economists, his model is often also referred to as the *neoclassical* growth model.

3.4.1 The Production Function

The simplest form of the Solow model specifies a general production function in which output, Y, is a function of the quantity of capital, K, and labor, L, or

(3-9) $Y = F(K,L)$

Solow assumed that his production function was a standard neoclassical production function in which individual inputs were subject to diminishing returns. On the other hand, he also assumed production was subject to *constant returns to scale*, so that for any positive constant λ

(3-10) $\lambda Y = F(\lambda K, \lambda L)$

In its simplest version, the Solow model assumes that only K changes and labor is a contant. Hence, we can let $\lambda = 1/L$, which gives us

(3-11) $Y/L = F(K/L, 1)$

The production function can then be conveniently rewritten as

(3-12) $y = f(k)$

where $y \equiv Y/L$ and $k \equiv K/L$, and the function $f(k)$ is equivalent to $F(k,1)$. Equation (3-12) describes output per worker as a function of capital per worker, which accords with most economists' definition of economic growth as the change in *per capita* output, so that economic growth occurs only when y, not Y, increases. Finally, Solow assumed diminishing returns to individual factors, that is, the first derivative of y with respect to k is positive, or $f'(k) > 0$, and the second derivative is negative, or $f''(k) < 0$.

3.4.2 Saving and Investment

Output is divided between consumption, C, and investment, I:

(3-13) $Y = C + I$

For simplicity, the usual aggregate demand equation $Y = C + I + G$ is not used here. We effectively assume that government purchases consist of either consumption goods or investment goods and allocate them to C or I. Again, dividing by L to put all variables in "per worker" terms gives us

(3-14) $$y = c + i$$

where $c \equiv C/L$ and $i \equiv I/L$. The amount of capital that appears in the production function depends on investment, and investment is limited by society's willingness to save. As in the Harrod-Domar model, Solow assumed consumption and saving to be constant fractions of income. If the savings rate, σ, has a value between zero and one, then

(3-15) $$c = y - s = (1 - \sigma)y$$

and

(3-16) $$i = s = \sigma y$$

Like the Harrod-Domar model, Solow assumed that saving always translates into new productive capital, albeit with diminishing returns.

The Solow model differs from the Harrod-Domar model in that it recognizes that the stock of capital is subject to *depreciation*. Solow assumed that the amount of the capital stock that depreciates is a constant percentage of the existing capital stock. Defining such a constant rate of depreciation as δ implies that the change in the capital stock is the difference between investment and depreciation, or

(3-17) $$\Delta K = I - \delta K$$

In per worker terms, the equation (3-17) becomes:

(3-18) $$\Delta k = i - \delta k = \sigma y - \delta k = \sigma f(k) - \delta k$$

If $\sigma f(k) > \delta k$, the capital-labor ratio k and per capita output $y = f(k)$ will increase. On the other hand, if $\sigma f(k) < \delta k$, then Δk will be negative, and k and y will decline.

This simple version of the Solow model thus concludes that if the production function exhibits (1) constant returns to scale and (2) diminishing returns to any single input, and (3) the values of the parameters σ and δ are constants, then in the long run the capital-labor ratio settles at the equilibrium value of k* and per capita income settles at the equilibrium value of y*. This stable equilibrium represents a *steady state* where the growth rates of k and, therefore, $f(k) = y$ are zero. For those who embraced the logic of the Harrod-Domar model and saw growth as a direct consequence of investment, this result was surprising. Despite a constant rate of saving and investment, in the Solow model growth eventually comes to a stop.

3.4.3 The Graphic Version of the Solow Model

In most introductory textbooks, the Solow model is presented graphically as in Figure 3-3. Diminishing returns implies that the production function f(k) rises at a diminishing rate. Under the assumption of a constant saving rate σ, the saving curve σf(k) is just a diminished version of f(k) that also increases at a decreasing rate. On the other hand, under the assumption that total depreciation is a constant proportion of the capital stock, the depreciation function is the straight line δk with a slope δ.

In the graphic model, the steady state occurs at the level of capital k*, which is where the saving function intersects the depreciation function. Where the saving function lies above the depreciation line, or where σf(k) is greater than depreciation δk, the stock of capital per worker grows. This occurs at the capital/labor ratio k_1, for example. On the other hand, if investment is less than depreciation, which is the case where σf(k) < δk, then k declines. Hence, k tends toward a stable steady state equilibrium

Figure 3-3
The Solow Model's Steady State

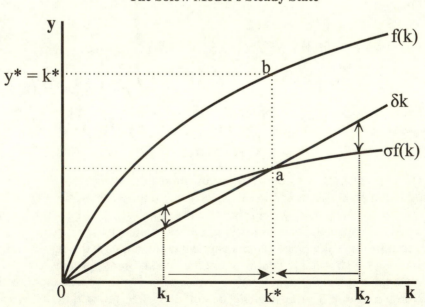

level k* and y tends toward a stable steady state equilibrium level of output at y* = f(k*).

The Solow model shows that once the capital stock adjusts fully to its steady state, only a change in the parameters can change per worker capital and output. Increasing the rate of saving, σ, would change the economy's steady state. For example, Figure 3-4 shows that an increase in the rate of saving from $σ_1$ to $σ_2$ shifts the saving function upward and raises the intersection of the saving and depreciation curves to the steady state capital-labor ratio k_2*. This increase in the saving rate will, therefore, cause medium-run growth as the capital-labor ratio and per capita income both increase. However, once the economy reaches that higher steady state, growth again ceases. Further increases in the rate of saving would cause further increases in the steady state level of output. However, since there is obviously a limit to how far the rate of saving can be raised, permanent growth is not possible by means of continual increases in the rate of saving.

The Solow model described here does not seem to be able to explain long-run economic growth. This makes the model unrealistic, because since 1820, many countries have been able to increase per capita incomes year after year for extended periods of time. The United States, for

Figure 3-4
The Medium-Run Growth Effect of an Increase
in the Saving Rate

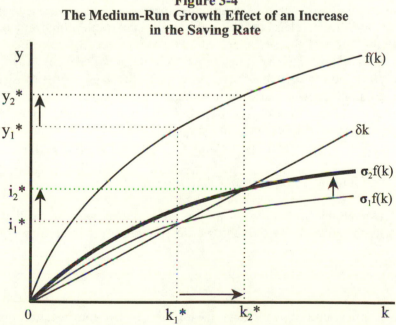

example, has grown almost continually for 200 years. The Solow model can in fact explain long-run economic growth if we augment it to include a variable for technology.

3.4.4 Population Growth and the Solow Model

Suppose that population growth causes the labor force to grow at the constant rate of n, that is, $\Delta L/L = n$. Now, equation (3-17) no longer correctly describes the change in the capital-labor ratio, $k = K/L$. For k to remain constant when the labor force L grows, investment minus depreciation must grow at the same rate as L because investment must cover not only the amount of capital that depreciates, but it must also equip new entrants to the labor force. The direction of change in k depends on whether the amount of investment per worker, $i = \sigma f(k)$, is greater than or less than depreciation per worker plus the amount of additional capital needed per new worker. Total depreciation is still equal to the depreciation rate times the stock of capital. And the amount of new capital per worker is equal to the population growth rate times the stock of capital. The change in the capital-labor ratio k is thus

(3-19) $$\Delta k = i - \delta k - nk = \sigma f(k) - (\delta + n)k$$

Compared to an economy with no population growth, an economy where n > 0 does experience continuous increases in *total* output in the steady state. Because k is constant in the steady state, both capital and total output must grow at the rate of growth of the labor force, n. Investment in effect does not suffer from diminishing returns if the capital stock grows in exact proportion to the labor force. And, with constant returns to scale, when all inputs grow at the same rate output also grows at that rate: $G_Y = G_K = G_L = n$. But, a positive rate of population growth does not cause the Solow model to generate continuous economic growth. In the steady state, per capita output is equal to $G_y = (G_Y - G_L) = 0$ and $G_k = (G_K - G_L) = 0$.

3.4.5 Technological Progress and the Solow Model

If we assume that technological progress is *labor-augmenting* in that it increases the productivity of labor, we can restate our production function as

(3-20) $$Y = F[K, (L \cdot E)]$$

where E is defined as the *efficiency* of each worker. Defining technological progress as being exclusively labor-augmenting permits us to conveniently redefine our variables in terms of *effective labor*, which is the product of L and E. In the case of the "simple" Solow model above, E was implicitly assumed to be constant and equal to one. In general, the level of labor augmenting technology grows at some rate z, which can be greater than zero, zero, or less than zero.[43]

By defining k as K/(L·E), y as Y/(L·E), and i as I/(L·E), we can show the changes in the capital stock per effective worker in a familiar format:

(3-21) $\Delta k = i - (\delta + n + z)k = \sigma f(k) - (\delta + n + z)k$

The steady state occurs where y and k are constant. Defining $y = Y/(L\cdot E)$ and recognizing that $G_y = 0$ in the steady state, it must be true that in the long run

(3-22) $G_y = G_Y - G_L - G_E = 0$

Since per worker output is y = Y/L, $G_y = G_Y - G_L$. Therefore, equation (3-22) implies that:

(3-23) $G_y = G_E = z$

Now, the Solow model generates continuous economic growth. In the steady state, the rate of growth of per capita real output is equal to the rate of labor-augmenting technological progress.

The full Solow model with investment, population growth, and technological progress is illustrated in Figure 3-5. For given rates of saving and depreciation, a constant rate of technological progress z continually raises the production function and therefore continually increases the

---

[43] The simplifying assumption that technological progress is purely labor augmenting is justified by the result that it is the only type of technological progress that can generate permanent growth in per worker output. All other things equal, capital-augmenting technological progress is subject to diminishing returns, just as is investment. In general, overall technological progress tends to affect all factors to some degree, but it generates permanent per worker output growth in the long run only to the extent that it raises effective labor supply. So we simplify and assume that only labor-augmenting technological progress occurs.

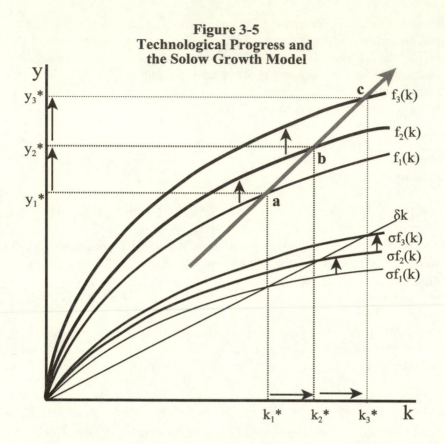

Figure 3-5
Technological Progress and
the Solow Growth Model

economy's steady state capital-labor ratio and per capita real output at the same rate z. Three such sequential steady states occur at the points a, b, and c, which combine the steady state sets of capital and output (k_1^*, y_1^*), (k_2^*, y_2^*), and (k_3^*, y_3^*). Technological progress raises per capita output along a straight upward-sloping line rather than along a single production function with diminishing returns. This full Solow growth model accurately depicts economic growth over the past 200 years. The rising standards of living that people in most countries have experienced have been the result of both *more* tools and machines and *better* tools and machines as well as better knowledge and production methods. These improvements in technology shift the production function up, and this enables the economy to avoid diminishing returns and stagnation. Note also that in Figure 3-5, the capital-labor ratio does continually increase. Hence, there is a correlation between increased capital and economic growth. However, it is not increased capital accumulation that fundamentally drives growth. Rather, it is technological progress that shifts the steady state capital labor ratios.

To convince yourself that technological progress is really necessary for economic growth, try imagining what our standard of living would have been like today if after 1800 we had only increased the number of horses rather than inventing farm tractors, used ever greater doses of cod liver oil rather than developing antibiotics to fight infections, and just made more and more slates and chalk rather than inventing word processors. Or, to put it in a more contemporary setting, do you think the earth can support twice as much electricity generation using coal fired plants with the same technology currently used, twice as many cars putting twice as much exhaust into the air, and twice as many acres devoted to growing our food? Obviously, for continued growth of output to be possible, we need to learn to get more output from the resources that are available to us. In other words, we need technological progress to keep growing.

3.4.6 Summing Up the Solow Growth Model

With population growth and technological progress now incorporated into the Solow model, we conclude the following:

- Increased saving and investment will shift the economy's steady state, causing medium-run growth as the economy transitions to the new steady state, but no permanent growth.

- An economy will experience permanent economic growth only if the economy experiences continual labor-augmenting technological progress.

The Solow model therefore explains how medium-run and long-run economic growth are related to investment and technological progress. The major shortcoming of the model is that it treats these variables as exogenous, determined outside the model. It does not explain why the savings rate σ and the rate of technological progress z are what they are or how economic policy might be able to influence them. Nevertheless, the Solow model provides a great service by showing where we need to look for the determinants of long-run economic growth.

The next step in building useful models with which to analyze economic growth and examine how trade in particular affects economic growth is to model how technology is created. We clearly need a model of technological progress to supplement the Solow model. That task will be taken up in the next chapter. In the meantime, in the remainder of this chapter we examine how trade fits into the Solow model.

3.5 The Gains from Trade According to the Solow Model

Trade's effect on economic growth can be analyzed using the Solow model. As detailed in this section, several economists have recently analyzed the growth effect of international trade within the framework of the Solow model. In light of what we concluded above, intuition should enable you to predict that for trade to generate permanent economic growth in the Solow model, it must be linked to technological progress.

3.5.1 Baldwin's Application of the Solow Model

Recall from Chapter 1 how standard models of international trade point out how a shift from complete autonomy to free trade increases total real income. One simple version of the Heckscher-Ohlin model illustrates the increase in real income by means of a production-possibilities curve diagram where an economy is assumed to produce two commodities, X and Y, as in Figure 3-6. In the absence of

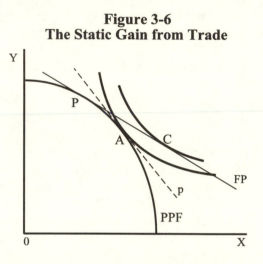

Figure 3-6
The Static Gain from Trade

trade, the economy can do no better than to produce the combination of commodities represented by point A. In the case of free trade however, production shifts to point P, which generates real income that, according to international prices, can be allocated to the combination of X and Y at the point C. The point C provides a higher level of total welfare than the combination of X and Y at the point A because it lies on a higher indifference curve. Similar conclusions are reached in partial equilibrium models of trade and in models of imperfect competition where industries enjoy increasing returns to scale.

Baldwin (1992a) showed that within the framework of the Solow growth model, a one-time improvement in welfare from a shift from restricted trade to free trade results in a secondary improvement in real output. Specifically, a shift to free trade effectively improves the economy's efficiency with which it transforms its available inputs into welfare-enhancing final products. That is, free trade effectively shifts the production function in the Solow model, and this generates economic growth while the economy shifts up to a higher steady state equilibrium level of capital and output.

Figure 3-7 depicts the trade-induced shift in the production function from f(k) to g(k). The shift from f(k) to g(k) changes the economy's steady state capital-output ratio and per capita income from k_1^* and y_1^* to k_2^* and y_3^*, respectively. These changes are the result of an immediate increase in per worker output from y_1^* to y_2^* before the capital-output ratio begins to change. This is the traditional static gain

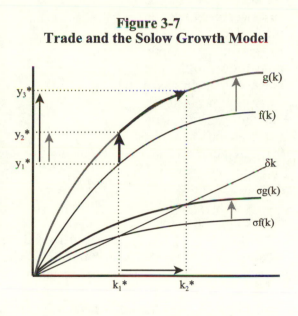

Figure 3-7
Trade and the Solow Growth Model

from trade, as shown in Figure 3-6. But assuming a constant rate of saving, the increase in real income raises the economy's saving function as well. Therefore, the steady state equilibrium shifts up and generates a secondary spurt of medium-run growth that gradually moves to the new steady state equilibrium at k_2^* and y_3^*. The traditional gain from trade does not cause permanent economic growth according to the Solow model, however, because the economy eventually settles at the new steady state equilibrium.

3.5.2 Does It Matter What a Country Trades?

Mazumdar (1996) qualifies Baldwin's seemingly straightforward analysis of trade's growth effect in the Solow model. Mazumdar pointed out that a country may not be able to increase its rate of growth in the medium run if it exports capital goods and imports consumer goods. His reasoning is based on the standard result from the trade model presented in Figure 3-6, namely that the shift to free trade changes the relative prices of the export and import goods. If the export good Y in Figure 3-6 is a capital good and the import X is a consumption good, then the price increase of capital goods will be reflected in a rise in the depreciation line. The rise in the price of domestic capital raises the cost of replacing depreciated capital, thus effectively making the cost of depreciation greater. Figure 3-8 illustrates the special case where the rise in the price of capital happens to be exactly proportional to the rise in real output. In such a case, the depreciation line shifts up by exactly the same amount that the savings function shifts up, as shown by the line $\delta_2 k$ in Figure 3-8. The steady state level of k remains at k_1^* and

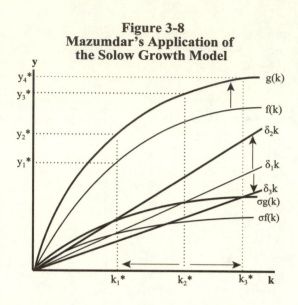

Figure 3-8
Mazumdar's Application of the Solow Growth Model

y rises from y_1^* to y_2^* only. The gain in per capita output is exclusively the effect of the rise in the production function; there is no medium-run growth because there is no increase in the amount of capital per worker, k.

On the other hand, if a country imports capital goods and exports consumer goods, then Mazumdar's analysis concludes that medium-run growth will be greater than Baldwin suggested. With trade lowering the cost of capital goods, fewer savings are required to replace depreciated capital. An example of such a case is also shown in Figure 3-8 in the form of a decline in the depreciation line from $\delta_1 k$ to $\delta_3 k$ and a shift in the steady state all the way to k_3^* and y_4^*, instead of just k_2^* and y_3^* in Baldwin's case illustrated in Figure 3-7.

No economy exports or imports exclusively consumption goods or capital goods, of course. But, since developing economies tend to export relatively fewer capital goods than developed economies because the production of capital goods is relatively physical capital intensive and human capital intensive, Mazumdar's analysis effectively distinguishes a potential reason why international trade can cause incomes across countries to become more similar. Poor developing economies may gain more from international trade than high-income developed economies. Supporting Mazumdar's model is Eaton and Kortum's (2001) estimate that about 25 percent of productivity differences across countries are caused by variations in the prices of capital goods, and about half the variation in the prices of capital goods are a direct result of trade restrictions. The authors of this book, in Lewer and Van den Berg (2001, 2003a) and Lewer (2002), have also found that the composition of trade between consumer and capital goods is a statistically significant and positive determinant of economic growth. Xu and Wang (1999) show that in OECD countries capital goods imports are a significant determinant of a country's technological progress.

3.5.3 The Gains from Trade in the Solow Model

Baldwin (1992a) calls the secondary spurt in growth that is induced by the rise in the per worker capital stock a "multiplier" on the static effect of trade. He estimated that for five European countries this multiplier ranges from a low of 30 percent for France to a high of 129 percent for Germany. Baldwin thus concludes that a static improvement in welfare from trade liberalization may induce an overall improvement in welfare that may be more than double the initial static welfare effect. Keuschnigg and Kohler (1996) used Austrian data to estimate the effect of lower production costs on the accumulation of capital, and they found that international trade indeed increases the economy's capital stock and thus generates a secondary effect on real income beyond the initial static gain from trade. Baldwin and Seghezza (1996) concluded that protectionist policies reduce the level of investment, all other things equal, just as the Solow model in Figure 3-7 predicts. Other estimates of the Solow model's medium-run growth spurt include Harrison, Rutherford, and Tarr (1996) and Baldwin, Francois, and Portes (1997). However, Rodrik (1997) corrected Baldwin, Francois, and Portes for ignoring the short-run opportunity costs of the investment necessary to support the medium-term growth. Rodrik argued that a proper accounting of investment costs lowers the dynamic medium-term gains to under 5 percent of GDP, compared to the 10-20 percent gains found by some of the authors cited above.

The logical results of inserting the static income gains from international trade into the Solow growth model are thus as follows:

- An increase in international trade, brought about by a shift in trade policy or an improvement in the means of transportation will, all other things equal, shift the economy's steady state, causing medium-run growth as the economy transitions to the new steady state.

- The medium-run growth spurt may be influenced by the composition of trade, namely, whether a country's comparative advantage lies in producing capital goods or consumption goods.

■ However, according to the Solow growth model, an increase in trade cannot generate permanent economic growth unless the economy experiences continued technological progress.

■ Hence, international trade can only contribute to permanent economic growth if it directly influences an economy's rate of technological progress.

The latter of the above conclusions is especially important for developing a consistent explanation for the positive correlation between international trade and economic growth. We clearly need to find out how trade improves our capacity to come up with better ideas and new knowledge.

3.6 East Asia and the Solow Model

Hong Kong, Korea, Singapore, and Taiwan have experienced extraordinary rates of economic growth during the latter half of the twentieth century. These four *Asian tigers*, as they came to be called, have raised the average per capita incomes of their citizens from among the lowest in the world some fifty years ago to developed country levels today. According to Maddison's (2001) comparative income data, Hong Kong and Singapore currently enjoy real per capita incomes of over $20,000, placing them ahead of most European countries. Korea increased its real per capita income from less than $1,000 in 1950 to over $13,000 by 2000. Taiwan similarly raised its per capita income from $900 in 1950 to over $15,000 in 2000.

3.6.1 The East Asian Miracle

A simple extrapolation of recent trends suggests that East Asian economies will soon enjoy per capita incomes above those of the U.S. and Europe. The power of compounding means that, at recent growth rates, Hong Kong and Singapore will pass U.S. per capita income around 2015. Taiwan and Korea will require less than two decades to catch up to the United States. A decade ago, in a popular article entitled "The Myth of Asia's Miracle," Paul Krugman (1994b) argued that the rapid economic growth of the Asian tigers would not continue at the pace of the recent past, so simple extrapolation of past trends was misleading. In place of extrapolation of past patterns, Krugman applied the logic of the Solow model to conclude that there would inevitably be a slowdown in the growth rates of the Asian tigers.

Krugman relied on research by Alwyn Young (1992, 1995), who had estimated that the rate of technological progress was near zero in Singapore. Krugman also emphasized the fact that factor accumulation was extraordinary in East Asia. Savings rates were about 40 percent of income in Singapore, for example. The labor force also grew rapidly because the labor force participation rate of women increased substantially. And, the "quality" of the labor force improved rapidly due to the rapid increase in schooling. The average years of schooling of workers entering the labor forces in Hong Kong, Singapore, South Korea, and Taiwan are today similar to developed country levels. This compares to the East Asian tigers' average of less than three years of elementary school education in the early 1950s. Krugman thus concluded:

> The newly industrializing countries of the Pacific Rim have received a reward for their extraordinary mobilization of resources that is no more than what the most boringly conventional economic theory would lead us to expect. If there is a secret to Asian growth, it is simply deferred gratification, the willingness to sacrifice current satisfaction for future gain.[44]

Krugman's "boringly conventional economic theory" is obviously the Solow growth model. According to Krugman, East Asia's large jump in saving and factor accumulation indeed caused a substantial amount of medium-term growth. But, because the Asian tigers cannot continue to increase their savings rates and expand factor accumulation, the steady state will soon stop shifting out and diminishing returns will kick in. Eventually, the rate of economic growth will approach the rate of technological progress, which Krugman claimed was not very high in East Asia. Krugman therefore concluded that the East Asian economies were unlikely to catch up to and surpass the United States and Western Europe.

3.6.2 The Reaction to Krugman's Analysis

Krugman's article was severely criticized in many Asian countries. It also stimulated a great deal of research. Subsequent studies disputed some of Krugman's conclusions. Krugman relied on research by Alwyn Young (1992, 1995), who had estimated that the rate of technological progress was near zero in Singapore. Krugman did not emphasize that the other Asian tigers had experienced relatively fast technological progress in comparison to the G-7 industrialized countries. Table 3-2 presents data on productivity

---

[44] Krugman (1994b), p. 78.

for the G-7 countries as well as Young's data for the Asian tigers. Young's estimates of total factor productivity show that technological progress was actually relatively fast in three of the four Asian tigers. Estimates of total factor productivity using nonparametric estimation methods, which avoid the need to impose specific assumptions about underlying production functions, suggested that total factor productivity growth in East Asia, including Singapore, has actually been quite high. Iwata, Khan, and Murao (2002) show that total factor productivity growth in all of the four Asian tiger economies ranged from 3.4 to 3.8 percent over the period 1960-1995. Collins and Bosworth (1996), Klenow and Rodriguez-Clare (1997), Rodrigo (2000), and Easterly and Levine (2001) similarly found high rates of technological progress.

Table 3-2
Total Factor Productivity: G7 Countries and the Asian Tigers

Country	Years	Rate % per yr.	Country	Years	Rate % per yr.
Canada	1960-89	0.5	Hong Kong	1966-91	2.3
France	1960-89	1.5	Singapore	1966-90	0.2
Germany	1960-89	1.6	South Korea	1966-90	1.7
Italy	1960-89	2.0	Taiwan	1966-90	2.1
Japan	1960-89	2.0			
United Kingdom	1960-89	1.3			
United States	1960-89	0.4			

Sources: The G-7 countries estimates are from John C. Dougherty (1991), "A Comparison of Productivity and Economic Growth in the G-7 Countries," Ph.D. dissertation, Harvard University, and the Asian tiger estimates are from Alwyn Young (1995), "The Tyranny of Numbers: Confronting the Statistical Realities of the East Asian Growth Experience," *Quarterly Journal of Economics*, Vol. 104(3), pp. 641-679.

Krugman's reliance on Young's one estimate of TFP for Singapore appears to have led him to reach the wrong conclusion about future economic growth in the region. On the other hand, recent policy shifts by the government of Singapore suggest that it did not take Krugman's analysis lightly. The government of Singapore has begun providing incentives for high technology industries to locate in the city state. Tan and Phang (2005) provide an interesting description of Singapore's new incentives for firms that build "innovation infrastructure" in the country.

Furthermore, Singapore has invested heavily in higher education in order to improve the economy's capacity to advance knowledge and technology. Singapore has also created a Ministry for Entrepreneurship to oversee its efforts to stimulate technological progress. Even elementary and secondary education in Singapore, long noted for its efficient teaching of basic skills and rote learning, are being urged to encourage more original thinking and risk taking. According to a 2004 article in *The Wall Street Journal*:

> Singapore is hammering the message to its youngest citizens. Schools emphasize group projects, debates and assignments with open-ended questions, and have mandatory courses on entrepreneurship. An eight-hour module requires 13-year-olds to write business plans and market products such as friendship bracelets. Authors of the best plans win a one-week trip to Silicon Valley in California.[45]

Policy makers in Singapore seem to have moved beyond the Solow model to address the specific determinants of technological progress.

3.6.3 Avoiding Diminishing Returns

Findlay (1996) and Ventura (1997) use the conventional Heckscher-Ohlin theoretical model to show why economic growth in "follower" countries such as the East Asian tigers remained so rapid for so long: The well-known *factor price equalization theorem* derived from the Heckscher-Ohlin model states that in a single global economy the marginal rate of return to capital in all economies is determined not by the size of each country's capital stock, but by the world's total capital stock. Because they are small open economies that are closely linked to the global economy, the East Asian economies have therefore not experienced the gradual decline in the marginal rate of return to capital predicted by the Solow model. Instead, their returns to capital have remained similar to the returns to capital elsewhere in the world, and these have been quite steady over the latter half of the 20th century because worldwide technological progress has roughly offset diminishing returns to capital accumulation. Of course, to prevent a decline in returns to investment, the East Asian economies had to continually reallocate their growing capital stock and better educated labor force in accordance with its rapidly changing comparative advantage. In terms of the Heckscher-Ohlin model, the East Asian economies have

---

[45] Cris Prystay (2004), "Singapore Encourages Entrepreneurial Grit," *Wall Street Journal*, January 21.

increasingly specialized in capital-intensive products as their high rates of investment made physical and human capital more and more abundant.

Findlay (1996) or Ventura (1997) do not suggest that the East Asian tigers can continue to grow at rates that exceed their rates of technological progress in the long run, however. It is likely that when the small open Asian economies reach the capital-output ratios of the most developed countries, they will also in effect approach the cutting edge levels of world technology. This is likely because much of the world's technology is embodied in capital equipment, and the production methods that most intensively exploit physical and human capital similarly reflect cutting edge production technologies. Hence, Findlay and Ventura can be interpreted as implying that a small economy can grow continually at rapid rates but that it will suffer a sudden slowdown when their production methods and capital intensity approach the levels of the most capital abundant economies. East Asian policy makers' focus on incentives for innovation and educational reform therefore makes sense from this perspective as well. Growth can continue into the indefinite future only if there is continued technological progress.

3.7 Conclusions

The Solow model provides insight into where trade's influence on economic growth are to be found. For one thing, international trade's static gain in welfare is clearly an understatement of the true gain from trade. The extensions of Solow's neoclassical growth model by Baldwin, Mazumdar, and others make it clear that trade changes the economy's steady state equilibrium. Therefore, trade generates not only a one-time shift in economic efficiency but also medium-run growth because the economy adjusts its stocks of factors.

The Solow model also sheds some light on why Levine and Renelt (1992) found a close relationship between international trade and investment in their study on the robust determinants of economic growth discussed in the previous chapter. Figure 3-7 in this chapter shows that when the expansion of international trade shifts the economy's steady state equilibrium, the economy tends to raise its capital-labor ratio. In the case of developing countries that import physical capital, Mazumdar (1996) showed that both growth and the rise in the capital-output ratio are likely to expand at an accelerated rate in the medium run. Also, small developing economies open to international trade can avoid declines in the marginal products of capital if they continually shift production to more capital intensive industries.

The most important prediction of the Solow growth model is that permanent economic growth is only possible if there is continued technological progress. Factor accumulation by itself does not enable the economy to grow in the long run. For example, if we give a worker more and more identical shovels to work with, his or her ability to dig holes in the ground will not increase in proportion to the number of shovels. But, diminishing returns can be avoided if we give the worker a diesel powered backhoe. It costs at least 100 times as much as a good shovel, but the backhoe permits the worker to dig several 100 times as big a hole as she could dig with a shovel. Replacing shovels with a backhoe represents *technological progress*. Permanent economic growth is only possible when there is technological progress.

The Solow model's prediction about what causes economic growth is derived from logical reasoning and the initial assumptions of the model. Logic, by itself, does not make a model useful. The model does have to be shown to fit the facts before we can say that it is a useful theory. In this regard, Easterly and Levine (2001) provide a rigorous verification of the Solow model's prediction. They distinguish five general characteristics of economic growth over the past two centuries: (1) the growth residual (total factor productivity) explains most of the variation in growth rates across countries, (2) per capita income diverges over time, (3) factor accumulation has been much more similar across countries and over time than have growth rates, (4) economic growth is highly concentrated with all factors of production flowing to the countries that already have the highest incomes, and (5) national economic policies and institutions are closely correlated with national growth rates. Easterly and Levine then carefully show that all of these characteristics are compatible with technological progress, but not factor accumulation, serving as the dominant determinant of long-run economic growth.

The first characteristic of economic growth examined by Easterly and Levine is a straightforward confirmation of the Solow model's conclusion that technological progress drives economic growth. The second characteristic of growth provides more subtle support. The fact that per capita income has diverged, that is, has become less equal across countries, implies that something other than factor accumulation is driving growth. Factor accumulation would encounter diminishing returns, and thus cause incomes to converge, not diverge. With diminishing returns, an additional unit of capital will have a larger effect on output in a poor capital-scarce country than in a rich capital-abundant country; therefore, all other things equal, factor accumulation should cause a poor country to grow faster than a rich country. The third characteristic of economic growth, that growth rates cannot be explained by capital accumulation, is also straightforward. The fourth characteristic of economic growth, that returns to all factors of production are higher in rich countries, implies that technological progress must have shifted up the production functions in rich countries; otherwise returns to all factors would not be higher in some countries than others. This latter characteristic also effectively confirms that technological progress drives growth because in the absence of technological progress the inflows of factors would have resulted in diminishing returns and a decline in average incomes, as shown in Figure 3-2 earlier in this chapter. Finally, the fifth growth characteristic is the most complex evidence in favor of technological progress' role in the growth process. The discussion of technological progress in the upcoming chapters of this book will show more clearly how and why institutions are critical determinants of technological change.

The growth economist Paul Romer (2001) points out that Easterly and Levine's conclusions about the importance of technological progress over simple factor accumulation are very well founded because they bring in so much evidence to support their conclusions. According to Romer:

> For someone who wants to maintain an unreasonable prior assumption, the advantage of a narrow focus on one piece of data is that it does not threaten the convenient theoretical framework built on this prior. It is possible to go through the motions of doing science, testing various theories and rejecting some in favor of others. But far from advancing the science, this approach is a dead end. It does not allow for rejecting or modifying prior beliefs that simply turn out to be wrong.[46]

When economists confront models with one observed correlation or just a limited set of relationships, many models based on many different hypotheses end up being compatible with the specific evidence. For example, recall that both the Harrod-Domar and Solow models are compatible with the hypothesis that rising per capita GDP is correlated with a rising capital-labor ratio. Romer lauds Easterly and Levine's work because they confront the Solow model's hypothesis that long-run

---

[46] Romer (2001), p. 226.

economic growth requires technological progress with data on a number of different correlations. Just as a prosecutor in a criminal case wins her case when she is able to explain all of the facts before an objective jury, Easterly and Levine convincingly show that a large number of observed facts about economic growth are consistent with the Solow model's principal conclusion that growth is driven by technological progress.

The acceptance of the Solow model's conclusions means that we need to focus on the relationship between international trade and technological change. Unfortunately, after serving its valuable purpose of alerting us to the importance of technology, the Solow model is completely silent on what determines an economy's rate of technological change. The Solow model simply assumed a rate of technological progress z and then logically concluded that in the long run the entire economy would grow at the rate of z. But, why is the rate of technological progress equal to the rate z and not some other rate? And, most important for our discussion in this book, how does international trade influence z? The Solow model points us in the right direction, but it does not take us to our destination.

Fortunately, beginning with Adam Smith some two centuries ago, economists have investigated the sources of technological progress. We have already discussed Smith's contributions, especially his suggestion that international trade, by promoting specialization, contributes substantially to technological progress. Recall also Smith's discussion of entrepreneurs, the process of learning-by-doing, institutions, and infrastructure. There have been many further contributions to our understanding of innovation, technological progress, and the accumulation of knowledge by economists since the time of Adam Smith. Especially in the past 25 years, there has been very lively research activity in the optimistic spirit of Adam Smith to develop models that explain long-run economic growth. The next chapter begins our examination of how economists explain the process of technological progress. We will also show how international trade is likely to fit into the process.

Appendix to Chapter Three

The Convenient Cobb-Douglas Production Function

The Solow growth model specifies a neoclassical production function of the general form $Y = F(K,L)$, in which Y is output, K is capital, L is labor, and F represents the functional relationship between output and the inputs. The Solow model further assumes that the production function is characterized by constant returns to scale and diminishing marginal returns. A functional form that matches the assumptions of the Solow model and also has very convenient mathematical properties is the so-called *Cobb-Douglas* production function

(3-1A) $$Y = AK^{\alpha}L^{1-\alpha}$$

in which Y is output, A represents the level of technology, K is capital, L is labor, and $0 \leq \alpha \leq 1$. The sum of the exponents of the inputs K and L, α and $1 - \alpha$, is equal to one: $\alpha + (1 - \alpha) = 1$.

The Cobb-Douglas production function can also be conveniently written in *per worker* terms, as is done in this chapter. Dividing equation (3-1A) by L gives us

(3-2A) $y = Y/L = AK^{\alpha}L^{1-\alpha}/L = AK^{\alpha}L^{1-\alpha}L^{-1} = AK^{\alpha}L^{1-\alpha-1} = AK^{\alpha}L^{-\alpha} = Ak^{\alpha}$

where $k \equiv K/L$. It should be clear that for any $0 < \alpha < 1$, the function Ak^{α} looks like Figure 3-3. (If you are not convinced, use your calculator and insert any positive value for A, some value between 0 and 1 for α, and several increasing values for k, and graph the result for $y = Ak^{\alpha}$)

Constant Returns to Scale

To prove that the Cobb-Douglas production function exhibits constant returns to scale, multiply each factor by a constant c and enter those new quantities into the Cobb-Douglas function (3-1A):

(3-3A) $A(cK)^{\alpha}(cL)^{1-\alpha} = Ac^{\alpha}K^{\alpha}c^{1-\alpha}L^{1-\alpha} = c^{\alpha+1-\alpha}AK^{\alpha}L^{1-\alpha} = cY$

Note that constant returns depend on the coefficients α and $(1-\alpha)$ adding up to exactly one. If the coefficients of K and L in equation (3-1A) were α and β instead and $(\alpha + \beta) > 1$, then $A(cK)^{\alpha}(cL)^{\beta} = c^{\alpha+\beta}Y > cY$. This represents a case of *increasing returns to scale* because the proportional increase in output is greater than the proportional increase in each of the inputs. For the Cobb-Douglas production function to fit the Solow model, therefore, the coefficients must be specified to sum to one.

Diminishing Marginal Returns

The marginal products of the inputs can be found by taking the *partial derivative* of Y with respect to labor and capital:

(3-4A) $$\partial Y/\partial L = A(1-\alpha)K^{\alpha}L^{-\alpha} > 0$$

and

(3-5A) $$\partial Y/\partial K = A\alpha K^{\alpha-1}L^{1-\alpha} = A\alpha K^{\alpha-1}L^{1-\alpha} > 0$$

The second derivatives $\partial^2Y/\partial L^2$ and $\partial^2Y/\partial K^2$ are negative, as required for diminishing returns:

(3-6A) $$\partial^2Y/\partial L^2 = -A(\alpha - \alpha^2)K^{\alpha}L^{-\alpha-1} < 0$$

and

(3-7A) $$\partial^2Y/\partial K^2 = A(\alpha^2-\alpha)K^{\alpha-2}L^{1-\alpha} < 0.$$

The terms $(\alpha - \alpha^2)$ and $(\alpha^2-\alpha)$ are greater than and less than one, respectively, because $0 < \alpha < 1$. Therefore, each individual factor is subject to diminishing returns.

In *per worker* terms, the partial derivatives are

(3-8A) $$\partial y/\partial k = A\alpha k^{\alpha-1} > 0$$

and

(3-9A) $$\partial^2y/\partial k^2 = A(\alpha^2-\alpha)k^{\alpha-2} < 0$$

which confirms that the Cobb-Douglas function matches the assumptions of the function drawn in the graphic version of the Solow model used in this chapter.

Constant Factor Shares

The Cobb-Douglas function has another characteristic that is particularly convenient. To uncover this characteristic, we first need to go through the intermediate step of rewriting total output as a function of L and k. Specifically:

(3-10A) $\quad Y = AK^{\alpha}L^{1-\alpha} = LAK^{\alpha}L^{1-\alpha}L^{-1} = LAK^{\alpha}L^{-\alpha} = LAk^{\alpha}$

Under perfect competition in the factor markets, each factor is paid its marginal product. This means that the *share* of total output that is earned by capital is equal to the amount of capital times its marginal product, all divided by total output. Or, from (3-5A) and (3-10A), and remembering that K/L = k, capital's share of total product is

(3-11A) $\quad K(\partial Y/\partial K)/Y = [K(A\alpha K^{\alpha-1}L^{1-\alpha})]/Y = [K(A\alpha k^{\alpha-1})]/(LAk^{\alpha})$
$$= A(A)^{-1}\alpha(k)(k)^{\alpha}(k)^{-\alpha}(k)^{-1} = \alpha$$

And labor's share is the amount of labor multiplied by its marginal product, all divided by Y. Using (3-4A) and (3-10A), we find that labor's share is

(3-12A) $\quad L(\partial Y/\partial L)/Y = L(A\alpha K^{\alpha-1}L^{1-\alpha})/Y = LA(1-\alpha)k^{\alpha}]/(LAk^{\alpha}) = 1-\alpha$

Thus, the exponents of the inputs in the Cobb-Douglas production function are the share of that input in the total product. And, because α is a constant, factors shares are constants in the Cobb-Douglas model.

Example: Thailand's Increase in Saving

For simplicity, suppose that A = 1, so that the per worker Cobb-Douglas production function is

(3-13A) $\qquad\qquad\qquad y = k^{\alpha}$

To make things even easier, suppose $\alpha = 0.5$. Therefore,

(3-14A) $\qquad\qquad\qquad y = k^{0.5} = \sqrt{k}$

According to the Solow model, in the steady state $\Delta k = 0$ and $\sigma f(k^*) = \delta k^*$. Therefore

(3-15A) $\qquad\qquad\qquad k^*/f(k^*) = \sigma/\delta$

Note, however, that

(3-16A)
$$k^*/\sqrt{k^*} = \sqrt{k^*}$$

which implies that

(3-17A)
$$k^* = (\sigma/\delta)^2$$

If we know the values of σ of δ we can calculate k^* and the steady state income $y^* = f(k^*)$. Let's assume that depreciation is 10 percent, or $\delta = 0.1$.

Let's use Thailand as an example. According to World Bank data, Thailand increased its savings ratio from 21 percent in 1970 to 35 percent in 1997. Inserting these values for σ into (3-17A), we see that in 1970 k^* = $(.21/.1)^2$ = 4.41 And, in 1997, k^* = $(.35/.1)^2$ = 12.25. Then applying equation (3-14A), in 1970 y^* = 2.1 and in 1997 y^* = 3.5. With the assumptions for δ, α, and the production function as specified in equation (3-16A), the model predicts that Thailand should have experienced a $(3.5 - 2.1)/2.1 = 67\%$ increase in per capita output as, all other things equal, its economy went through the transition from the steady state in which the saving rate was 21 percent to the one where the rate was 35 percent.

Actually, Thailand's real per capita income grew by over 200 percent between 1970 and 1997! The increase in the rate of saving thus accounts for only part of Thailand's 1970-1997 economic growth. Perhaps the specific form of the production function that we assumed in this example is incorrect. Perhaps the Solow model is inaccurate. Most likely, the saving rate was not the only variable that changed between 1970 and 1997. You may also wonder why we analyzed the period 1970-1997 and did not extend the analysis to include more recent years for which data is available. Actually, Thailand suffered a severe financial crisis and deep economic recession after 1997. Thailand's growth was sharply negative in 1998, and by 2005 had barely recovered its 1997 per capita income level. The process of economic growth is complex.

Chapter Four

Overcoming Diminishing Returns:
Technology as an Externality

It is naturally to be expected...that some one or other of those who are employed in each particular branch of labour should soon find out easier and readier methods of performing their own particular work.
    (Adam Smith, 1776)[47]

T he Solow growth model predicts that, in the absence of technological progress, factor accumulation is subject to diminishing returns and an economy sooner or later settles at a steady state where economic growth ceases. The fact is that, over the past 200 years, the majority of the world's economies have not declined into economic stagnation. Rather, the last two centuries have been characterized by unprecedented and accelerating economic growth. Therefore, it must be the case that diminishing returns have not proven to be as serious a problem as the Solow model predicts or the world has been able to overcome diminishing returns by continually generating technological progress. Economists have sought to reconcile the Solow model with observed evidence in two different ways: (1) show how economies can avoid diminishing returns to investment within the framework of the Solow model, and (2) develop new models of technological progress. The second approach has proven to be much more useful for understanding how an economy achieves long-run economic growth, but the first approach has also provided useful insights into where the fundamental sources of economic growth might be found.

This chapter covers the first approach to explaining permanent economic growth. The first section introduces a special case of the Solow model known as the "AK" model. This is followed by a discussion of

---

[47] Adam Smith (1776[1976]), Vol. 1, p. 13.

technology and technological progress. The remainder of the chapter covers models in which technological progress occurs as an *externality* to investment, production, or international trade. These models have the advantage of explaining permanent economic growth without abandoning the basic assumptions and structure of the Solow growth model.

4.1 Factor Accumulation without Diminishing Returns

It is not entirely correct to conclude, as we did in the previous chapter, that the Solow model cannot generate permanent growth in the absence of technological progress. There is a special case in which the Solow model *can* generate growth indefinitely even if technology does not continually shift up the production function. An understanding of this special case is helpful in understanding the Solow model and other models of technological progress.

4.1.1 The AK Model

Suppose that the economy can be represented by the constant returns to scale Cobb-Douglas production function discussed in the previous chapter

$$(4-1) \qquad\qquad Y = AK^{\alpha}L^{1-\alpha}$$

But, instead of assuming $0 < \alpha < 1$ as usual, suppose that $\alpha = 1$. This assumption effectively implies that there are no fixed or exogenous factors, that all factors can be increased by investment, and that all factors are subject to depreciation. With $\alpha = 1$, equation (4-1) becomes

$$(4-2) \qquad\qquad Y = AK^{1}L^{0} = AK$$

In the case of $\alpha = 1$, the per worker form of the model, $y = Ak^{\alpha}$, is

$$(4-3) \qquad\qquad Y/L = y = A(K/L) = Ak$$

For obvious reasons, this model has become known as the "AK" model of economic growth. It is attributed to Sergio Rebelo (1991).

The AK model is related to the more general Solow model. Figure 4-1 shows the per worker Cobb-Douglas function. The closer the capital share α is to 1, the closer to a straight line is the production function. For two economies starting with the same capital-labor ratio k_1, the economy with the higher capital share enjoys a longer transition to the higher steady state value. If α_1

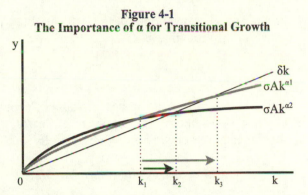

Figure 4-1
The Importance of α for Transitional Growth

> α_2, the economy whose capital share is α_1 transitions to k_3 while the economy whose share is α_2 transitions to k_2. A higher value of α implies diminishing returns take effect more gradually and economic growth takes longer to slow down. As the capital share α approaches 1, the production function approaches a straight line. In the AK model, α = 1 and the production function is a straight line. Permanent economic growth is now possible. Specifically, economic growth will occur as long as saving exceeds depreciation, or as long as

(4-4) $$\Delta k = \sigma Y - \delta k = \sigma A k - \delta k = (\sigma A - \delta)k > 0$$

Figure 4-2 depicts the AK model on a diagram similar to the one used to illustrate the Solow model. When $\sigma A > \delta$, the amount of new capital created exceeds the amount of new capital needed to replace depreciated capital. Growth can proceed without limit because the saving function σAk never bends over to intersect the straight depreciation line. In fact, the growth of the ratio of capital to labor is a constant function of the

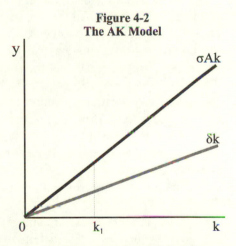

Figure 4-2
The AK Model

difference between σA and δ. Specifically, dividing equation (4-4) gives us the growth rate of k:

(4-5) $$\Delta k/k = g_k = \sigma A - \delta$$

Since A is a constant and the growth rate of a *product* of two variables is the *sum* of the growth rates of the two variables, per worker output y = Ak grows at the same rate as k:

(4-6) $\Delta y/y = g_y = \Delta(Ak)/Ak = g_A + g_k = 0 + g_k = g_k$

The AK model thus generates permanent economic growth despite the absence of technological progress. Clearly, diminishing returns is a fundamental reason why growth eventually stops in the Solow model.

4.1.2 Are All Factors Really Reproducible?

The AK model in effect assumes that *all* factors can be increased through investment. Rebelo's (1991) justification for the AK model is that, in the real world, few factors are truly fixed. Indeed, many factors that we think of as being fixed in quantity are at least partially reproducible.

Natural resources are not fixed in supply. Rather, they are a function of investment in exploration, research, and development. Since we have not yet scoured every piece of the earth, investments in searching for mineral deposits will, no doubt, continue to increase our stock of usable resources. Labor consists partly of *human capital*, which is created by the economy through education, training, and experience. In high income economies, human capital is more important than basic labor as a source of income. The average number of years of education in the developed economies of North America, Europe, and the Asia-Pacific region is about 12 years.[48] This suggests that the return to human capital greatly exceeds the return to basic physical labor. For example, Psacharopoulos (1994) has estimated that education augments basic labor by 7.7 to 12 percent for each year of education. Thus, in the hypothetical case where the income for basic labor is equal to 100, in developed economies the return to the combination of labor *and* human capital are at least $100(1.077)^{12} = 244$ and possibly as much as $100(1.12)^{12} = 390$. In the latter case, the return to human capital is nearly three times as large as the return to basic labor.

In other ways, factors and resources *are* limited, however. Even though labor consists of mostly human capital, human capital literally needs to be *embodied* in people, and people do not exist in unlimited supplies nor are they costless. It takes quite an investment to raise a child to adulthood and then to keep that adult alive. Also, human capital is limited by a

---

[48] OECD (1998), *Human Capital Investment*, Paris: Centre for Educational Research and Innovation, OECD.

person's finite lifetime. It makes little sense to devote anything close to our entire lifetimes to acquiring human capital; we would never reap the returns to our investment in human capital. Further advances in medicine and genetic engineering are likely to extend our longevity in the future, which will let us have more years to *both* invest in human capital *and* reap the rewards of our investment. Nevertheless, in the absence of infinite lives, we will continue to face diminishing returns to human capital investment.

The AK model's biggest weakness is its inability to explain *all* characteristics of world economic growth over the past 200 years. The return to capital has remained nearly constant over the past two centuries. This could be taken as evidence supporting the AK model and the constant slope of its production function. But, if we also consider that technology has improved immensely over the past 200 years, the AK model cannot be accurate. In the absence of diminishing returns to capital, improving technology should have caused the return to capital to increase. The combination of technological progress and a constant return to capital is consistent with continual upward shifts of a production function subject to diminishing returns to capital, exactly as the Solow model hypothesizes.

In sum, it may be true that the share of reproducible factors in the Cobb-Douglas production function is greater than the 0.25, 0.3, or even 0.4 values usually assumed for the capital coefficient. At the same time, the capital share is certainly not equal to one. Hence, in the long run there are diminishing returns to investment and technological progress is required to generate continuous economic growth. Technological progress neutralizes diminishing returns by raising the marginal product of factors even as factor accumulation diminishes factors' marginal returns. Interestingly, we will find that technological progress effectively makes the economy behave *as if* it has an AK production function.

4.2 Technology

Modeling the growth of technology has not been an easy task for economists, in part because of the ambiguity surrounding the meaning of *technology*. The definition of technology that covers a seemingly endless variety of innovations makes it difficult to model technological progress. On the one hand, technological progress consists of marginal improvements in the design of familiar tools and machines. On the other hand, it consists of abstract ideas such as quantum physics. Technological progress is the very diverse process that generates the new ideas, products, methods, systems, processes, designs, theories, etc. that are fundamental to increasing human welfare. Despite the enormous diversity of what we call technology, this section provides some general characteristics of technology that will prove useful for understanding the models of technological progress discussed later in this chapter and in the following three chapters.

4.2.1 Defining Technology

Technology is indeed a very broad concept, covering a variety of new ideas, knowledge, methods, organizational structures, legal institutions, procedures, and other innovations that enable an economy to increase the value of output that can be produced from a given set of national resources. Some technology is incorporated in the productive factors, such as the specific design of a machine, the layout of a factory building, or a genetically engineered drought-resistant seed. Technology also consists of more general knowledge that determines how we use the various factors and resources to produce new products, such as how to operate machines, where to place the machines in the factory building, and how much water and fertilizer to apply to seeds planted in a field. Also included among what we call technology are the institutions that guide economic activity. An economy whose institutions lead people to concentrate on being productive and innovative will transform its resources into a greater amount of welfare-enhancing output than an economy where institutions permit widespread theft, destruction, or extortion.

Paul Romer (1993) prefers the broader term *ideas* over the traditional term *technology:*

> The word technology invokes images of manufacturing, but most economic activity takes place outside of factories. Ideas include the innumerable insights about packaging, marketing, distribution, inventory control, payments systems, information systems, transactions processing, quality control, and worker motivation that are all used in the creation of economic value in a modern economy. If one looks carefully at the details of the operations of a corporation like Frito-Lay, one sees that there are as many subtle ideas involved in supplying potato chips to a consumer as there are in making computer chips. In addition, the ideas involved in supplying potato chips are probably more important for successful development in the poorest countries.[49]

---

[49] Romer (1993), p. 543.

Romer effectively describes technological progress as any change that improves an economy's efficiency with which it transforms its available resources into welfare-enhancing output. Furthermore, his reference to economic development suggests that a complete definition of technological progress should cover its "second derivative," namely the *improvement* in the economy's *capacity to improve* the efficiency with which it transforms resources into welfare-enhancing output.

4.2.2 It's the Application of the New Ideas that Matters

Technological progress consists of more than just the creation of new ideas; it consists of the *application* of new ideas. Knowledge and ideas do not shift the production function until they are put to use. For example, in analyzing the accelerating rate of technological progress in the United States in the late 1990s, Robert Solow includes the "Wal-Mart factor" as a critical element:

> The technology that went into what Wal-Mart did was not brand new and not especially at the technological frontiers, but when it was combined with the firm's managerial and organizational innovations, the impact was huge....Productivity growth accelerated after 1995 because Wal-Mart's success forced competitors to improve their operations.[50]

The implementation of new ideas have been investigated by economic historians. For example, Cipolla (1978) describes the development and applications of the time clock over the centuries, David (1990) examines the development of the dynamo and the computer, and Macfarlane and Martin (2002) retrace the discovery, development, and applications of glass. Teresi's (2002) *Lost Discoveries* describes numerous new ideas that were not put to use for centuries. These histories of specific technologies make it clear that there is often a long lag between the discovery of a new idea and when that idea is actually applied to enhance human welfare.

4.2.3 The S-Curve of Technology Diffusion

A frequently observed characteristic of technological progress is that it tends to occur continuously in a long series of small steps. For example, in the early stages of the development of agriculture, societies still continued

---

[50] Quoted in Michael Shrage (2002), "Wal-Mart Trumps Moore's Law," *Technology Review*, March, p. 21.

to gather and hunt. Only gradually did societies switch almost entirely to the cultivation of the land. Despite the thousands of years that have passed, hunting and gathering are still undertaken today in various forms. Although fish farms have become more common in recent years, the fishing industry still mostly hunts, for example.

The introduction of new technologies seems to often follow a gradual pattern that looks like an "S-curve," as illustrated in Figure 4-3. Such a curve suggests that new ideas spread slowly at first, then are applied more quickly, but it takes a long time for a new technology to win over the last potential users and reach full 100 percent acceptance. The S-curve was first suggested by two sociologists, Ryan and Gross (1943), who conducted a study sponsored by the Iowa Agricultural Experiment Station to determine the pattern of adoption of new hybrid-seed corn by farmers in Iowa. The economist, Zvi Griliches (1957, 1958), also used data on the adoption of hybrid seed corn to estimate the parameters of an S-shaped logistical function for different states of the U.S. Mansfield (1961) examined industrial technologies and found that the S-shaped logistic curve also explained the diffusion of new industrial technologies quite well. Mansfield went beyond Griliches by separately examining the diffusion of technology across individual firms as well as industries.

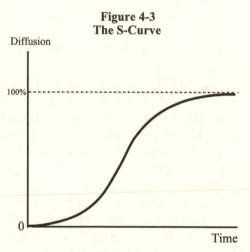

Figure 4-3
The S-Curve

Chong and Zanforlin (2002) provided a plausible theoretical model of technological diffusion that generates an S-curve pattern of technical adoption. Cohen and Levinthal (1989) argued that before any choices about acquiring foreign technology can be made, domestic resources must be expended to understand and evaluate the technologies available. David and Wright (1999) observed that, because the introduction of new technologies requires new plants and equipment, firms are often reluctant to abandon still serviceable manufacturing plants using older technologies. Rosenberg (1976) suggested that the uncertainty of technological change often makes it rational for potential users of technology to wait for further developments before they jump to a new path of technology.

There are in fact many examples of the S-curve pattern for technology adoption. For example, many years passed between the discovery of electricity and its major economic impact. A generator and electric lights were demonstrated in 1876 at Philadelphia's Centennial Exposition. It was not until six years later that Thomas Edison opened the first commercial generator to power electric lights in the Wall Street district of New York. And, it was not until decades later that electricity was readily available in all U.S. cities and towns. Only in the 1930s, 60 years later, did the Rural Electrification Act provide the financing to bring electric power to most rural areas of the United States. Of course, rural areas in many countries of the world still lack electric power today. Similarly, the patent for the internal combustion engine was filed in 1877. But it was not until the late 1920s, fifty years later, that half of all households in the richest country of the world, the United States, owned an automobile. And, like electricity, there are many countries in the world where most households still do not have an automobile. The birth of the computer in often set in the late 1940s, when Bell Laboratories invented the first semiconductor–the transistor–and IBM built its Selective Sequence Electronic Calculator. But, it has taken about fifty years for half the homes in the United States to have a computer. Just like the case of electric motors, there was early skepticism about the viability of the new technology: Even Thomas Watson, the President of IBM, foresaw no commercial possibilities for the first computer that his company had built under government contract fifty years ago. It took many other innovations, such as the miniaturization of transistors, the development of the personal computer, and the Internet, before computers became common household appliances. In most countries of the world, only a small minority of households have computers.

Figure 4-4 is from a recent report on technology by the Federal Reserve Bank of Dallas, and it shows S-curves for the diffusion of a number of path-breaking products, such as electricity, the refrigerator, radio, television, the automobile, home computers, and, most recently, the cell phone. While these examples all suggest that the spread of technology is far from quick, casual observation suggests that the process has gradually accelerated over time. It took millennia for farming and animal husbandry to replace hunting and gathering, but the more recent development of electricity has reached most corners of the world in about a century. Comin and Hobijn (2003) studied the diffusion of 20 different technologies across 23 countries over the period 1788-2001, and they found that the speed of diffusion has accelerated sharply since World War II. They also concluded that human capital and a country's social and economic institutions determine the rate of diffusion.

Figure 4-4
S-Curves of Technological Diffusion

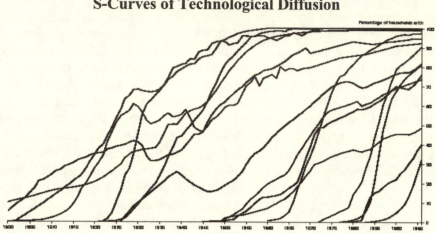

In order of introduction: range, telephone, electricity, automobile, radio, refrigerator, clothes washer, air conditioning, clothes dryer, dishwasher, color television, microwave, VCR, computer, cellphone.

4.2.4 The Geographic Diffusion of Technology

There is also ample evidence that suggests new technologies are slow to spread geographically. The concentration of information technology firms in Silicon Valley, financial firms in London, and the automobile industry in Detroit are often given as evidence that applications of new technologies tend to agglomerate close to where they were initially developed. Glaeser et al. (1991) offer some simple intuition to explain agglomeration: "After all, intellectual breakthroughs must cross hallways and streets more easily than oceans and continents."[51]

Nearly a century ago, Alfred Marshall (1920) devoted an entire chapter of his popular economics textbook to the "Concentration of Specialized Industries in Particular Localities."[52] Marshall attributed concentration to three factors: (1) the availability of specialized labor, (2) the development of specialized suppliers of intermediate goods and services, and (3) the flows of technology between the industries. More recently, Fujita, Krugman, and Venables (1999) and Krugman and Venables

---

[51] Glaeser, Kallal, Scheinkman, and Schleifer (1991), p. 1.

[52] Marshall (1920), Chapter 10.

(1995) presented theories to explain the development of cities, urban concentration, and the often-sharp differences in the economic development across regions of a country.[53]   Davis and Weinstein (2001) find that differences in productivity of Japanese industries across regions are directly related to the size of the regions and, mostly, to the local costs of production.   They argue that agglomeration makes economic sense by means of a counterfactual simulation that shows that Japan's real GDP would be 20 percent lower if production were evenly distributed throughout the country. This suggests that the gains from agglomeration of production in the regions that enjoy comparative advantage were quite large. Carlino, Chatterjee, and Hunt (2001) found that per capita patents increase by 20 to 30 percent for every doubling of population density in U.S. urban areas.

4.2.5 Technological Progress Is a Combinatoric Process

New knowledge generally builds on previous knowledge by *combining* existing ideas and knowledge in order to create new ideas and knowledge. According to Weitzman (1996): "An abstract case could be made that *all* innovations, being expressions of human imagination, are in a sense combinatoric."[54] The observation that the creation of new knowledge is a combinatoric process is very important for our understanding of technological progress. A combinatoric process can grow explosively.

Table 4-1 provides a simple example of a combinatoric process of technological progress. Suppose that in each successive period of time, the number of new ideas created is equal to the number of all possible combinations of pairs of ideas created in the previous period. Then, if the initial stock of knowledge in an economy consists of, say, four ideas, numbered 1 through 4 in Table 4-1, all the possible combinations of the initial four ideas result in six new ideas, labeled A through F in the table. Thus, after one period of innovation, this *combinatoric* process has expanded four ideas into six new ideas, which implies a total stock of knowledge equal to 10 ideas, an increase of 150 percent over the previous stock of four ideas. In the third round of innovation, the combinatoric process will increase the six ideas A through F into 15 even newer ideas. In the fourth period, the previous period's 15 new ideas are combined into

---

[53] For a general introduction to spatial economics, see Isard (1975) or Hoover and Giarratani (1984).

[54] Weitzman (1996), p. 212. See also Weitzman (1998) and Glaeser, Kallal, Scheinkman, and Schleifer (1991).

105 new ideas. In the fifth period, there are 5,460 combinations of the previous period's 105 new ideas. Clearly, this combinatoric process is explosive. If combinations between old ideas and new ideas are also possible in each period, then the number of ideas would have grown even faster. In this case, period three would be able to combine 10 ideas, not the six shown in Table 4-1, for example. The explosive nature of combinatoric processes implies that, so long as there are no impediments to bringing ideas together, technological progress is likely to accelerate over time.

The above examples are unrealistic. The state of knowledge obviously consists of more than four ideas. Given that knowledge Probably consists of millions or even billions of ideas, the combinatoric process of

---

Table 4-1
A Combinatoric Growth Process[1]
(new idea = the unique combination of two old ideas)

			New Ideas	Accumulated Ideas	Percentage Growth
Period 1	Begin with		4	4	
Period 2	4!/(2!·2!)	=	6	10	150%
Period 3	6!/(4!·2!)	=	15	25	150%
Period 4	15!/(13!·2!)	=	105	130	420%
Period 5	105!/(103!·2!)	= 5,460	5,590	4,200%

Period 1	*Period 2*	*Period 3*		
1	1,2 = A	A,B	B,C	C,E
2	1,3 = B	A,C	B,D	C,F
3	1,4 = C	A,D	B,E	D,E
4	2,3 = D	A,E	B,F	D,F
	2,4 = E	A,F	C,D	E,F
	3,4 = F			

---

[1] The number of combinations for n ideas taken r at a time is n!/[(n-r)!·r!]; we take n as the number of ideas generated in the previous period and combine them 2 at a time, so r = 2. The symbol "!" represents a product of descending integers beginning with the number preceding the !, e.g., 5! = 5·4·3·2·1 = 120.

technological progress must clearly be very explosive. On the other hand, knowledge can also be forgotten or lost, in which case the combinatoric process is less explosive. Resources must be employed to teach each successive generation of people the knowledge that was already accumulated by previous generations. Societies must also create the conditions that permit the combinatoric process to work. When new ideas are suppressed or people with different ideas are socially intimidated, few combinations will occur. Also, not all combinations of previous ideas produce useful new ideas. However, the greater the stock of knowledge, the more combinations are possible and, in all likelihood, the greater the number of useful combinations that will be created.

The combinatoric nature of knowledge also helps to explain why technological progress appears to be a *path dependent* process, in which each new step follows previous steps.[55] Path dependency means even momentous technological advances, such as the development of agriculture, gunpowder, the factory system, or electricity, naturally followed previously acquired knowledge, experiments, and technological change. However, history suggests the path of technological progress can take many twists and turns.

The noted twentieth century economist, Joseph Schumpeter (2005), has pointed out that *novelty* within a path dependent on combinatoric process is difficult to explain. "How do we explain the changes in Florentine painting that happened between the thirteenth and fifteenth century?" write Becker et al. (2005) in an introduction to Schumpeter's article. On the other hand, novelty may not be as difficult to explain as Schumpeter suggests. All new things seem revolutionary, or even completely out of context, to the casual observer. It is not surprising that Schumpeter takes an example of "novelty" from art. Art is especially likely to move with the whims of a particular artist. But closer examination usually finds that the artist's whims were driven by past experience, sometimes an unpleasant experience. What the earlier mentioned works tracing the development and application of clocks, glass, and electric motors make clear is that the process of technological change is really a series of minute events. Only when they are observed from afar, unfortunately the vantage point of most people, do they seem like a stunning, radical change. Technological progress, and the combinations of existing knowledge that it consists of, often follows paths that are neither smooth nor consistently

---

[55] For a very simple and interesting discussion of path dependency, see N. Gregory Mankiw (1998), "Why We Don't Speak Esperanto," *Fortune*, October 12.

upward sloping, but detailed evidence invariably shows that with every episode of technological progress there was a deterministic path that can be understood.

4.2.6 Technology Is a Nonrival Good

Technology is different from most products produced in an economy. Most products are *rival goods*. For example, if I buy and wear a new coat, someone else cannot buy and wear that same coat. Only one person at a time can wear it. If another person wants a coat, he is going to have to take one away from someone who has one or, preferably, pay for the costs of producing another one. But, technology is at least partially *nonrival*. If one person uses an idea or method, another person can use it without diminishing the first person's use or having to produce that same idea from scratch. Once the wheel has been invented, we do not have to "reinvent the wheel" every time we need another wheel. The marginal cost of applying a particular form of technology is sometimes very close to zero. This has the important implication that once a certain type of knowledge was available, competitive market forces would drive its price toward zero. But, at such a low price, why would anyone devote the effort, resources, and time to create new knowledge?

Even though they are nonrival in nature, new ideas may still be *excludable* in that the creator of a new idea may be able to prevent people from using it. Excludability gives the creator the power to limit supply and charge for the use of her ideas. Patents and copyrights that give the creator of an idea, product, or process exclusive use for a given number of years are often applied to make *nonrival* ideas *excludable*. There are many other ways to exclude others from using a new idea. For example, the unique way that a new idea is incorporated into a product may give the innovator some market power with which to recoup the costs of innovation. It often also takes time for others to copy new ideas and apply them, especially more complex modern technologies. Some things may be impossible to copy exactly, such as the formula for Coca Cola. The Coca Cola Company opted to keep its formula secret rather than revealing its formula to gain a patent. Many innovators use marketing and brands to give their creations greater value and thus increase profits to cover the costs of their efforts.

4.2.7 Not All Technology Is the Same

Research to generate new technology is often divided into *basic research* and *applied research*. It is commonly suggested that basic research precedes the use of that knowledge in practical applications, and many justifications for government funding of science are based on this perception. It is not clear that this is the natural sequence of knowledge creation, however. Technological progress may come from experimentation by engineers employed to raise factory output, "tinkering" by amateur inventors motivated by personal curiosity, ambitious entrepreneurs seeking to make a fortune with a "better mousetrap," or workers seeking shortcuts to make their job easier. Throughout the industrial revolution, such "unscientific" innovation repeatedly brought results well before scientific research finds the full explanation for what was discovered.

An example of innovation preceding basic scientific research is steel production in the latter half of the 19th century. Steel producers discovered, through trial and error, that minute variations in inputs greatly affected the quality and durability of steel. Experimentation led to the *Bessemer process*, which lowered the cost of producing steel more than tenfold and made steel a viable material for a vast new array of products. According to Nathan Rosenberg (1994), "even well into the twentieth century, metallurgy can be characterized as a sector in which the technologist 'got there first,' that is, developed powerful technologies, or alloys, *in advance of* systematized guidance by science."[56]

Technology is also often classified as either *codified* or *non-codified*. Codified technology is knowledge that can be written down in a recipe or a blueprint that others can follow. Studies of technology invariably show, however, that often only the broad ideas are codified, but according to Polanyi (1958), most knowledge is best described as "tacit." Polanyi suggests that tacit knowledge requires that it be passed on "by example from master to apprentice."[57]

In fact, the classifications of *basic* and *applied* or *codified* and *non-codified* may still be too broad for so complex a process as technological progress. Furthermore, the difficulties of classification come on top of the basic differences between generating knowledge and applying knowledge, as discussed above. In any case, the diversity of the things that we call technological progress makes modeling difficult. How we model technological progress depends on precisely what kind of new knowledge we have in mind. Can we come up with one model to explain the

---

[56] Rosenberg (1994), p. 20.

[57] Polanyi (1958), p. 53.

Pythagorean theorem, the efficient financial system of the United States, and Toyota's "just-in-time" parts supply system?   Each of these improvements in "technology" contributed to improving human welfare, but each was motivated by a different set of forces. Designing a single model that captures the incentives for creating each of these types of knowledge is a challenge.

4.2.8 International Trade and Technological Progress

The various characteristics of technological progress discussed here hint at some potential roles that international trade could play in the process of economic growth. First of all, the nonrival nature of technology implies that it takes an integrated global economy to maximize the benefits of new ideas. Also, international trade increases competition between firms and industries, which could decrease the lag between the creation of new ideas and their application. The increased contacts between people and firms in different countries is also likely to increase the speed at which new ideas are spread across industries, economic sectors, and countries. Tacit ideas are likely to travel better when they are accompanied by trade or foreign direct investment.

The fact that much of what we call knowledge or technology is not codified so that it can be easily learned and copied also implies an important role for international trade. Trade enables countries to import products and equipment that already incorporate knowledge and technology. When a country imports a machine, the technology embodied in the machine can be applied by simply turning on the machine. This is clearly easier than learning about the technology and applying it to the creation of a tool or machine from scratch. Furthermore, if applications of technology also require tacit knowledge, international trade helps to build the contacts between people that are necessary for transferring the tacit knowledge.

The combinatoric nature of technological progress also suggests that international trade's opening of communications between different societies is likely to increase the stock of knowledge available to innovators and, hence, to stimulate the explosive combinatoric process.   Different countries are likely to have developed different sets of knowledge because technological progress is likely to have followed slightly different paths in different countries.   The combinations of more distant ideas may be especially fruitful. The noted French mathematician/physicist Jules Henri Poincaré wrote: "To create consists precisely in not making useless combinations and in making those which are useful....Among chosen combinations the most fertile will often be those formed of elements drawn from domains which are far apart."[58]

In summary, given the characteristics of technological progress, an open economy is likely to enjoy a faster rate of technological progress than a closed economy. As Robert Solow said about economic development in a recent interview:

> The essence here is a poor country learning and becoming able to do (it's more than just learning) what rich countries already do. There I think the case [for globalization] is clear. The notion that the poor countries of the world can in any reasonable interval achieve rich-country incomes without trade and capital flows is utterly implausible. If the poor countries of the world...have to develop by themselves the skills and technology they need to become rich by our standards, it's going to take forever.[59]

This idea that technology makes open economies more likely to generate faster technological progress will be supported when international trade is introduced into rigorous models of technological progress. The next section begins the discussion of models of technological progress.

4.3 Technological Progress as an Externality

The assumption of perfect competition that underlies neoclassical models such as the Solow model presents a serious problem when trying to model technological progress. Perfect competition implies that the price of a product is equal to the cost of the inputs used to produce it. If this is true, then in perfectly competitive markets, firms earn only enough to cover the costs of production and have nothing left to repay the up-front costs of innovation necessary to develop the product in the first place. Perfect competition leaves nothing to cover the costs of conducting research and development activities, costly experiments, market research, and the time, effort, and other opportunity costs incurred by entrepreneurs and

---

[58] From Poincaré (1908), "Mathematical Creation," quoted in D.K. Simonton (2004), *Creativity in Science: Chance, Logic, Genius and Zeitgeist*, Cambridge: Cambridge University Press., p. 42.

[59] Interview by Robert Solow in the Federal Reserve Bank of Minneapolis' quarterly magazine, *The Region*, September, 2002, p. 27.

innovators. Models that explicitly make technological progress a function of costly research or entrepreneurial activities are not logically compatible with the assumption of perfect competition in which a product's price exactly covers production costs. Imperfect competition is not easy to model, however. Economists therefore sought to model technological progress in a way that did not require them to abandon the neoclassical framework of perfect competition. They accomplished this by assuming that technological progress is a costless *externality* to some variable that is endogenous to the Solow model. This section examines several of these so-called *externalities models* of technological progress.

4.3.1 Technology and Investment

New technologies can be *embodied* in new tools and machines. De Long and Summers (1991, 1992) point out that technological progress normally requires new investment in plant and equipment. Not long after first publishing his growth model, Robert Solow (1960) wrote:

> It is as if all technical progress were something like time-and-motion study, a way of improving the organization and operation of inputs without reference to the nature of the inputs themselves. The striking assumption is that old and new capital equipment participate equally in technical change. This conflicts with the casual observation that many if not most innovations need to be in new kinds of durable equipment before they can be made effective.[60]

For example, a mainframe IBM computer in 1970 was capable of 12.5 million instructions per second (MIPS). In 2005, personal computers costing just a few hundred dollars are capable of nearly 500 MIPS. The general knowledge available today cannot make that 1970 IBM computer run any faster. Today's hardware is needed to compute at 500 MIPS.[61]

Sakellaris and Wilson (2001) used plant level data to estimate the scope of embodied technological change. They found that over the years 1972-1996 in the United States, one year's capital equipment was about 12 percent more productive than the previous year's. This is a very high rate

---

[60] Solow (1960), p. 89.

[61] This information on technological progress in the computer industry is from Gort, Greenwood, and Rupert (1999).

of technological progress, enough to account for about two-thirds of overall productivity gains in manufacturing. Hobijn (2001) used a different estimation method and also found that in U.S. manufacturing embodied capital became more productive at an annual rate of 12 percent. Bahk and Gort (1993) had earlier found similar high rates of embodied technological change in capital equipment in the 1980s, although Gordon (1990) estimated embodied technological change to be only three percent per year. Hornstein and Krusell (1996) and Gort and Wall (1998) argued that Gordon's price-based estimates are likely to have understated actual embodied technological change, however.

Also indicative of the importance of embodied technology is a study by Hendricks (2000) showing that differences in equipment investment and prices account for a significant portion of variations in growth rates across countries. Gort, Greenwood, and Rupert (1999) broke down GDP growth into total factor productivity and factor growth, and among their conclusions was that 37 percent of economic growth was driven by technological improvements in equipment and 15 percent from new structures.

4.3.2 Technological Progress as an Externality to Investment

The close link between investment and technological change has been used by some theorists to design a neoclassical growth model that generates permanent economic growth. To arrive at such a model, one more assumption is needed: investment by one firm generates positive externalities in the form of technology spillovers to the rest of the economy.

The intuition behind the *investment externality model* of technological progress can be illustrated using the modified Cobb-Douglas production function that assumes technology is labor augmenting

(4-7) $$Y = K^{\alpha}(E{\cdot}L)^{1-\alpha}$$

Recall that E is the stock of knowledge that augments labor. Suppose that there are many competitive producers, each with an increasing cost function. Hence, there is no tendency for monopolies to develop. Suppose also that the labor force is a constant, as assumed for the simple Solow model in the previous chapter. Finally, suppose that investment in physical capital increases the level of non-rival labor-augmenting technology in the overall economy, but individual investors do not notice any increase in their own level of technology as a result of their own investment in equipment because as one of a very large number of producers, their contribution to the spillovers is minuscule. That is, each individual competitive producer takes investment's technology spillovers as exogenous, unaffected by their own decisions to invest in new capital. This particular set of assumptions is necessary to maintain the assumption of perfect competition that underlies the neoclassical model. If producers could enhance their own productivity through their own investment, they would have an incentive to invest and grow larger, thus undermining perfect competition. Those who invested first would drive less efficient firms out of the market.

Suppose that the economy-wide labor-augmenting technology available to each producer is related to the economy's total capital stock according to

$$(4\text{-}8) \qquad\qquad E = BK$$

where $B > 0$. This simple linear relationship between the level of technology and the capital stock reflects the assumption of the Solow model that in the steady state the economy must replace a constant proportion of the capital stock that depreciates. Notice that, unlike the Solow model that simply assumes technology grows at some given rate, this model *endogenously* determines the level of technology because E is a function of another variable in the model, the capital stock. Substituting (4-8) into (4-7) and defining the constant $A \equiv (B \cdot L)^{1-\alpha}$, equation (4-3) can be written as

$$(4\text{-}9) \qquad Y = K^{\alpha}(E \cdot L)^{1-\alpha} = K^{\alpha}(B \cdot K \cdot L)^{1-\alpha} = B^{1-\alpha} L^{1-\alpha} K^{1-\alpha} K^{\alpha}$$
$$= B^{1-\alpha} L^{1-\alpha} K = (B \cdot L)^{1-\alpha} K = AK$$

Equation (4-9) shows output as a constant function of the capital stock. Hence, capital accumulation is not subject to diminishing returns and investment can permanently cause output to grow.

Dividing equation (4-9) by L puts the technology-augmented production function into per worker terms

$$(4\text{-}10) \qquad Y/L \equiv y = K^{\alpha}(E \cdot L)^{1-\alpha} L^{-1} = (B \cdot L)^{1-\alpha} KL^{-1} = Ak$$

In equation (4-10), the small case y and k are again defined as per worker output and the capital-labor ratio, respectively. Equation (4-10) shows per worker output as a constant function of the capital stock and the capital-labor ratio, respectively. Investment can permanently cause output or per worker output to grow.

4.3.3 Increasing Returns to Scale and Economic Growth

The above result that technology externalities to investment *exactly* offset diminishing returns and effectively create an AK model out of the general neoclassical model depends critically on the specific assumption that E = BK. However, even in the case where technology externalities are not a linear function of the capital stock, permanent growth through factor accumulation is still possible. Suppose that more generally

$$(4\text{-}11) \qquad\qquad\qquad E = BK^{\varphi}$$

where B and φ are constants such that $B > 0$ and $0 < \varphi < 1$. Substituting (4-11) into (4-7) then yields

$$(4\text{-}12) \qquad Y = B^{1-\alpha}K^{\alpha}K^{\varphi(1-\alpha)}L^{1-\alpha} = B^{1-\alpha}K^{\alpha+\varphi(1-\alpha)}L^{1-\alpha} = AK^{\alpha+\varphi(1-\alpha)}$$

if we again assume that B and L are constants and define $A \equiv (B \cdot L)^{1-\alpha}$. In per worker terms,

$$(4\text{-}13) \quad y = Y/L = B^{1-\alpha}K^{\alpha}K^{\varphi(1-\alpha)}L^{1-\alpha}L^{-1} = B^{1-\alpha}\,L^{-\alpha}K^{\alpha}\,K^{\varphi(1-\alpha)} = B^{1-\alpha}\,k^{\alpha}\,K^{\varphi(1-\alpha)}$$
$$= B^{1-\alpha}\,k^{\alpha}\,K^{\varphi(1-\alpha)}\,[L^{\varphi(1-\alpha)}/\,L^{\varphi(1-\alpha)}] = B^{1-\alpha}L^{\varphi(1-\alpha)}k^{\alpha+\varphi(1-\alpha)} = Ak^{\alpha+\varphi(1-\alpha)}$$

In this case, output or per worker output is not a simple linear function of the capital stock or the capital-labor ratio, respectively. Recall, also, from our discussion of the Cobb-Douglas production function in the Appendix of the last chapter that in this function the returns to scale are equal to the sum of the exponents of the inputs K and L. Because $0 < \varphi < 1$ and $0 < \alpha < 1$, it must be that $\alpha + \varphi(1-\alpha) < 1$, which means K and k are subject to diminishing returns. Diminishing returns are not as strong as in the absence of the technology externalities because $\alpha < \alpha + \varphi(1-\alpha)$, but continued investment still cannot generate permanent growth of output or per worker output because $\alpha + \varphi(1-\alpha)$ is still less than 1.

On the other hand, if $\varphi > 1$, then $\alpha + \varphi(1-\alpha) > 1$, and there are *increasing* returns to scale to k. In this case, the growth of k causes per capita output y to grow as well. This case, in which case technology externalities to investment are an increasing function of the stock of capital, permits per capita income to continue to grow as the capital stock expands. In fact, growth is explosive. In sum, the assumption that technological progress occurs as an externality to investment enables the Solow model to generate permanent economic growth, provided that the externality effect is a linear or increasing function of the capital stock.

4.3.4 Investment Externalities and International Trade

The finding that technology is often embodied in capital goods not only implies that permanent economic growth become more easily attainable, but international trade plays a major role in transferring technology across borders. Capital equipment can be traded internationally, and when technology is embodied in the capital, technology is effectively traded as well. Hence, a country whose level of technology is below that of the rest of the world can effectively buy "off-the-shelf" foreign technology by importing foreign capital goods. Recall from the previous chapter's discussion of international and the Solow growth model that Lewer (2002) and Lewer and Van den Berg (2001, 2003b) found evidence that imports of capital goods increase economic growth more than imports of consumer goods. The potential technology externalities from importing capital goods also implies that tariffs and quotas on capital imports affect a country's economic growth. All other things equal, when technology is embodied in capital, trade restrictions slow the economy's rate of long-run growth.

4.4 Learning-By-Doing

Where the above model linked technological progress to investment, another popular way to model technological progress has been to assume it is an externality to production. These models essentially build on the observation over two hundred years ago by Adam Smith, quoted at the start of this chapter, that specialization increases the amount of *learning-by-doing* because people more rapidly accumulate experience in performing a given task. The idea behind these models is straightforward: The more people work at doing something, the more they improve their methods, their tools, and the product they are producing. Hence, the overall level of technology will improve as production accumulates. As in the case of investment externalities above, the overall improvements in the economy's level of technology is not taken into consideration by any of the numerous competitive producers. They take technology as a given and seek to maximize profits by producing products at the least cost. But, if we suppose that their production also has unintended positive externalities in the form of learning that is not perceived by an individual producer but stealthily increases the amount of knowledge available to everyone in the economy, then permanent growth again becomes possible even in a neoclassical growth model subject to diminishing returns to individual factors.

4.4.1 The Early Studies

The classic example of *learning-by-doing* is the World War II production of Liberty Ships, first described by Rapping (1965). Production costs declined steadily over the four-year production of nearly 3,000 identical 8,000-ton transport ships. Rapping found that the number of hours of labor required per ship fell by 12 to 24 percent for each doubling of cumulative output. Alchian (1963) took data from 22 airframe factories during World War II and derived a similar learning curve. These authors noticed that unit costs were correlated with *cumulative* production, not just the *level* of production, which they interpreted as evidence that learning is a function of experience. The evidence on the learning process also showed, however, that unit costs fall at a diminishing rate. Irwin and Klenow (1994) find such a learning curve in the semi-conductor industry. A *learning curve*, as the curve relating unit costs of production to its cumulative production in Figure 4-5.

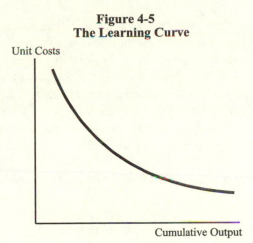

**Figure 4-5
The Learning Curve**

Unit Costs

Cumulative Output

4.4.2 Modeling Learning-by-Doing

Learning by doing can be modeled the same way as investment externalities were modeled above, except that the externalities are linked to output rather than the capital stock. Suppose that the level of technology, as represented by E in the production function, is directly related to the level of total output by the function

$$(4\text{-}14) \qquad\qquad E = BY$$

where $B > 0$. Substituting (4-12) into the augmented-labor version of the Cobb-Douglas production function from equation (4-7) yields

$$(4\text{-}15) \qquad Y = K^{\alpha}[E{\cdot}L]^{1-\alpha} = B^{1-\alpha}K^{\alpha}Y^{1-\alpha}L^{1-\alpha}$$

Dividing the equation by $Y^{(1-\alpha)}$ and isolating all the Y terms on left side of equation gives us

(4-16) $$Y \cdot Y^{-(1-\alpha)} = Y^{\alpha} = B^{1-\alpha}K^{\alpha}L^{1-\alpha}$$

Then, raising everything to the $1/\alpha$ power, assuming $(B^{1-\alpha}L^{1-\alpha})^{1/\alpha}$ to be a constant, and defining $A \equiv (B^{1-\alpha}L^{1-\alpha})^{1/\alpha}$, we again end up with the AK model:

(4-17) $$(Y^{\alpha})^{1/\alpha} = Y = (B^{1-\alpha}L^{1-\alpha})^{1/\alpha} (K^{\alpha})^{1/\alpha} = (B^{1-\alpha}L^{1-\alpha})^{1/\alpha}K = AK$$

In per worker terms, equation (4-17) becomes

(4-18) $$Y/L = y = (B^{1-\alpha}L^{1-\alpha})^{1/\alpha}(K/L) = Ak$$

When technology is a linear function of the level of output, production generates externalities that raise the overall economy's level of technology just enough to offset diminishing returns. Permanent economic growth is therefore possible. Just as in the case of the investment externalities model above, an exponential function such as $E = BY^{\varphi}$ can also permit permanent economic growth when $\varphi > 1$. When there are linear or increasing technology externalities to output, permanent per capita output growth is possible even with a standard neoclassical production function.

4.4.3 Recent Research on Technology Externalities

More recent studies using production data have led to some refinements and qualifications of previous research on learning-by-doing. For example, Mishima (1999) examined in detail the records at one of the 22 World War II airframe factories that Alchian (1963) studied. Mishima focused on the B-17 bomber production in Boeing Plant No. 2 in Seattle, Washington. He found that:

> The agent of learning is the core managers of control functions in the plant, that is, those who *coordinate* various aspects of the plant operation to ensure that work in progress flows smoothly....The hardware of production has little to do with learning in airframe fabrication and assembly. In Plant No. 2 the learning effect took place long after capital investment was suspended.[62]

Mishima thus finds that the learning process in the wartime airframe industry occurred separately from investment.

---

[62] Mishima (1999), p. 175.

In another study of the aircraft industry, Benkard (1999) concludes that some, but not all, learning carries over from one generation of aircraft to another. Benkard argues that learning can only be accurately explained if "forgetting" is included in the model. As time passes, accumulated learning "depreciates." Thus, a process of "learning-by-doing-and-forgetting" may be a more accurate description of efficiency gains in the aircraft industry. Such a process would help to explain the apparent slowdown in learning as illustrated by learning curves of the shape shown in Figure 4-5.

Other researchers have questioned whether the phenomenal increases in labor productivity were really due to on-the-job learning. Bell and Scott-Kemmis (1990) found many other sources of the productivity increases in shipbuilding during World War II. Thompson (2001) reexamined the data on the Liberty Ship program, and he noticed that development of new and better equipment by the manufacturers of equipment could account for much of the efficiency gains during the three years of Liberty Ship production. The detailed government records of Liberty Ship production also showed that production methods became more capital intensive, which implies there was a deliberate change in production technology as production progressed. This intentional innovation and investment was driven by explicit contractual clauses that called for rewards to shipbuilders when they accelerated output, improved quality, and lowered costs. The combination of newly-developed equipment and the switch to more labor-intensive technologies "reduces the estimated size of the learning effect by fifty percent."[63] The efficiency gains in the Liberty Ship program were to a substantial degree the result of intentional efforts to raise productvity, not unintended externalities from learning-by-doing.

4.4.4 Learning-by-Doing-With

Recall from the discussion about technology earlier in this chapter that Polanyi (1958) suggested that tacit knowledge requires that it be passed on "by example from master to apprentice."[64] The need for personal contact to facilitate the transfer of knowledge implies that technological progress is not so much learning-by-doing as it is *learning-by-doing-with*. In this case, international trade's role in transferring technology may be more related to after-sales activities and service than to the delivery of the

---

[63] Thompson (1999), p. 133.

[64] Polanyi (1958), p. 53.

product itself. Of course, the tacit nature of knowledge also implies that other forms of global economic activity, such as foreign direct investment by multinational enterprises may be more important than trade in transferring technology across borders.

Also important for transferring tacit knowledge is foreign direct investment. This book is primarily concerned with the role of international trade in stimulating growth, so an extended discussion of foreign direct investment is not appropriate here. However, it is worth noting that international trade and foreign direct investment are closely related. Mundell (1957) famously used standard static international trade theory to show that international trade and international factor movements are substitutes, not complements. The fact that we have for decades observed trade and immigration growing together suggests that either traditional trade theory does not capture all aspects of the relationship between trade and immigration, or the observed correlation is spurious, driven by third forces or a common trend. These results do not support Mundell (1957), who showed that in the classic Heckscher-Ohlin model of international trade, factor movements are substitutes for trade. Rather, they support recent studies by Clausing (2000) and Lewer and Terry (2003), who found a strong positive relationship between foreign direct investment (FDI) and international trade. The results also reflect the fact that trade data show multinational firms are involved in nearly all international trade. For example, Hipple (1990) noted that in 1982, 95.9 percent of total U.S. exports were made by U.S. multinational firms and U.S.-based affiliates of foreign multinational firms. Zeile (1997) used more recent data to confirm that the share of multinational firm trade had changed little over the two decades preceding his study.

With international trade growing faster than world GDP, and with multinational firms maintaining their dominant presence in international commerce, a positive correlation between foreign direct investment and trade flows is to be expected. It may, therefore, be difficult to separate the growth effects of international trade and foreign direct investment.

4.5 Learning-by-Trading

Exporting has been linked to increased efficiency and productivity. As discussed in Chapter 2, Feder (1982) specified a regression model in which the export sector of the economy generates positive externalities for the entire economy. Those externalities may be the result of the learning-by-doing process because trade expands output. According to Baldwin's (1992a) adaptation of the Solow model, detailed in the previous chapter, international trade increases the steady-state levels of k and real output. Or, they may be the result of investment externalities. For example, Lee (1995) extends Mazumdar's (1996) suggestion that trade may reduce the cost of capital goods and shows that falling costs of imported capital stimulates investment and, hence, creates potential investment externalities. International trade is also a source of increased competition. Porter (1990), Aghion, Dewatripont, and Rey (1999), and Semenick Alam and Morrison (2000) all suggest that there will be more "learning" when the "doing" is done under more competitive free trade. Another possible explanation for the observed direct relationship between exports and productivity is that trade generates international technology flows, either because foreign buyers provide technology to exporters or because foreign marketing requirements force exporters to apply foreign technologies. Chapter 8 will detail the many empirical studies that have found a close relationship between bilateral trade flows and technology flows. Included among these studies are, for example, Sjöholm (1996), who used information from the Swedish patent office to trace the international flow of ideas. He found these technology flows to be closely related to Sweden's international trade flows. Caselli and Coleman II (2001) examined the spread of computer technology across a large sample of countries between 1970 and 1990, and they found that openness to trade has a strongly positive effect on the diffusion of computer technology.

4.5.1 Learning-by-Exporting

Suppose, again, that producers in the economy all produce according to the production function in equation (4-7) above. Suppose also that exporting increases the level of labor-augmenting technology according to

$$(4\text{-}19) \qquad\qquad E = bxY$$

where $x > 0$ is the proportion of output that is exported and $b > 0$ is the coefficient that determines the strength of the external benefits that the export industry gives the rest of the economy. Substituting equation (4-19) into the Cobb-Douglas production function (4-7) yields

$$(4\text{-}20) \qquad\qquad Y = K^\alpha[E{\cdot}L]^{1-\alpha} = (bx)^{1-\alpha}K^\alpha Y^{1-\alpha}L^{1-\alpha}$$

Dividing by $Y^{(1-\alpha)}$, isolating all Y terms on left side of equation, raising everything to the $1/\alpha$ power, and defining the constant $A \equiv (bx^{1-\alpha}L^{1-\alpha})^{1/\alpha}$

simplifies equation (4-20) as follows:

$$(4-21) \qquad (Y^\alpha)^{1/\alpha} = Y = [(bx)^{1-\alpha}L^{1-\alpha}]^{1/\alpha} (K^\alpha)^{1/\alpha} = AK$$

Externalities to exporting can therefore, like investment and production, also make the economy behave as if its production function is an AK function. As in the previous cases of externalities, any form of increasing returns permits permanent per capita output growth provided the fixed factor (labor) grows over time.

4.5.2 Testing the Learning-By-Exporting Hypothesis

Clerides, Lach, and Tybout (1998) rigorously tested the *learning-by-exporting* hypothesis using data on individual exporting firms in Colombia, Mexico, and Morocco. They found that export industries exhibit falling costs, but it was not the gains in efficiency by exporters from foreign technology transfers that caused the fall in costs. Rather, costs fell through a self-selection process in which high-cost firms stopped exporting and low-cost firms increased exports. This finding suggests that importing firms in developed countries do not necessarily transfer technology to make their foreign suppliers more efficient; they may simply learn to place their foreign orders with relatively more efficient firms. They "learn-by-importing" to find the best sources of foreign supply. International trade may thus serve the function of rewarding efficient firms and causing the inefficient ones to contract, which can certainly be seen as a positive contribution to the growth process. Bernard and Jensen (1999a, 1999b) and Aw, Chung, and Roberts (2000) similarly found that exporting has no direct effect on plant efficiency, but overall industry efficiency improves with exporting because the more efficient plants exported and grew at the expense of the less efficient plants.

The selection process found by Bernard and Jensen, Clerides, Lach, and Tybout, or Aw, Chung, and Roberts is not compatible with the export externalities hypothesis. The selection process has nothing to do externalities. Rather, the shift in resources from less efficient plants to more efficient plants within an export industry is more akin to the shift in resources from one entire industry to another as predicted by the traditional Heckscher-Ohlin model of international trade. There is technological progress as long as there are shifts in resources, and, according to the Solow model, there will even be medium-run growth as the economy's steady state shifts. But the selection process, per se, does not generate permanent technological progress and economic growth.

In his survey of technology diffusion, Keller (2004) concluded:

> The conventional wisdom today is that learning-by-exporting effects
> are non-existent. This position is consistent with current evidence,
> but at the same time there are a number of issues which in my view
> are worth further research before the question should be considered
> settled.[65]

For one thing, Keller suggests that aggregation across firms and sectors of the economy may have masked industry-specific and firm-specific learning in many studies. There is, in fact, some evidence that exporting does improve productivity in individual exporting firms. Blalock and Gertler (2004) estimated productivity changes for a panel of Indonesian firms for the years 1990-1996, and they found that Indonesian firms experienced jumps in productivity after starting to export. Hahn (2003) shows that changes in Korean exporting firms' total factor productivity is explained by both self-selection and learning-by-exporting. Learning-by-exporting effects are especially large immediately after firms first start exporting. Van Biesebroeck (2003) similarly found both self-selection effects and gains from increasing scale among South African exporters. Fernandes and Isgut (2005) found that young firms learn much more from exporting than do old firms, with recently established firms increasing their productivity by 4 to 5 percent for each year the firm has exported.

Some studies have uncovered evidence of technology transfers from foreign buyers and domestic exporters. According to a World Bank study on Korea by Rhee, Ross-Larson, and Purcell (1984):

> The relations between Korean firms and foreign buyers went far
> beyond the negotiation and fulfillment of contracts. Almost half of
> the firms said they had directly benefitted from the technical
> information foreign buyers provided: through visits to their plants
> by engineers or other technical staff of the foreign buyers, through
> visits by their engineering staff to the foreign buyers, through the
> provision of blueprints and specifications, through information on
> production techniques and on the technical specifications of
> competing products, and through feedback on the design, quality
> and technical performance of their products.[66]

---

[65] Keller (2004), p. 767.

[66] Rhee, Ross-Larson, and Purcell (1984), p. 61.

Hou and Gee (1995) similarly find substantial technology transfers to supplier firms in Taiwan from importers in developed economies. Pack and Saggi (1999) investigate why importing firms, or "upstream firms," are willing to transfer technology to foreign suppliers when externalities benefit many other firms in the exporting economy. They explain that importers gain from the increased competition among exporters and are able to capture many of the gains from the technology they transfer through lower prices and better quality. That is, foreign importers who supply foreign suppliers with technology effectively capture some of the technology externalities in the form of lower prices offered by the more competitive foreign suppliers.

4.5.3 Enclaves, Maquiladoras, and Spillovers

Export industries have not always been seen as conduits through which foreign technology transfers to the rest of the economy. For example, in the 1870s several large British mining firms established operations in the arid, unpopulated desert region of northern Chile. These firms operated far out of sight of most Chileans, who lived in the central part of the country one thousand miles to the south. The mining firms built their own port facilities and rail connections, and they employed relatively few Chileans in their capital-intensive industry. All equipment and supplies were imported from Britain. There were few opportunities for technology spillovers to the local economy, and the huge profits derived from the very low production costs and the high world prices for nitrate accumulated largely to the British mining firms. The Chilean nitrate industry is a classic example of what is termed an *enclave industry*, a foreign-owned industry that largely imports from and exports to the rest of the world and has few transactions with the domestic economy.

Modern examples of enclave industries that are largely isolated and have few spillovers to local economies are mostly mining industries. Another example of enclave industries are the Mexican *maquiladoras* along the northern border with the United States. Maquiladoras are assembly industries operating near Mexico's northern border with the U.S., which were actively promoted by the Mexican government in order to increase domestic employment. Critics have argued that the rules governing the maquila industries practically guaranteed that they would be *enclaves* with few externalities or technology spillovers to the Mexican economy. Recent studies of export processing zones in Central America and Asia by Jenkins, Esquivel, and Larraín B. (1998) and Madani (2000) have also criticized these special arrangements for their lack of spillovers and externalities.

There are ways to turn what appear to be enclaves into industries with externalities. For example, in the late 1800s, the Chilean government began to extract larger tax revenues from foreign mining firms. These very substantial tax revenues helped to fund education and infrastructure that made Chile one of the wealthier countries in Latin America. The potential downside of using taxation to spread the benefits of trade is that the government in Chile grew to be a very large participant in the economy, eventually making the government the owner of much of Chile's heavy industry. And, when the prices of copper exports collapsed in the depression years of the 1930s, the government ran into severe budgetary problems. Mexico has made the maquiladoras less like enclaves by joining a free trade area with the United States and Canada, the North American Free Trade Area (NAFTA). Foreign firms can now locate anywhere in Mexico and import parts and raw materials freely, exporting or selling locally as the market demands. Now that NAFTA has been operational for over ten years, it should be possible for researchers to begin examining whether the many industries that have located throughout Mexico in response to trade opportunities associated with NAFTA generate more technology spillovers to the rest of the Mexican economy.

4.5.4 Learning-by-Importing

Many researchers have hypothesized that it is imports, not exports, that provide the greatest stimulus for economic growth. Imports of new products and services are a very direct channel through which technology is transferred from abroad. The investment externalities model suggests that the introduction of new capital equipment is accompanied by the introduction of new ideas. In fact, for developing economies imported capital equipment will be much more likely than domestically produced capital to incorporate new ideas, methods, and procedures. Imports of services such as foreign travel and foreign education are often accompanied by the introduction of new ideas and technologies. People who travel abroad will be exposed to things that they would not otherwise see, and students who study abroad do so explicitly to acquire knowledge that is not available at home.

It is easy to model learning-by-importing. All that is necessary is to assume that importing increases the level of labor-augmenting technology in the overall economy according to the function

(4-22) $$E = amY$$

in which m > 0 is the proportion of output (real GDP) that is imported and a > 0 is the coefficient that determines the strength of the external benefits that imports provide to the economy. You will notice that this equation is nearly identical to equation (4-19) above, which specified the learning-by-exporting process. You can perform the usual substitutions into the Cobb-Douglas model to end up with an AK function as in equation (4-21).

4.5.5 The Role of Import Competition

It is often suggested that imports increase a country's rate of economic growth because they increase competition that pressures producers in the economy to innovate more rapidly, to adopt new ideas more rapidly, and to apply cost-cutting measures more quickly. There is research to support this suggestion. For example, the McKinsey Global Institute (1993) noted how the competition from Japanese automakers forced U.S. automakers to improve their productivity. Dertouzos, Lester, and Solow (1990) used data from several U.S. industries to documented how foreign competition improved productivity, and Lawrence and Weinstein (1999) showed that imports served an important role in raising productivity in Japan and Korea. Levinsohn's (1993) data that spanned the dramatic market opening in Turkey in 1984 showed that trade enhanced productivity.

MacDonald (1994) looked at a large sample of U.S. industries and analyzed the effect on labor productivity in each industry as a result of an increase in competing imports. He specifically differentiated the effect of foreign competition on industries that were less concentrated (having a greater number of competing firms) and those that were more concentrated and thus less competitive. According to MacDonald:

> The results are striking. Import shocks have a small, positive and weakly significant association with later productivity growth in less concentrated industries. But in highly concentrated industries, import shocks have large and highly significant effects on next period productivity growth–a five percentage point increase in import share is associated with a 3.7 percentage point increase in annual labor productivity growth....That increase is quite large either compared to the overall mean (2.75 percentage annual growth), or to predicted growth of 4.15% in a highly concentrated...industry.[67]

---

[67] MacDonald (1994), p. 727.

Thus, import competition seems to promote innovative behavior to improve productivity.

It is not obvious, however, that a correlation between imports and firm productivity implies that there are externalities. Imports may simply embody foreign technology, and thus trade implies the importation of technology. There is nothing "external" about this process. Nor is it even necessarily true that foreign competition necessarily stimulates innovation. The next chapter details Joseph Schumpeter's model of technological progress in which firm profits provide the incentive for innovation. Profit will tend to be diminished by increased competition.

Finally, a word of caution about learning-by-trading. The empirical results that relate exports or imports to productivity in exporting or importing industries do not prove that either exporting or importing drive innovation. As Levine and Renelt (1992) write:

> if one substitutes imports or total trade for exports in cross-country growth or investment regressions one obtains essentially the same coefficients estimate and coefficient standard error. Thus, researchers who identify a significant correlation using an export performance measure should not associate this result with exports per se, because it could be obtained using a corresponding measure of imports or total trade.[68]

Abba Lerner's (1934) *symmetry theorem* long ago made it clear that exports and imports always tend to move in tandem. Exchange rates, resource allocation, and price levels all serve to keep exports and imports correlated. Lerner's proof that a tax on imports serves as a tax on exports as well was distinguished by Irwin (1996b) as one of the most important principles of international economics. If exports and imports are closely correlated, it will not matter much which of the two are put into a regression to explain technological progress. The results reported above from various studies that claim to have uncovered a link between either exporting and technological progress or importing and technological progress may have found little more than what so many of the empirical studies reviewed in Chapter 2 found, which is that international trade and economic growth tend to be correlated. Interpreting the results of the studies reported just above as indicating that exporting or importing directly causes technology externalities may be stretching what the data actually reveals.

---

[68] Levine and Renelt (1992), p. 953.

4.6 Conclusions

This chapter has detailed one of the ways in which economists have sought to model technological progress. By assuming that technological progress is an unintended by-product, or externality, of investment, production, exporting, or importing, it becomes possible to graft technological progress onto the Solow growth model. The external technological progress turns the Solow model into an AK model or a model with increasing returns to scale, both of which are capable of explaining permanent economic growth.

Growth economists have not been entirely satisfied with the externality models, however. One weakness of the models is that they do not link the creation of new ideas and knowledge to any specific incentives that guide human behavior. Externalities are by definition external to decision makers. The externality models also effectively assume that the creation of new technology is an unnoticed and costless process. These models therefore tell us little about how technological progress is generated. In our case, these models are of limited use in determining how international trade is likely to influence economic growth. Also, Bloom, Canning, and Sevilla (2002) recently uncovered evidence that there are no externalities to aggregate production functions.

More important, beginning with Schmookler's (1966) classic study of innovation, researchers have consistently found that there are costs associated with innovative activity and that innovative activity only occurs when ways are found to cover those costs. New ideas do not "just happen" as an unintended by-product of some other activity. The evidence overwhelmingly shows that, for technological progress to occur, someone has to decide to think, to apply resources toward research and development, and to be willing and able to upset the status quo to put new ideas and technology into practice. Economists have, therefore, increasingly embraced the more direct approach of modeling technological progress as an intentional choice by innovators to apply scarce, costly resources to the task of creating new ideas. This second approach to modeling technological progress is intuitively more appealing and potentially much more useful for economic policy because it explicitly distinguishes the causes of incentives that drive innovation. It is also more difficult than grafting technological progress onto the Solow model as an externality. Fortunately, the gains have been well worth the effort, and we today have a set of insightful models of growth and technological progress. The next chapter examines the popular model of innovation based on Joseph Schumpeter's concept of creative destruction.

Chapter Five

Technological Progress
as Creative Destruction

The problem that is usually being visualized is how capitalism administers existing structures, whereas the relevant problem is how it creates and destroys them.
(Joseph Schumpeter)[69]

Innovation and the application of new ideas is generally the result of intentional and costly effort. Most innovation emerges from research and development departments of corporations, from government-funded projects, or from long years of experimentation by individuals and organizations. New knowledge and technology do not suddenly appear to us as miraculous revelations or in dreams. Virtually all breakthroughs in knowledge can be traced back to years of study and preparation. As Thomas Edison is said to have remarked, innovation is "10 percent inspiration and 90 percent perspiration."

Another feature of innovation is that it is costly, which means that it can be carried out only if there is some way of covering the costs. Schmookler's (1966) classic study of innovation in U.S. industries found that, invariably, inventions and discoveries were the result of profit-seeking behavior rather than mere individual curiosity or accidental discoveries. Further research has confirmed Smookler's findings. More recently, Acemoglu and Linn (2003) found that innovation in the pharmaceutical industry is directly related to market size and prospective profits. A recent OECD study on industrial productivity notes that most investment in new

---

[69] Schumpeter (1934), p. 34.

equipment by producers is intentionally undertaken in order to acquire the technology embodied in the capital.

Recall also that Thompson's (2001) reexamination of the World War II Liberty Ship program reveals that the persistent cost reductions were the result of intentional efforts effectively paid for by U.S. government bonus payments for improved quality and speed of delivery. Other efficiency gains in the Liberty Ship program were the result of new capital equipment developed by equipment makers who supplied the shipyards. In other words, profits motivated intentional research and development activities that produced gains in efficiency. The alleged "learning curve" did not represent the gratuitous by-product of unintended learning-by-doing at all, the declines in costs over time were the straightforward result of intentional efforts to lower costs. Expenditures on research and development by firms throughout the world constitute further proof that new technology is not exogenous. UNESCO estimates that during the 1990s research and development expenditures in the United States averaged 2.55 percent of GDP. A similar percentage was reported for Switzerland, and even higher portions of GDP were spent on research and development in Japan, Korea, and Sweden.[70]

Growth models must accurately reflect the intentional nature of innovation. Research, experimentation, analysis, planning, designing production equipment, and all the other activities related to the creation and application of new ideas, products, methods, procedures, and organization, require real resources that must somehow be paid for. When innovation has direct costs, technological progress becomes more like a costly investment undertaken to achieve expected future gains. Models that describe the process of innovation must, therefore, identify the *incentives* that induce people to incur the up-front costs of innovation. The need to recover the up-front costs of innovation makes the assumption of perfect competition particularly awkward for modeling technological progress because the convenient assumption of perfect competition is no longer appropriate. Perfect competition results in prices that exactly cover the costs of production, which means a competitive equilibrium leaves nothing to cover the up-front costs of research and development activities. Growth economists have therefore had to abandon the comfortable world of perfect competition and static efficiency.

---

[70] As reported in The World Bank (2002), *World Development Indicators*, Washington, DC: World Bank, Table 5.11, pp. 322-324.

Some of the most popular modern models of technological progress assume that innovation is driven by entrepreneurs who seek to introduce new products and new methods in order to earn profit. These models specifically assume that innovation serves to give innovators market power that permits them to charge prices above their marginal production costs. These models are often referred to as Schumpeterian models, in honor of the twentieth century economist Joseph Schumpeter, who described technological progress as a process of profit-driven *creative destruction*. Creative destruction is a dynamic process whereby innovators continually apply costly resources to create new products and methods that give them a competitive advantage over existing producers. Schumpeterian models have proven to be very useful because they can be generalized to cover a broad set of circumstances and incentives relevant to most types of innovation. For our purpose, Schumpeterian models also can incorporate international trade and provide us with very useful insights into how trade affects a country's long-run rate of economic growth.

5.1 Joseph Schumpeter's Creative Destruction

During the first half of the twentieth century, when mainstream economics focused on resource allocation using static "all other things equal' analysis, Joseph Schumpeter (1912, 1934) presented a very different model of economic growth. Schumpeter was viewed as a radical for his description of the capitalist system as a dynamic system that continually generates change and technological progress. The neoclassical view of the market system is that it is inherently *stable*, always moving to a stationary *equilibrium*. Schumpeter described the capitalist system as an evolutionary process that never reverts to a stationary equilibrium. He saw an ever-changing economy in which innovative activities set in motion changes that cause further disruptive innovations. Schumpeter's model is a truly *dynamic* one in that he described a continually changing economy, not the stable equilibrium described by the familiar supply and demand models popular in mainstream microeconomics.

5.1.1 The Process of Creative Destruction

Schumpeter criticized mainstream economists for concentrating their analysis on resource allocation. He complained that "the problem that is usually being visualized is how capitalism administers existing structures, whereas the relevant problem is how it creates and destroys them."[71] Schumpeter described the capitalist economy as a "perennial gale of creative destruction" in which each firm sought to gain an advantage in the marketplace through innovation. Each innovation, such as a more attractive design, a lowering of production costs, a new product, a new source of supply of inputs or raw materials, or an improved management method, was pursued because it held the possibility of generating higher profit for the innovating firm. Such *creative* activity also *destroyed* the market power that other firms had gained by means of their earlier innovations. Hence, each innovator's gain is only temporary because the creative innovation of competitors will, sooner or later, destroy newly conquered market power. This continual creation and destruction prevents permanent monopolies from developing. More important, society enjoys continuous technological progress. Creative destruction was, according to Schumpeter, the source of economic growth and the enormous increases in living standards observed in the early 1900s. Such a dynamic concept did not fit well with the static models economists used at that time.

Schumpeter's idea of *competition* was also radically different from the price competition that economists normally promote as the source of economic efficiency. Schumpeter saw ferocious competition among firms, but it was technological competition, not price competition. Competition to develop new products and production processes created the temporary monopoly profits that induced innovators to incur the up-front costs of innovation, but these profits were eventually eliminated by the "creative destruction" of competing innovators. Everyone in society benefitted from the technological progress, wrote Schumpeter. Hence, Schumpeter rejected the conclusion of standard microeconomic theory that monopoly profit is a form of "market failure" that creates costly deadweight losses (the well-known "Harberger triangles") for society and shifts income from workers to capital owners. Schumpeter contended that profits were in fact necessary for the economy to grow and raise standards of living. It is no wonder he was not viewed as a mainstream economist in the early twentieth century, when popular sentiment supported anti-trust legislation and forced breakups of monopolies to reduce the market power of large firms. People were more concerned with the "robber barrons" than they were with a slowdown of technological progress.

---

[71] Joseph Schumpeter (1934), p. 84.

5.1.2 The Role of the Entrepreneur

Central to Schumpeter's process of creative destruction is the *entrepreneur*, the person who initiates, organizes, and manages the process of innovation. According to Schumpeter, the entrepreneur is the one who recognizes and grasps the opportunities for introducing a new product, changing a firm's management organization, exploiting a new market, finding a new source of raw materials, cutting the costs of production, or motivating the labor force. Entrepreneurs are the people who see the economic potential of inventions. They may not themselves be the owners of a new venture, nor are they necessarily the inventors of specific technologies. Rather, entrepreneurs often employ inventors on behalf of those who provide the funds for the enterprise. But it is the entrepreneurs who have the ambition, the vision of profit, and the organizational skills to bring projects to fruition.

Schumpeter attached great importance to the *social climate* within which entrepreneurs have to operate. Since the rate of technological progress of an economy depends on how aggressively and competently entrepreneurs employ resources to innovate, the incentives and barriers they face are critical to the process of economic growth. Among the critical institutions are society's attitude toward business success, the prestige of business activity, how well the education system prepares potential entrepreneurs, and how much freedom "mavericks" have to pursue their ambitions. Schumpeter actually referred to entrepreneurs as "social deviants" who often clash with tradition and certainly act counter to the wishes of vested business and social interests. This need for the entrepreneur to break with tradition can explain the apparent lack of entrepreneurs in some societies. Schumpeter pointed out that entrepreneurs are often immigrants and minority groups, such as the Jews in Europe and expatriate Chinese in Southeast Asia, where natives were, on average, much less entrepreneurial. He suggested that the same Chinese who were entrepreneurial in Singapore, Malaysia, and Trinidad were not nearly as entrepreneurial in their native societies. Only when they left China and were freed from the traditions of their society and less inhibited by how people saw them did they become entrepreneurs. Schumpeter argued that societies that tolerate people who break with tradition, think differently, and challenge vested interests will have higher levels of technological progress than societies that restrict economic and social freedoms.

Rothbard's (1995) and Formani's (2001) interesting histories of entrepreneurship make it clear that Schumpeter was not the first to elevate the entrepreneur to a position of importance in the economy. The early

French economist, Richard Cantillon wrote in 1730 that producers in an economy consisted of two classes: hired people who received fixed wages and entrepreneurs with non-fixed, uncertain returns. Other early French economists, such as François Quesnay and Jean-Baptiste Say, also discussed entrepreneurs. Recall, also, from Chapter 3 that as early as 1776 Adam Smith had described "philosophers and men of speculation" who greatly increased "the quantity of science." The concept of the entrepreneur gradually disappeared from the economics literature in the 1800s with the dominance of neoclassical microeconomics. Schumpeter is correctly credited with reintroducing the entrepreneur to the economics literature in the early twentieth century. While still too often absent from mainstream microeconomics, thanks to Schumpeter the entrepreneur has gained prominence in growth theory. The teaching of "entrepreneurship" has, of course, become standard fare in U.S. business colleges.

5.1.3 The Role of the Financial Sector

Schumpeter also emphasized the critical role of an economy's financial sector in enabling the economy to generate technological progress. Innovation is similar to investment in that future gains come long after current expenses. Entrepreneurs must therefore find ways to finance their research and development costs. According to Schumpeter, without a financial sector to channel funds from savers to the most capable entrepreneurs, to monitor the projects, and to spread risk for savers, innovation is not possible, and economic growth would cease. Schumpeter was not unique in his appreciation of the importance of the financial sector; John Hicks (1969) stated unequivocally that the Industrial Revolution could not have occurred without the concurrent development of financial markets.

Schumpeter's concern with the role of the financial sector contrasts with many growth models that assume savings are somehow automatically channeled to productive investment. The Harrod-Domar model, the Solow model, and even the externalities models of technological progress all simply assume that saving and investment are equivalent. Intertemporal transactions, in which something of value today is exchanged for something with an expected value in the future, are much more difficult to complete than contemporaneous transactions in which two things of equal value are exchanged at one point in time. The future is never perfectly predictable, even the roughest predictions require large amounts of information, and there are perverse incentives that undermine efforts to deliver the promised results in the future. The well-known problems of *risk*, *adverse selection*, and *moral hazard* often prevent mutually-beneficial intertemporal transactions from being completed even in countries with the most sophisticated financial markets.

5.1.4 Creative Destruction and Economic Growth

Joseph Schumpeter's concept of *creative destruction* captures a basic characteristic of economic growth, which is that doing something new requires that some existing activity ceases to be done. In a growing economy, new products replace old products, new jobs replace old jobs, and new production methods replace what most people had come to view as the normal way of producing things. Growing economies are characterized by *structural change*.

As Dwight Lee and Richard McKenzie (1993) write in their book *Failure and Progress: The Bright Side of the Dismal Science:*

> an understanding of scarcity keenly focuses attention on the fundamental and pervasive cause of failure: people's absolute inability to have everything that is desirable and the pervasive necessity of their making choices.... Failures occur frequently because the successes that are occurring in the economy deny resources to the ventures that fail. When the automobile was invented, many producers of horse-drawn buggies could not continue to operate. Resources were diverted into the production of cars, as buggy makers were no longer able to offer buggies at prices that were attractive to consumers and pay the wages and input prices necessary to compete against automobile producers for resources.[72]

The need for structural change is a direct consequence of the fundamental economic principle of scarcity. In the long run, economic growth *reduces* scarcity and continually increases the economy's capacity to convert resources into welfare-enhancing output, but it does not *eliminate* scarcity and the need to make choices in the short run. The resources needed to produce automobiles had to be taken away from other productive activities, such as building horse-drawn buggies. Of course, the costly process of innovation itself requires reducing output elsewhere in the economy. The opportunity cost of innovation is the output that could have been produced with the resources used instead to generate new ideas and technologies.

---

[72] Lee and McKenzie (1993), p. 17.

5.2 The Schumpeterian R&D Model

Romer (1990), Grossman and Helpman (1991b), Rivera-Batiz and Romer (1991), and Aghion and Howitt (1992) are among those who developed models of endogenous growth around the assumption that innovative activities are carried out by profit-seeking entrepreneurs. There are subtle differences between the many models that have been developed, but all of them incorporate the following five fundamental ideas:

1. Innovations are generated by intentionally employing costly (scarce) resources to create new products, ideas, methods, etc.

2. Profit-seeking innovators must compete with producers to employ the economy's scarce, and thus costly, resources.

3. Innovation creates new products or techniques that are better, cheaper, more attractive, or in some other way better than existing products, which gives the new activities and products an advantage over existing producers and products.

4. Just as their innovations "destroyed" earlier innovators' profits, innovators also know that further innovations by competing innovators will eventually eliminate the profits of their innovations.

5. Innovators rationally weigh the costs of innovation and the discounted expected future profits of innovation.

The "Schumpeterian" models of technological progress depict technological progress as an ongoing activity engaged in by individuals, firms, organizations, universities, or governments that have an incentive to employ scarce resources to generate new knowledge, ideas, methods, forms of economic organization, and other economic changes to increase the value of the economy's output.

This section introduces a simplified graphic Schumpeterian model of technological progress. The following section will present an alternative mathematical version of a Schumpeterian model.

5.2.1 Imperfect Competition and Profits

In the traditional microeconomic model of a firm, an imperfectly competitive producer faces a downward-sloping demand curve. To simplify the analysis without losing generality, suppose that the marginal cost of production is constant at the wage level w. This assumption means the marginal cost (MC) curve is a horizontal line at price w. As shown in Figure 5-1, the profit-maximizing producer increases production up to the point where marginal revenue equals marginal cost. The traditional static microeconomic model of an imperfectly competitive market, shown in Figure 5-1, therefore prescribes a profit-maximizing output level of q sold at price p. The difference between the price and the marginal cost (p−w) is the markup μ, which generates profit in excess of variable production costs equal to the product of the quantity of products sold q and the markup μ. Profit is thus equal to the shaded box in Figure 5-1.

A feature of the diagram in Figure 5-1 is that it does not have a time dimension. It says nothing about how long the firm with monopoly market power can continue to reap profits. In dynamic models of creative destruction, profits from innovation depend critically on how long a producer can reap the profit. Innovators hope that the future stream of

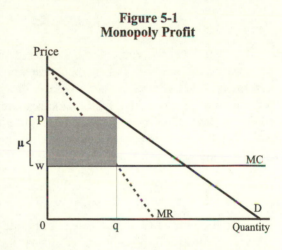

Figure 5-1
Monopoly Profit

profits following an innovation is large enough and continues long enough to exceed the costs of innovation. The duration of the profit stream of course depends on how quickly other innovators *destroy* the latest creation. We therefore need a more dynamic model than the static Figure 5-1.

5.2.2 A Model of Costly Innovation Driven by Profits

The models of endogenous technological progress usually model technological progress as the stream of products x_1, x_2,..., x_n, where each new product replaces the product preceding it because it is in some way superior to its predecessor. The models generally assume that innovators engage in innovative activity up to the point where the expected marginal gains from innovation equal the marginal costs of innovation. Suppose that the world consumes one product, denoted as x_t, at time t, and that the innovator who created x_t reaps a profit because the innovation made x_t preferable to x_{t-1}. This latter assumption implicitly includes the assumption that all consumers are identical (they are not distributed all along a downward-sloping demand curve) and that the markup is marginally less than the increase in value provided by the latest innovation (so that consumers no longer demand any more x_{t-1} after the creation of x_t).

In the Schumpeterian environment of *creative destruction*, profit from innovation depends on (1) the profit markup μ, (2) the level of production X, which is the quantity of the product x_t produced during one period of time, say one day, and (3) the number of periods (days) τ that the innovator can produce and enjoy the profit markup before her market position is *destroyed* by a subsequent innovation. Thus, profit π is equal to

(5-1) $$\pi = \mu X \tau$$

The level of production, X, depends on how many resources are devoted to production rather than research and development (R&D) activities. That is, daily production of x_t is directly related to the economy's total amount of productive factors and resources, R, and inversely related to the fraction of those resources devoted to innovation, n, during the day. Specifically, the total resources devoted to innovative activity during the day are equal to

(5-2) $$N = nR$$

Suppose for simplicity, but no loss of generality, that one unit of resources R *produces* one unit of output x_t. The total level of production during the day is therefore

(5-3) $$X = (1-n)R$$

5.2.3 Innovation Requires Costly Resources

The rate of innovation can be found by solving a maximization problem that takes into consideration the costs of innovation and the expected benefits of innovation. Innovating firms seeking to create a new product x_{t+1} must purchase labor and other productive resources in competition with the producer who demands resources to produce the most recently-developed product, x_t. The opportunity cost of innovation is the lost production of products x_t caused by shifting scarce resources to innovative activities.

The cost of resources will be lower, all other things equal, the greater is the supply of resources, R, in the economy. And, all other things equal, the cost of resources will be higher, the greater is innovative activity. Along with the level of output, the level of innovative activity determines the demand for resources. The price of resources is therefore a function of R and N as follows:

(5-4) $$w = g(\overset{+}{N}, \overset{-}{R})$$

The signs over the independent variables show their directions of influence, that is, the signs of their partial derivatives with respect to w.

The process of innovation is subject to a high degree of uncertainty. Devoting resources to R&D activity does not guarantee that something useful will actually be created, nor is there normally a neat time schedule that says how long it will take to make a new scientific discovery or when the search for a more attractive product will actually result in a successful creation. In short, there is a large degree of uncertainty associated with innovative activities. It is difficult to incorporate some unknown level of uncertainty into the maximization problem that we are trying to model, so we must make some simplifying assumptions. Suppose that new products are developed according to an R&D process that has a known average outcome around which actual outcomes vary. Suppose, furthermore, that the average time it takes to come up with a new product or technology is a direct function of the amount of resources devoted to innovative activity and that the exact timing of any one R&D project fluctuates randomly around the average timing predicted by the amount of resources devoted to R&D activity in the economy. Since we are interested in modeling the long-run growth process, we can legitimately solve for the average outcome. A further justification for our simplifying assumptions is that potential innovators can reasonably be assumed to have *rational expectations*, which means that they predict the future correctly *on average*. The assumption of rational expectation permits us to substitute *expected values* for future values.

Another simplifying assumption that we make is that each innovator is a perfect competitor in the market for resources and in the innovative process, and that each entrepreneur employs resources to the point where marginal expected cost of innovation is equal to the expected future profits from innovation. That is, we assume competitive entrepreneurs who use innovative activity to compete for temporary profits. The economy's average cost and profit functions are therefore viewed as the marginal functions by each individual innovator. Note that, with this assumption, we also effectively assume that innovators are risk-neutral and they do not require a premium to induce them to undertake the inherently risky innovative activities.

Suppose that it takes, on average, β units of resources to produce an innovation. We are here assuming that the production function of innovations is linear with respect to the amount of productive resources, R, employed in innovative activity. The average cost of innovation, CoI, that entrepreneurs expect to incur in generating an innovation is therefore

(5-5) $CoI = w\beta$

This function specifies that the more research is undertaken, the more labor and other resources need to be hired. If the total supply of productive factors and resources are fixed at R, increasing innovation increases total demand for factors and resources, which drives up the prices of factors and resources. Hence, the cost of innovation, CoI, increases as innovative activity increases. Figure 5-2 shows a typical upward-sloping CoI curve relating marginal costs of innovation to the amount of factors and resources used in innovation, N. All other things equal, the CoI curve shifts up if β, the average amount of resources needed to generate an innovation, increases, and it will shift down if R, the total supply of resources, increases. In general notation, the cost of innovation is

(5-6) $CoI = h(\overset{+}{N}, \overset{-}{R}, \overset{+}{\beta})$

Whether it is worthwhile to incur the costs of innovation of course depends on the gains from innovative activity, which we will examine next.

A brief note on the assumption of a linear R&D function is in order. There is no obvious reason why the R&D function should be linear. Good reasons can be found to assume the R&D function is non-linear, perhaps subject to diminishing returns. On the other hand, the function could enjoy increasing returns if innovation is a combinatoric process of

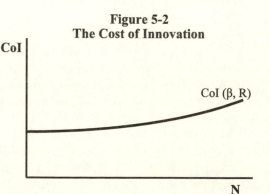

Figure 5-2
The Cost of Innovation

some sort; the more researchers are probing new ideas and communicating their findings, the easier it is for everyone to make progress toward finding new ideas, products, methods, etc. It is reasonably certain that the R&D function is an increasing function of the resources entrepreneurs devote to innovation. We therefore appeal to simplicity and assume that the positive function is linear. This does not in any way reduce the generality of the qualitative results derived from the model.

5.2.4 The Present Value of Innovation

In accordance with equation (5-1), the expected profit from an innovation is a positive function of the average markup μ, the amount of output produced, X, and the length of time τ that an innovator expects to enjoy the monopoly profit. The length of time τ depends on how fast new innovations are created. Since we have assumed that it takes β units of resources to generate an innovation, the expected number of innovations, **q**, during a day is

(5-7) $$\mathbf{q} = (1/\beta)N.$$

Figure 5-3 provides a graphic illustration of the relationship between the amount of resources devoted to innovation, N, and the average quantity of innovations **q** generated per day. It follows from equation (5-3) that the number of days that an innovator expects to enjoy his/her profit is equal to

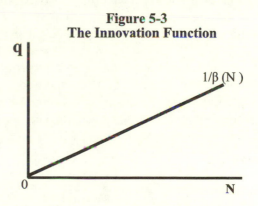

**Figure 5-3
The Innovation Function**

(5-8) $$E(\tau) = 1/\mathbf{q} = \beta/N.$$

For example, if **q** = .01, it takes 100 days before a new innovation "destroys" the current product's market position. According to equation (5-8), expected future profit is therefore a direct function of β and an inverse function of N.

Expected future profit also depends on the amount of production X, which competes for the use of resources. The more resources are expected to be used for innovation, the fewer are available for producing profitable products derived from the innovations. Hence, there are two reasons why the present value of an innovation is inversely related to N: (1) a higher N leads to a faster destruction of prior creations and (2) a higher N reduces the amount of resources available to produce profit-generating output. An increase in total resources, R, permits more future production X, which implies that expected profits are positively related to R.

Finally, because innovations require *current* expenditures on research and development (R&D) that must be paid for from *future* profits, expected future profits must be discounted. The annual interest rate is r; the higher the interest rate, the more rapidly future earnings are discounted, and the less is the present value of an expected innovation. In general, the present value of future profit from innovation, denoted as PVI, takes on the following general form:

(5-9) $$\text{PVI} = f(\overset{+}{\mu}, \overset{+}{R}, \overset{-}{N}, \overset{+}{\beta}, \overset{-}{r})$$

A more specific relationship can be derived by defining the right-hand variables in (5-1) more precisely. According to equations (5-1), (5-3), and (5-7), the expected profit, $E(\pi)$, accruing to an innovation is

(5-10) $$E(\pi) = \mu X/q = \mu(R-N)(\beta/N)$$

The exact rate at which the future profit is discounted to the present of course depends on exactly when and how long the profit occurs. The present value of innovation thus consists of a series of future profits, each one discounted to the present. Hence, the PVI takes on the form:

(5-11) $$\text{PVI} = \sum_{j=1}^{(\beta/N)} 1/(1+r)^j \, \mu(R-N)(\beta/N)$$

PVI declines as N increases and more resources are applied to innovative activity because profit is destroyed more quickly the greater is N, all other things equal. This negatively-sloped function is drawn in Figure 5-4. As specified by the signs in equation (5-9), an increase in μ, R, or β raises the entire PVI curve. An increase in r lowers the curve.

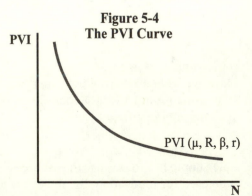

Figure 5-4
The PVI Curve

PVI

PVI (μ, R, β, r)

N

5.2.5 The Equilibrium Level of R&D Activity

Figure 5-5 combines Figures 5-2, 5-3, and 5-4. The top portion of Figure 5-5 combines Figures 5-2 and 5-4. The intersection of the CoI and PVI curves determines the equilibrium N, the amount of resources that competitive entrepreneurs devote to innovative activity. The bottom half of Figure 5-5 is simply the Figure 5-7 turned upside down and conveniently attached along the horizontal axis that it shares with Figures 5-2 and 5-4. The $1/\beta$ curve translates N into the number of innovations per day. Given the values of the parameters that determine the CoI and PVI curves in the upper half of Figure 5-5 and the productivity of the innovative process as given by β, the economy produces **q** innovations per day.

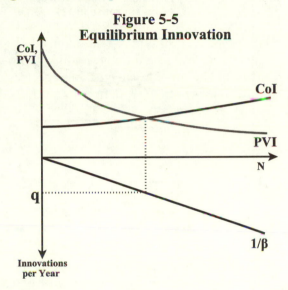

Figure 5-5
Equilibrium Innovation

5.2.6 Changes in μ, r, R, and β and Innovation

The graphic model in Figure 5-5 can be manipulated to find the effects of changes in μ, R, β, or r on the number of innovations **q**. For example, Figure 5-6 shows that, *all other things equal*, an increase in the markup μ shifts the PVI curve up to PVI₁, as suggested by equation (5-11). As a result, the equilibrium N, the number of resources devoted to innovative

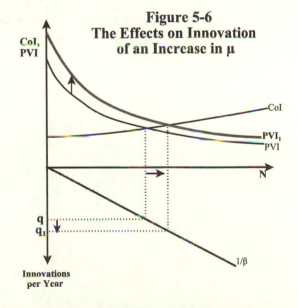

Figure 5-6
The Effects on Innovation
of an Increase in μ

activity, increases. The increase in N, in turn, raises the number of innovations per day to q_1. On the other hand, an increase in the discount (interest) rate r lowers the PVI curve and, therefore, reduces the average number of innovations per day.

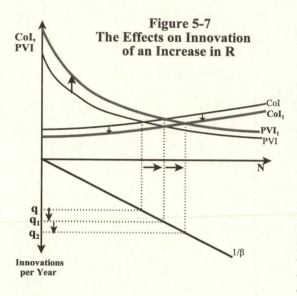

Figure 5-7
The Effects on Innovation
of an Increase in R

Figure 5-7 illustrates how a change in R affects innovation through shifts in both the CoI and PVI curves. For example, an increase in R lowers w, which, according to equation (5-6), shifts the CoI curve down to CoI_1, causes the equilibrium value of N to increase, and thus increases the number of innovations to q_1. However, an increase of R also shifts up the PVI curve because an increase in productive resources implies more production of new products and, therefore, more profits, all other things equal. This effect increases N further, and thus the number of innovations rises further to q_2.

A change in β is even more complex because it affects all the curves in Figure 5-5. Suppose, for example, that β declines, which implies an increase in the efficiency with which the economy generates and applies new ideas. First of all, a decrease in β shifts the 1/β line relating N and **q** clockwise, as shown in Figure 5-8. Second, the CoI curve shifts down, as suggested by equation (5-6). Finally, equation (5-9) indicates that the PVI curve also shifts down; all other things equal, if it gets less costly to innovate, then creative destruction occurs more frequently and any given innovation enjoys profits for a shorter period of time. The net result of these shifts appears to be ambiguous because a fall in β not only reduces the marginal cost of innovation, but it also reduces expected profits because the lower costs of innovation imply that the destruction side of the creative destruction process occurs more quickly. However, the net effect on innovation of a decline in β is likely to be positive when all is said and done.

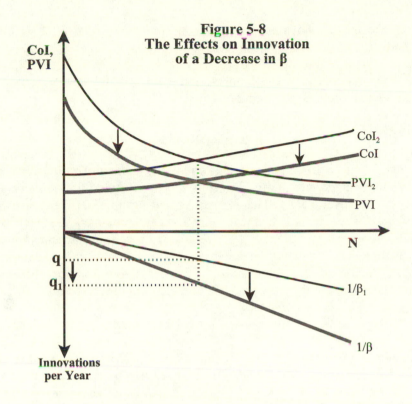

Figure 5-8
The Effects on Innovation
of a Decrease in β

If the the PVI and CoI curves are specified as given by equations (5-5) and (5-11), then the intersection of the CoI and PVI curves defines the equilibrium condition

$$(5\text{-}12) \qquad PVI = CoI = \sum_{j=1}^{(\beta/N)} 1/(1+r)^j \, \mu(R-N)(\beta/N) = w\beta$$

Since β enters into both the CoI and PVI curves as a simple multiplicative factor, the partial derivatives of CoI and PVI with respect to β are

$$(5\text{-}13) \qquad \partial PVI/\partial\beta = \sum_{j=1}^{(\beta/N)} 1/(1+r)^j \, \mu(R-N)(1/N) = w = \partial CoI/\partial\beta$$

Thus, a decrease in β causes equal downward shifts in the CoI curve and the PVI curve. These offsetting effects keep N unchanged after a decline in β, and therefore the remaining shift in the q= (1/β) curve in the bottom portion of the diagram determines the net effect of a decline in β on innovation. Thus, we conclude that, under the plausible conditions, an improvement in the efficiency of innovation will raise the amount of innovation in the economy.

In summary, the Schumpeterian R&D model of endogenous technological progress can be represented as

$$(5\text{-}14) \qquad\qquad q = f(\overset{+}{\mu}, \overset{+}{R}, \overset{-}{r}, \overset{-}{\beta})$$

This model states that, all other things equal, the number of innovations in an economy is greater (1) the larger is the profit markup at which the successful innovator can sell her innovative new product, (2) the greater is the supply of resources available to innovators and producers, (3) the more highly innovators value future gains relative to current costs, and (4) the more efficient are innovators in employing the economy's scarce resources toward generating new innovations. Figure 5-5 thus captures the key elements of most of the recent models of technological progress.

5.2.7 Some Further Observations on the R&D Model

Equation (5-5) suggests that the amount of innovation depends on the total amount of resources. The higher the supply of resources, the lower is the opportunity cost of employing resources for R&D activity and, all other things equal, the less costly it is to innovate. This result suggests that wealthier societies will, all other things equal, experience faster rates of technological progress and, hence, faster economic growth. This result furthermore suggests that large countries will grow faster than small countries. And, it suggests that countries with larger populations will grow faster than countries with small populations. In short, the model would predict that the United States will grow faster than Bolivia.

There is no evidence that suggests a direct relationship between population size and economic growth or between population size and per capita output, however. Many small countries have grown very rapidly, and many very large countries have had below-average growth performances. One possible reason why small countries can grow rapidly despite having a small stock of entrepreneurs and thinkers is that technology moves across borders. To the extent that international trade moves technology by letting products embodying technology cross borders, international trade enhances the growth of smaller, poorer countries.

The Solow growth model shows that population growth reduces the economy's steady state level of output because rising population growth creates a drain on savings similar to that of depreciation of the capital stock. In the absence of new investment, population growth reduces per worker output because the capital stock must be spread across more workers. Thus, population growth is just like depreciation in that it requires new investment to keep the per worker capital stock the same as before. The Schumpeterian model ignores this burden created by population growth and focuses instead on population growth's role in increasing productive and innovative resources. The Schumpeterian model suggests that, all other things equal, population growth is good for innovation and economic growth. The Schumpeterian model sees people as the source of new ideas. In the words of William Petty, a seventeenth century English intellectual: "...it is more likely that one ingenious curious man may rather be found among 4 million than among 400 persons."[73]

5.3 A Mathematical Version of the Schumpeterian Model

Growth models are normally presented exclusively in mathematical form, not the graphic form of the previous section. In this section, we present an exclusively mathematical growth model that follows logic similar to that of the graphic model of the previous section, albeit with one important difference. Rather than making the assumption that each successive innovation (new product) replaces earlier innovations (products), the model in this section assumes that innovation consists of new products that are added to the existing stock of products. This model treats technological progress as a continual accumulation of knowledge rather than the pure process of creative destruction in which new products eliminate and replace old products. In the growth literature, these two types of models are often referred to as "quality ladder" models and "expanding variety" models.[74] The dichotomy between the two types of models is not as great as it seems; as shown below, the conclusions of the models are nearly identical.

5.3.1 Innovation and Profit

Suppose that each act of innovation consists of creating a new firm that produces a new product. We start with n firms in the economy, each

---

[73] Petty (1682), p. 474.

[74] In their advanced graduate level textbook on economic growth, Barro and Sala-i-Martin (2004) devote separate chapters to these two groups of models of endogenous technological progress.

producing one of n different products. Suppose also that one unit of labor is required to produce a product; this implies that the marginal (and average) cost of producing each good is equal to the wage rate, w. Because each product is different, each producer enjoys some degree of market power so that each firm faces a downward-sloping demand curve. For simplicity, suppose that each firm faces an identical demand curve, which means that each firm sets the same price equal to

(5-15) $$p = w(1/\gamma)$$

where $0 < \gamma < 1$ and the price markup $p - w = \mu = [(1-\gamma)/\gamma]w$. Since $w = p\gamma$, profit per unit is $p(1-\gamma)$. Because entrepreneurs face downward-sloping demand curves, they can set a price above the marginal cost of production w and, potentially, recover the cost of innovation.

The total value of output is GDP, and therefore total profits in the economy are equal to

(5-16) $$\Pi = GDP(1-\gamma)$$

The profit of any one of the n identical firms is

(5-17) $$\pi = [GDP(1-\gamma)]/n$$

The present value of the earnings of a successful innovation is equal to the discounted stream of future profits, or

(5-18) $$PV = \sum_{j=0}^{\infty} \rho^i \pi_{t=i}$$

where ρ is the discount factor $1/(1+r)$, where r is the interest rate, and the $\pi_{t=i}$ are the future profits in each future time period t. The present value of all future profits can be thought of as the stock market or equity value of the firm.

5.3.2 The Equilibrium Level of Entrepreneurial Activity

Entrepreneurs will innovate and enter the market so long as the present value of future profits, PV, exceeds the current cost of product development. Suppose that β is equal to the units of labor required to develop each new product. The cost of developing a new product is thus $w\beta$. Assuming that there is a fixed number of workers in the economy, the more workers that are hired by firms to develop new products, the higher will be w, the opportunity cost of those workers' marginal product in producing goods. Innovation will stop expanding when the discounted future earnings from producing the nth good are exactly equal to the cost of creating the nth good. Putting together the costs and profits from innovation, the *innovation profit*, defined as θ, is

(5-19) $\theta = PV - w\beta$

If there is competitive innovation, meaning that all prospective entrepreneurs can demand resources for innovation and, if successful, market their new products, then $\theta = 0$ and

(5-20) $PV = \beta w$

Equation (5-20) represents the equilibrium condition for innovation profits. This equilibrium condition is similar to the intersection of the CoI and PVI curves in Figure 5-5.

5.3.3 The Equilibrium Rate of Technological Progress

We assume that firms live forever, even though their profits are gradually eroded by the entry of new firms with new products. In the case of an endless flow of future profits, the discounted value of future profits can be approximated by π/r, where π is the average future profit and r is the interest rate. If the growth of products is zero, or $g = 0$, the total stock market valuation of a firm is

(5-21) $(PV) = [GDP(1-\gamma)]/nr$

where r is the rate of interest and n is the total number of firms and products. The total capitalization of the economy's stock market is thus

(5-22) $n(PV) = [GDP(1-\gamma)]/r$

If innovation is profitable, the number of products increases, however. For simplicity, suppose that (1) total output, or GDP, stays the same when new firms develop new products and (2) each new firm has to share a fixed amount of labor in the economy. Thus, the profit of any single firm $[GDP(1-\mu)]/n$ will decrease if the number of firms increases. Specifically, profit will continually decline by the growth rate of new products/firms $g = \Delta n/n$. If $g > 0$, then the market valuation of *existing* firms is

(5-23) $n(PV) = [GDP(1-\gamma)]/(r + g)$

The equilibrium rate of innovation, g, can be found manipulating the above results. First, combining (5-15) and (5-20) gives us

(5-24) $p = w/\gamma = PV/\gamma\beta$

Using (5-23), equation (5-24) can be rewritten as

(5-25) $p = PV/\gamma\beta = [GDP(1-\gamma)]/\gamma\beta n(r + g)$

Since it takes one unit of labor to produce each unit of output of old and new products, the total amount of labor devoted to production is exactly equal to the total quantity of output of products, which is equal to GDP/p. The amount of labor devoted to research and development is equal to the number of new products, ng, times the amount of labor required to create a new product, or βng. If the quantity of labor available in the economy is R, then the growth rate of new products must be compatible with

(5-26) $\beta ng + GDP/p = R$

Using equation (5-25) to substitute for p in equation (5-26) yields

(5-27) $\beta ng + [\gamma\beta n(r + g)/(1-\gamma)] = R$

Multiplying all terms in (5-27) by (1-γ) and dividing everything by βn:

(5-28) $g(1-\gamma) + \gamma r + \gamma g = R(1-\gamma)/\beta n$

Equation (5-28) can be further simplified to:

(5-29) $g + \gamma r = R(1-\gamma)/\beta n$

Isolating g, the growth of new products, on the right-hand side of the equation gives us a result that is very similar to the graphic Schumpeterian model of the previous section:

(5-30) $g = [R(1-\gamma)/\beta n] - \gamma r$

That is, the growth rate of new products, which is really intended as a proxy for the creation of new ideas and technology, depends directly on the amount of resources R and inversely on γ, β, n, and r.

The partial derivatives of g with respect to R, γ, β, n, and r are: $\partial g/\partial R = (1-\gamma)/\beta n > 0$, $\partial g/\partial \gamma = -R/\beta n - r < 0$, $\partial g/\partial r = -\gamma < 0$, $\partial g/\partial \beta = -[R(1-\gamma)]/(\beta)^2 n < 0$, and $\partial g/\partial n = -[R(1-\gamma)\beta]/(\beta n)^2 < 0$. The signs of the derivatives suggest that the rate of technological progress depends directly on the amount of productive resources R and inversely on γ, β, n, and r. Note that γ is inversely related to $\mu = [(1-\gamma)/\gamma]w$, or $\partial \mu/\partial \gamma = [-w(1-\gamma)/\gamma^{-2} - w/\gamma] < 0$. Therefore, given the result above that $\partial g/\partial \gamma < 0$ and the chain rule $\partial g/\partial \mu = (\partial g/\partial \mu) \cdot (\partial \mu/\partial \gamma)$, it follows that $\partial g/\partial \mu > 0$. Hence, the results here are compatible with the graphic Schumpeterian model in the previous section, in which we found that $\partial g/\partial \mu > 0$.

5.4 The Long-Run Trend in the Costs of Innovation

The mathematical model above concludes that $\partial g/\partial n < 0$. That is, all other things equal, as technological progress increases the number of products, n, the rate of technological progress slows down. Figure 5-5 in Section 5.2 has a similar implication for long-run technological progress: the equilibrium constant quantity of innovations each period, q, actually implies that the *rate* of technological progress slows down in the long run. For the *rate* of technological progress to remain constant, the *number* of innovations per year must increase in proportion to the rising level of technology. Hence, the models of endogenous technological progress we have built seem to not generate permanent economic growth! Such a conclusion is not warranted, however. There are very good reasons why the slowdown in technological progress is far from inevitable.

5.4.1 How the Models Avoid a Technology Slowdown

There are two ways in which the slowdown in technological progress can be avoided. First of all, both the graphic and mathematical models presented above assume that total demand for output remains constant. Specifically, in the graphic model profit is assumed to remain the same, and in the mathematical model total GDP is assumed to remain the same. This was done to avoid the complexity of solving dynamic models in which everything changes over time. But if technological progress causes economic growth, real incomes and, hence, demand will increase. Recall that in fact the Solow model suggests that the growth of real income will be equal to the rate of technological progress in the long run. Thus, demand for output and profits is likely to rise in proportion to technology, and the incentive to innovate will increase over time, thus ensuring that the growth process will not weaken over time.

The slowdown in the rate of technological progress can also be avoided if the cost of research and development decline as technology expands. For example, Romer (1990) specifically assumes that cost of research and development β is not a constant, but a variable related to the size of the economy. That is, he assumes that it becomes easier to create new products as more products are created and as knowledge accumulates. In terms of the mathematical model, Romer assumed that

(5-31) $\beta = c/n$

where c is a constant. Clearly β declines the larger is n. Substituting (5-31) into (5-30) yields

(5-32) $g = R(1-\gamma)/c - \gamma r$

The variable n is no longer a determinant of the rate of growth. In this equation, if R, γ, and r are constants, then the growth rate of new and better products will also be constant. Thus, there is no obvious tendency for the rate of innovation, or technological progress, to slow over time. But note that the constancy of g depends on the specific assumption of declining costs of research and development as specified in equation (5-29). Romer's assumption is equivalent to shifting the curve $1/\beta$ in the bottom half of Figure 5-5 to gradually become steeper so that the quantity of new innovations per period of time grows over time.

How justified is Romer in making this assumption about the productivity of R&D activity? A number of authors have attempted to determine the trend in R&D productivity. The next section reviews some of the evidence uncovered.

5.4.2 Do R&D Costs Rise or Fall over Time?

There are very compelling reasons why the number of innovations **q** is likely to increase as technological progress raises the level of technology over time. First of all, technological progress itself increases the effective stock of productive resources R. According to Baumol, Batey Blackman, and Wolff (1989):

> measured in terms of their prospective contribution to human welfare, the available quantity of our exhaustible and non-reproducible natural resources may be able to rise unceasingly, year after year. Rather than approaching exhaustion with continued use,

their effective inventories may actually be growing and may never come anywhere near disappearance. In short, our society's growing per capita output, rather than constituting a case of profligacy in which society "lives off its capital," may in fact involve what amounts to a net saving of finite natural resources, so that their *effective stocks* are constantly expanded by the same family of technological developments that underlie the growth in real per-capita income since the Industrial Revolution....this is no mere abstract possibility....[This] is, at least to some degree, happening now.[75]

To put Baumol, Batey Blackman, and Wolff's point into a more familiar perspective, recall that technological progress is essentially an upward shift in the economy's production function and represents an improvement in the economy's ability to produce more real output from a given set of resources. If we define productive resources in terms of the amount of output they can effectively produce, then clearly *effective resources* increase as innovations improve the economy's level of technology. As the total stock of effective resources grows, the opportunity cost of R&D activity falls (w declines), which shifts the COI and the PVI curve up and thus raises the equilibrium level of N and q as shown earlier in Figure 5-7.

Paul Romer (1990) suggested that it gets easier to create new ideas the more ideas we already have to build on. According to Romer:

every generation has underestimated the potential for finding new recipes and ideas. We consistently fail to grasp how many ideas remain to be discovered. The difficulty is the same one we have with compounding. Possibilities do not add up. They multiply.[76]

For example, the 18th century discovery of the steam engine led to many unforeseen developments. First used to pump out flooded mines, the steam engine was then applied to other stationary applications such as milling and sawing. In the 19th century, the steam engine caused a transportation revolution by drastically lowering the cost of hauling goods and people over land. Eventually, steam engines were used to generate electricity, which replaced many of the direct uses of steam in factories as well as enabling the

---

[75] Baumol, Batey Blackman, and Wolff (1989), pp. 211-212.

[76] From Romer's website www.stanford.edu/~promer/Econgro.htm.; also published as Romer (1998).

introduction of labor-saving home appliances. In short, ideas multiply as each new idea breeds other ideas. But Romer also seems to imply that technological progress is likely to accelerate the more knowledge is accumulated. That is, the more we discover, the more we find out how much we do not yet know and the more potential research projects beckon for our attention.

5.4.3 Evidence on the Cost of Technological Progress

While few scientists and researchers today agree with the former director of the United States Patent Office who at the end of the nineteenth century said that "we must certainly have discovered everything there is to discover by now," not everyone agrees with Romer either. There is evidence that suggests innovation is becoming more difficult. For example, in France, Germany, Japan, the United Kingdom, and the United States, the number of scientists and engineers engaged in research and development activities has grown between two-fold and four-fold over the past thirty years, but the number of patents issued has not shown any tendency to increase. Actual expenditures by manufacturers on R&D activities in these same countries show increases of similar magnitude. Keller (1996) and Segerstrom (1998) interpreted this increase in expenditures with constant results as evidence that it must be getting harder, not easier, to create new ideas. Ulku (2004) examined the relationship between R&D expenditures and patents in 20 OECD countries and 10 non-OECD countries, and found no evidence of increasing or even constant returns to innovation measured in terms of inputs.

Griliches (1990) presents a thorough assessment of what the evidence on patents and R&D activity really tells us. The number of patents issued does not necessarily reflect actual new ideas created or innovative activity. The criteria for issuing patents have changed over time and they are certainly not uniform across countries. The motivation for seeking a patent may have changed as well, since the time and cost of applying is considerable. In a later work, Griliches (1994) suggests that the "quality" of patent applications has changed to where only the better ideas are presented for patents. That is, the percentage of new ideas that are patented has gone down, and, thus, the number of patents understates the amount of new ideas created. The number of scientists and engineers employed in research and development may also not be an accurate measure of research effort. Modern economies are much more specialized than they were in the past, and thus more people are classified as "researchers" today than in the past. The scientist and writer Thomas Barlow (2001) reports that a more thorough accounting of the resources applied to research and innovation shows that 25 years ago knowledge increased at a rate that doubled the total stock of human knowledge every 14 years but today is increasing at a rate that doubles the stock of knowledge every five years.[77] Guellec and Van Pottelberghe de la Potterie's (2001) OECD data for 1980-1998 showed that business R&D has become more efficient in raising productivity since the early 1980s.

Given the difficulty of measuring knowledge and the resources that are applied to the creation of knowledge, all estimates of the rate of technical innovation must be taken with some degree of skepticism. There is no clear evidence that technological progress is slowing, but neither can we rest assured that technological progress will continue to accelerate in the future.

5.5 Conclusions and Remaining Issues

Economists have modeled technological progress in two fundamentally different ways. The earlier models assumed that technological progress is an unintentional by-product, an *externality*, of some other activity such as investment or production. Most of the more recent models have recognized that most new knowledge is created by intentionally applying scarce and, therefore costly, resources to innovative activities. Romer echoes many growth economists when he suggests that this second set of endogenous growth models is most valuable for understanding technological progress. Romer himself developed *externality* models, his best known appeared in Romer (1986), before he published his well-known 1990 model on which this chapter's graphic model is based. In 1994 he wrote: "When I look back on my work on growth, my greatest satisfaction comes from having rejected the first round of external effects models that I tried."[78]

Despite the popular story of Sir Isaac Newton being inspired to come up with his theory of gravity after being hit on the head by a falling apple, there are very few examples of knowledge falling from the sky! Newton was able to translate the experience of the falling apple into a theory of gravity because he had already devoted considerable time and resources to investigating gravity and other related topics. Surely other people had been hit on the head with falling fruit, but not having devoted

---

[77] Barlow (2001).

[78] Romer (1994b), p. 20.

much prior thought to the concept of gravity, they did not think to derive the formula for gravity from their experiences. The thinking of Joseph Schumpeter has inspired the recent growth models, and further refinements of Schumpeter's ideas promise to further improve our models. Baumol's (2002) book on innovation is a good recent example.

By modeling technological progress as driven by intentional efforts to create new ideas, better products, more efficient production processes, etc., policy makers are better advised to focus on how to provide better incentives to stimulate such activities. How can entrepreneurs be encouraged? What institutions lead entrepreneurs to innovate? Can other organizations generate and disseminate new ideas where entrepreneurs fail to act? How can the costs of innovation be reduced? What resources are most appropriate for creating new ideas? How can developing economies adapt existing ideas and technologies more efficiently to their specific circumstances? Recognizing that technological progress is the result of costly effort is an important precondition for finding the answers to these and many other important questions.

In this chapter we did not follow our earlier procedure of inserting international trade into the models we develop. Given the importance of the endogenous models of technological progress, we elected to focus on just presenting the models. It is clearly time to examine how international trade can enhance economic growth when technological progress is driven by intentional and costly innovative activity as described by the Schumpeterian models of this chapter. This will occupy the entire next chapter.

Chapter Six

International Trade
and
Technological Progress

The international trading system...has enhanced competition and nurtured what Joseph Schumpeter a number of decades ago called "creative destruction," the continuous scrapping of old technologies to make way for the new.
          (Alan Greenspan)[79]

This chapter continues the discussion of the Schumpeterian model. The Schumpeterian model describes innovation and the application of new ideas as the result of deliberate effort that requires the use of scarce, and thus costly, resources. The rate of technological progress depends on the expected eventual rewards from innovation relative to the costs of innovation. These rewards and costs, in turn, depend on the size of the market for innovations, the availability of resources needed to generate innovations, the productivity with which societies generate innovations, and how societies are willing to allocate resources between present consumption and innovative activities. This chapter focuses on the role of international trade in the Schumpeterian model. Specifically, the model will reveal how international trade affects the size of the market for innovations, the availability of resources needed to generate innovations, the productivity with which societies generate innovations, and how societies are willing to allocate resources between present consumption and innovative activities.

---

[79] Alan Greenspan (2001), "Testimony of Chairman Alan Greenspan Before the Committee on Finance," U.S. Senate, April 4 (Federal Reserve Bank Web site: www.frb.org, April 5, 2001).

The Schumpeterian model of technological progress suggests that international trade stimulates technological progress and, therefore, economic growth. International trade tends to enhance technological progress because it (1) increases the expected gains from innovation by making innovations available to more people in more countries, (2) increases the efficiency with which new ideas are created because its helps to spread technology and knowledge across borders, and (3) increases the world's effective resources that can be allocated to innovative activities. The Schumpeterian model also points to where international trade might hinder economic growth, and these possibilities need to be analyzed. The process of economic growth is complex, and there are many ways in which international trade may affect the costs and benefits of innovation. Overall, however, the Schumpeterian model supports the hypothesis that international trade enhances economic growth.

6.1 International Trade and the Schumpeterian Model

Our quest for an explanation of international trade's role in the economic growth process leads us logically to the Schumpeterian model of technological innovation for several reasons. The Solow growth model showed that long-run economic growth cannot be maintained by means of factor accumulation alone. Also, recall from Chapter 2 that statistical analysis by Levine and Renelt (1992), Edwards (1998), Frankel and Romer (1999), Wacziarg (2001), and Easterly and Levine (2001) found evidence showing that international trade's effect on economic growth operates through technological progress. The Schumpeterian model of technological progress is therefore an appropriate model for analyzing international trade's long-run effect on economic growth.

6.1.1 Creative Destruction in an Integrated World Market

A convenient way to illustrate the growth effects of international trade in the Shumpeterian model is to assume that two identical economies are combined into one. This approach is reasonable because international trade is a form of arbitrage that effectively integrates previously distinct markets into a single market.

The effect on profit from combining two identical isolated economies with two identical sets of consumers into a single integrated market is shown in Figure 6-1, which builds on Figure 5-1 from the previous chapter. Total demand doubles from D to D_T, and the profit area also doubles in size. Trade lets entrepreneurs sell their innovative new products to many more users. For this reason, international trade shifts up the PVI curve in the Schumpeterian model, all other things equal. This is just the first effect of economic integration that international trade brings about, however.

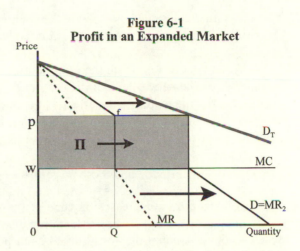

Figure 6-1
Profit in an Expanded Market

All other things do not remain equal when the economy effectively doubles in size. In an integrated economy, the combination of two identical economies doubles the supply of resources that are available for production and innovative activity. The slope of the CoI curve declines because the larger stock of resources in the combined economy means that a given absolute increase in innovation has less effect on the price of productive resources than would an identical increase in innovative activity in single isolated economy.

Figure 6-2 shows the net effects of doubling the size of the economy. The PVI shifts up from PVI to PVI_2 and the CoI curve shifts down to CoI_2. As a result, the amount of resources employed in R&D activity increases from **a** to **b**, which in turn increases the number of innovations per day from q_1 to q_2. Thus, all other things equal, the doubling of demand for output and the doubling of resources imply that

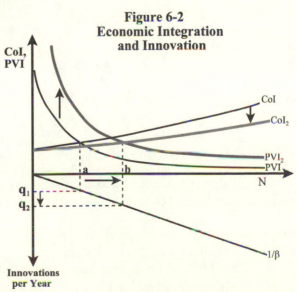

Figure 6-2
Economic Integration and Innovation

two economies integrated by trade will experience more rapid innovation than either of the two economies would in isolation.

The conclusions from the graphic model above can be duplicated using the mathematical model from the previous chapter. Because international trade increases the effective stock of productive resources, R, the derivative of resources with respect to trade is positive, or $\partial R/\partial \text{Trade} > 0$. Since it was already shown in Section 5.3 that $\partial g/\partial R > 0$, it follows that

$$(6\text{-}1) \qquad (\partial g/\partial R) \cdot (\partial R/\partial \text{Trade}) > 0$$

Similarly, since trade increases the size of the market faced by potential innovators, $\partial \mu/\partial \text{Trade} > 0$. From Section 5.3 we also have that $\partial g/\partial \mu > 0$, where μ is the amount of profit gained each period of time. It therefore follows that

$$(6\text{-}2) \qquad (\partial g/\partial \mu) \cdot (\partial \mu/\partial \text{Trade}) > 0$$

That is, trade increases the rate of technological progress g by increasing R and μ.

6.1.2 An Integrated Economy Raises Income

The combined real income of an integrated world economy is greater than the sum of incomes of isolated nations. The traditional static gains from trade effectively raise the productivity of production and cause total real income to rise by more than the combined national incomes. Hence, average per capita real incomes rise. Of course, the distribution of the higher real income will be different in the integrated economy than it is in the isolated individual economies, as predicted by the Stolper-Samuelson theorem of the Heckscher-Ohlin model of trade, for example. An open economy is therefore likely to reach a different combined decision about how to allocate resources between production and innovation. The rise in average per capita income is likely to lead to an increase in demand for output. How this rise in demand for output changes the allocation of resources between production and innovation depends, in part, on the price and income elasticities of demand for output. It also depends on how much the rise in demand increases the potential for profiting from new innovations. If demand for output is highly income elastic, then producers will tend to allocate a greater proportion of the world's resources to production in response to the rise in demand fueled by the higher national income. On the other hand, a low price elasticity of demand for current output may induce producers to maximize profits at lower levels of output, and it becomes more likely that the rise in income and product demand will result in more resources being allocated to innovation.

6.1.3 Technology Transfers and Creative Destruction

There are other subtle channels through which international trade can affect the rate of growth of technology. One of these is trade's positive influence on international technology transfers. International trade and the accompanying activities of international marketing, market research, product planning, and international travel all serve to spread knowledge and technology. Thus, by integrating individual economies into a single global economy, international trade expands the knowledge and ideas that innovators can draw on.

This latter point, that trade expands the stock of knowledge available to innovators, implies that trade enhances economic growth. If technological progress is a multiplicative or combinatoric process, its growth rate depends directly on the amount of knowledge that already exists. The more knowledge we have, the easier it is to increase knowledge. If only a small proportion of combinations results in useful innovations, then there may be very large differences in the growth rates of a single isolated economy and an integrated world economy. To illustrate, suppose the economy begins with three ideas rather than the four ideas in the example presented in Chapter 4. In this case, illustrated in Table 6-1, the rate of technological progress actually *decreases* over time. Not illustrated is another interesting case: if the initial stock of knowledge consists of two useful ideas, then technological progress stops entirely after just two periods. These examples of combinatoric processes are obviously unrealistic. The state of knowledge certainly consists of more than three ideas, which suggests the combinatoric process of technological progress must always be explosive. However, it is unlikely that all combinations of previous ideas produce useful new ideas. Knowledge can also be forgotten. There may be institutional barriers against certain combinations, such as the formal and informal restrictions on stem cell research in the United States or the ban on genetically-modified foods in Europe. All other things equal, the greater the stock of knowledge, the more potential combinations there are, the less likely that the process stagnates. Casual observation suggests that technology is not the same in all countries. This gives international trade a role in expanding the number of ideas that can be combined into new ideas. The integration of economies through trade gives innovators in any country more knowledge to combine into new ideas.

Table 6-1
A Slowing Combinatoric Growth Process
(new idea = the unique combination of two old ideas)

	New Ideas		Accumulated Ideas	Percentage Growth
Period 1	Begin with	3	3	
Period 2	$3!/(1!\cdot2!)$ =	3	6	100%
Period 3	$3!/(1!\cdot2!)$ =	3	9	50%
Period 4	$3!/(1!\cdot2!)$ =	3	12	33%
Period 5	$3!/(1!\cdot2!)$ =	3	15	25%

The number of combinations for n ideas taken r at a time is $n!/[(n-r)!\cdot r!]$; we take n as the number of ideas generated in the previous period and combine them 2 at a time, so $r = 2$. The symbol "!" represents a product of descending integers beginning with the number preceding the !, e.g., $5! = 5\cdot4\cdot3\cdot2\cdot1 = 120$.

6.1.4 Creative Destruction and Comparative Advantage

Another reason why trade may increase technological progress is that it permits greater specialization in innovation. The principle of comparative advantage applies to innovative activity as well as productive activities. Given that countries have different endowments of resources and that different activities have different production functions, some countries will have a comparative advantage in innovative activity while others have a comparative advantage in producing goods. The percentage of highly educated people, the number of engineers, and the conditions that inspire entrepreneurial activity vary greatly from one country to another. Thus, by having countries specializing in either production or innovation, unlike an isolated economy that has to *both* produce *and* innovate, the worldwide amounts of production and innovation can both increase. Provided economies are closely integrated and the innovative new ideas and products become available throughout the world, it does not matter who produces and who innovates; everyone's consumption (real income) rises at a faster rate because of the faster rate of technological progress.

Innovative activity is in fact centered in a small number of developed economies, while very little measurable new technology is developed in developing economies. Research and development expenditures as a percentage of GDP vary greatly across countries.[80] Indicative of the concentration of R&D activity is Lewer and Van den Berg's (2001, 2003a) finding that the more developed countries, which are relatively abundant in human capital, tend to be net exporters of capital goods, whereas developing countries with their relatively lower levels of human capital tend to be net importers of capital goods.

The exploitation of comparative advantage in allocating the world's resources between innovation and production will reduce the average value of β in the world as a whole. To illustrate how the agglomeration of R&D activity in some countries affects overall technological progress, suppose that in a world consisting of two economies one of the two economies is more efficient at innovation than the other. Specifically, suppose that the second of the two countries requires twice as many resources to produce an innovation, on average, than the first economy. In terms of the models developed above, suppose that $\beta_2 = 2\beta_1$. In this case, the cost of innovation curve in the second country, CoI_2, lies above the first country's CoI_1 curve, exactly twice as high. The horizontal combination of the two curves into a single curve looks like the kinked CoI_W curve in Figure 6-3. The doubling of the market size still increases profits from innovation, just as in the doubling case above, and the PVI curve shifts up in proportion to the rise in profits. The quantity of innovations per year therefore rises from q_1 to q_2. The other effects of trade described just above reinforce the shifts in the curves; to avoid cluttering the diagram, we do not add them here. In this case of different economies, complete economic integration results in all innovation occurring in country 1 because the equilibrium where the PVI intersects the combined CoI_W curve is below the CoI_2 curve. Total innovation in the larger integrated economy is still greater than it would be in either isolated economy. So long as the benefits from innovation spread evenly throughout the integrated region, it does not matter who does the innovating. International trade's role is thus to spread technology and to spread the gains from the growing levels of production.

Bayoumi and Haacker (2002) show that international trade spreads the benefits of innovations across borders. They examined the information technology sector, and found that the users of IT captured a considerably

---

[80] See, for example, the data on R&D expenditures as a percentage of GDP given in UNESCO (2002), *Statistical Yearbook*, Geneva: UNESCO, or in World Bank (2002), *World Development Indicators*, Washington, DC: World Bank, Table 5.11, pp. 320-322.

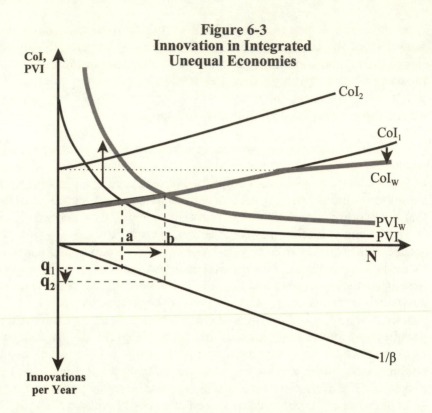

Figure 6-3
Innovation in Integrated
Unequal Economies

larger share of the total gains from innovation than did the innovators.[81] At the same time, there is also ample evidence that technology does not move promptly or costlessly from one country to another. The next two chapters examine these possibilities in greater detail in order to determine the "robustness" of this chapter's conclusions about international trade's positive effects on technological progress and economic growth.

6.2 The Size of Economies and Technology

The previous section's conclusion that a larger integrated world economy grows faster because it generates new ideas at a faster rate, all other things equal, is similar to the previous chapter's conclusion that technological progress is directly related to the size of an economy. Indeed, a positive relationship between economic growth and economy size is a logical

---

[81] For a popular description of Bayoumi and Haacker's results, see David Wessel (2002), "Technology Users Cash In, While Its Makers Founder," *Wall Street Journal*, September 12.

conclusion of models that recognize that (1) innovation has an opportunity cost because it requires the use of the economy's scarce resources, (2) new knowledge builds on existing knowledge, and (3) the gains from innovation depend on how many people make use of the innovation.

6.2.1 Kremer's Model of Trade and Technology

Kremer (1993) hypothesized that the change in technology, A, is a direct function of the population, P, the existing stock of knowledge, A, and the probability of each person thinking of a new idea, q:

(6-3) $$\Delta A = qPA$$

That is, the more people there are, the more they already know, and the better they are at thinking, the more new ideas are created. The rate of growth of technology g_A can be found by dividing both sides of (6-3) by A:

(6-4) $$\Delta A/A = g_A = qP$$

The implication of the Kremer's hypothesis of a direct relationship between technological progress and the size of the population is that, all other things equal, larger countries grow more rapidly than smaller ones.

6.2.2 The Role of Trade in Promoting Technology Flows

International trade can accelerate the economic growth of small countries by facilitating the movement of technology, often embodied in products, across borders. With trade, small countries can grow rapidly despite having a small stock of entrepreneurs and thinkers. International trade has over the centuries served as a major motivation for contacts among people of different countries and regions and the dissemination of new ideas and the transfers of new technologies. A good example of how contacts between regions of the world spread technological progress is the development of agriculture some 10,000 years ago. Evidence suggests that between 8000 or 7000 B.C. farming and animal husbandry developed along the Fertile Crescent in the Middle East. The new farming technologies eventually spread throughout Asia, Europe, and Africa over the next 2,000 years, first to the regions closest to the Middle East, then to the regions farthest away. Those regions not connected to the Middle East by existing trade routes did not benefit from the new technology. Spotty evidence suggests that people in the Western Hemisphere had to invent agriculture and animal husbandry all by themselves, and those practices did not appear there until several thousand years later.

Today, scholars read books from other countries, and the Internet makes the latest research in science and the latest achievements in the arts instantaneously available to the entire world. People can watch television from other countries and see how other people live, think, and behave in a great variety of real and fictional situations. Entrepreneurs travel to observe and copy ideas from other countries. Buying foreign books, watching foreign television programs, and traveling overseas to observe foreign production methods are, of course, forms of international trade.

6.2.3 Trade Helps Small Countries Most

Alesina, Spolaore, and Wacziarg (2000) conclude that in today's global economy the costs of being a small country have gone down.[82] Ades and Glaeser (1999) find that a variable representing a country's "openness" to trade serves as a substitute for a country's initial level of wealth as an explanatory variable in growth regressions. They interpret this as implying that market size has a significant effect on a country's rate of growth only if its economy is closed.

There is a clear trend away from large countries to small countries. In fact, the number of countries in the world rose from 74 in 1946 to 192 in 2000. And the total continues to grow as provinces and regions secede and nations fragment. Most new countries are relatively small. Almost half of all countries, 87 out of the 192 to be precise, have populations of less than 5 million; 35 had populations of under 500,000. The breakups of the Soviet Union and Yugoslavia, the split of Czechoslovakia into the Czech and Slovak Republics, the independence of East Timor from Indonesia, and the granting of political autonomy to regions within countries all suggest that the costs of smallness are not as high as they used to be. Where the consolidation of small political regions into large countries during the 18th and 19th centuries no doubt reflected the cost of smallness in the past, the current efforts to create more countries, and the willingness of large nations to go along with breakups and the creation of autonomous regions all suggest that smallness does not matter so much. Of course, for smallness not to matter, countries must link themselves to the global economy by permitting largely unrestricted international trade.

---

[82] For a very accessible discussion of this issue, see G. Pascal Zachary (1999), "An Era for Mice to Roar," *The Wall Street Journal*, February 25.

6.3 Leader-Follower Models of Growth

Robert Lucas (2000) performs a simulation exercise in which he assumes that countries gain the capabilities to imitate and innovate on a random basis, so that some countries begin to grow sooner than others and some countries begin to imitate and catch up sooner than others. By tweaking the parameters of his model, he is able to generate a pattern of international economic growth that is similar to what we have observed over the past 200 years, with increased income divergence as some countries spurt ahead and others remain behind. When he extends his model into the future using the same parameters that generated the growth pattern that matches recent history, his simulations suggest that over the next century, international inequality will decline, overall economic growth will increase, and the world will achieve accelerating rises in human welfare.

Lucas' prediction of *convergence* of living standards across countries rests on his assumption that it is less difficult to adopting existing technologies than it is to develop new technologies from scratch. This assumption is what makes it possible for lagging countries to catch up to the leading countries. Lucas also recognizes that the ability to adopt existing technologies depends on a country's institutions, and these institutions are also subject to a learning process. Some countries begin to catch up sooner than others because they develop the appropriate institutions sooner than others. Convergence eventually occurs for all countries, however, because of the "demonstration effect" that induces even the most stubborn follower economies to establish growth-friendly institutions.

Lucas' exercise borrows from a large set of models that explain technology flows from *leader* to *follower* countries. These leader/follower models generally assume that the creation of cutting edge technology is in some way different from the adoption of existing technologies. These so-called leader-follower models provide useful insights into how technology moves across borders and what the growth effects of such movements are. The characteristics of some of these models are detailed by Barro and Sala-i-Martin (2004).[83]

6.3.1 Vernon's Product Cycle Model

Raymond Vernon (1966) presented one of the earliest models of leaders and followers that exploits both the supply and demand sides of technological

---

[83] Barro and Sala-i-Martin (2004), Chapter 8.

innovation. Vernon's still-popular model is often referred to as the *product cycle model* because it describes how trade patterns change as a product goes through its life cycle. During a product's early life, production and consumption tend to be concentrated in the most developed countries where resources for innovation are relatively abundant and where the high income levels ensure that there are consumers who can afford the expensive new products. Then, as the new product becomes known throughout the world, an increasing proportion of production is exported from the countries where the product originated. As the product matures, domestic consumption growth slows and domestic production levels off. At the same time, production costs decline as production methods are perfected and standardized production equipment becomes available. Key components and parts are increasingly outsourced to other suppliers. This development of standardized production methods makes overseas production easier. Also, the originator of the new product may be more willing to license production by others as the more mature market results in slower growth of profits.

Every new product sooner or later becomes what Vernon calls a "standardized product," whose production technology becomes widely known and for which equipment can be easily acquired. Less skilled labor can do more of the production work, and comparative advantage shifts to low-wage countries. Eventually, production may cease altogether in the country where the product originated, and trade flows completely reverse themselves as low-wage countries export the product back to the country that originated the product. Producers in the origin country are, by this time, already producing and exporting new products, and they are performing the R&D for even newer products that will replace the products they are currently producing and exporting.

Figure 6-4 illustrates how production and trade evolve in a developed (leader) country according to Vernon's product cycle model. The most advanced economies with the best-educated labor force specialize in developing new products. They export new products to the rest of the world during the early phases of the product cycle, and they develop new products as the production of older, standardized products moves to developing economies. Low-wage countries eventually adopt the products that are produced and exported by the advanced economies. All countries gain from the continually-changing pattern of trade. The shifting patterns of international trade described by Vernon's product cycle model are often the result of multinational firms moving production from high-cost countries to low-cost countries when technology becomes easy to transfer.

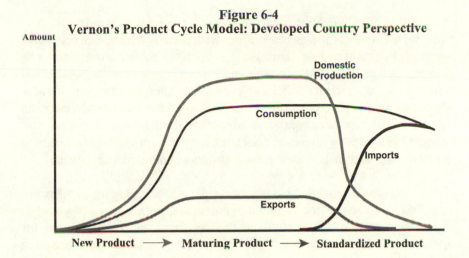

Figure 6-4
Vernon's Product Cycle Model: Developed Country Perspective

Figure 6-5 illustrates the Vernon model from the perspective of the developing (follower) economy. Low incomes keep consumption small during the early life of a new product, when the product is expensive. Consumption is at first satisfied entirely by imports. As the product matures, local production starts up in developing countries. Only when the product becomes a standardized product, and production technology becomes well-known, do the follower countries become exporters.

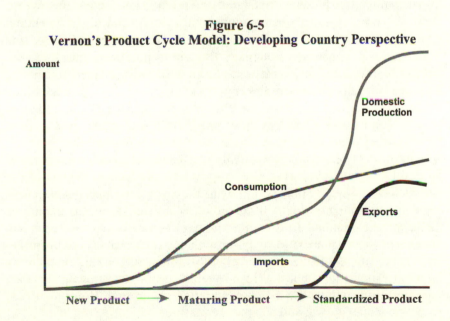

Figure 6-5
Vernon's Product Cycle Model: Developing Country Perspective

Although it is often presented as an alternative to standard models of trade, Vernon's model is compatible with the Heckscher-Ohlin general equilibrium model of trade because it effectively hypothesizes that trade patterns change in accordance with technology, and hence the production functions, over a product's life cycle. Advanced economies with highly-educated labor forces and sophisticated financial and scientific infrastructures have a comparative advantage during the early stages of a product cycle. Labor abundant countries have the comparative advantage in production later in the "standardized product" phase of the product cycle.

Vernon's model also describes a pattern of technology diffusion. First, the technology for producing the new product spreads to other developed economies, which have the resources most appropriate for adopting the new technology. Eventually, the new technology becomes standardized and becomes available in less developed economies. Product standardization implies that easy-to-use machinery is available, the production methods are well-known, and the various inputs, components, and raw materials are available through well-established trade channels. This means that the technology to produce the product can be acquired by economies with few specialized resources, located far from the large markets for the product, and little experience in producing similar products.

Examples of Vernon's product cycle are clothing and shoes in the nineteenth and early twentieth century, radios and televisions after World War II, and computers and computer chips at the end of the twentieth century. In each case, the leading industrial economy developed the products, techniques, and machinery to manufacture the products. These same countries were once great exporters of the products, which first moved to other developed economies but eventually moved to developing economies. Computer chip production moved from the United States to Japan, then to Taiwan, and, most recently, to China.

6.3.2 Other Leader-Follower Models

Baldwin and Forslid (1999) build what they call a *core-periphery model* that combines technology diffusion with the tendency for economic activities to agglomerate in order to exploit economies of scale and externalities. Agglomeration helps growth, but if technology spillovers are weak then there will be uneven growth around the world. Preventing agglomeration does not increase overall economic growth; in fact, agglomeration will tend to increase overall world growth. However, it also causes unequal growth and income inequalities.

Zhu (2005) uses a Heckscher-Ohlin model to show how technological innovation in skill-abundant, high-income economies and technology transfers to low-income economies affect wage inequality. The well-known Stolper-Samuelson theorem derived from the Heckscher-Ohlin model states that, if high-income countries are capital or skill abundant, then international trade will increase wage inequality in rich countries and decrease wage inequality in poor economies. However, there is ample evidence that wage inequality has increased in both poor and rich countries. Zhu shows that in the case where technological innovation continually increased the productivity of skill-intensive production in the advanced skill-abundant countries and older, relatively less skill intensive production is shifted to poor countries, the skill-intensity of production rises in both poor and rich countries and wage inequality increases everywhere, as observed in the world.

Leader-follower models bring out several important points about technology diffusion and economic growth. First of all, the worldwide pace of economic growth depends on the incentives for innovation in the leader countries and for technology adoption in the follower countries. These models, therefore, make assumptions about the costs of innovation versus the costs of copying and adopting existing technologies. Secondly, Vernon's model suggests that comparative advantage drives the shifting trade pattern over the life of a product, and Taiwan, Korea, and Singapore are examples of how countries can assume different positions in the product cycle as their factor endowments, and thus their comparative advantage, changes. For example, the average level of education in Taiwan in the early 1950s was three years; today it is approaching twelve years, about the same as in most developed countries. Hence, Taiwan is now a leader because it has developed a comparative advantage in R&D activity and new product introductions. Taiwanese computer chip manufacturers are now opening factories in China. Singapore similarly increased its human and physical capital stocks to where it is now promoting itself as a center for biotechnology research.

Some leader-follower models suggest that as long as there is technology diffusion, countries will tend to grow at similar rates in the long run. The absolute levels of technology will be quite different across countries, however, if the diffusion of technology is slow. Vernon's model is an example of such a model. On the other hand, Lucas suggests that growth can be faster in follower countries. If there was little diffusion of technology in the past but an acceleration of technology diffusion suddenly occurs, say by the liberalization of international trade or the improved absorptive capabilities in follower countries, then the opportunity to copy rather than invent technologies may permit follower countries to achieve higher rates of economic growth and catch up to the technology leaders. Models by Brezis, Krugman, and Tsiddon (1993) and Ben-David and Loewy (1998) even predict "leapfrogging" if the countries that catch up gain enough "momentum" to pass the leaders and reverse roles with them.

Leader-follower models often conclude that trade is good for both the leaders and the followers in that it raises both of their growth rates above what they would be in the absence of trade. The leaders gain from being able to concentrate on innovation while importing relatively less expensive products from the followers. The followers gain by specializing in production, for which they are better endowed, and importing technology from the leaders at a cost that is only a fraction of the cost of innovation. In their summary of leader-follower models, Barro and Sala-i-Martin (2004) also point out that the models suggest that foreign direct investment raises worldwide growth by permitting innovators to achieve additional gains from their innovations. International trade and foreign direct investment are closely related, of course; nearly all international trade involves a multinational firm on at least one side of the transaction.

6.4 Sources of Ambiguity about Trade's Growth Effect

The models of technological progress presented in this chapter seem to show that the empirical results of Chapter 2 can be theoretically justified by combining accepted models of international trade and economic growth. The logic behind the model that described the integration through trade of two identical economies is especially easy to grasp. One possible complication is trade's effect on the level of price competition. The Schumpeterian model gives profits an important role in generating innovation, and Schumpeter explicitly defended imperfect competition as providing the excess profits necessary to spur innovation. It is not difficult to imagine, therefore, that the increased price competition that accompanies trade could cause innovation to fall. This section examines this potential exception to the previous section's conclusion that international trade enhances economic growth.

6.4.1 Increased Competition in an Open Economy

It is often suggested that international competition is good for growth. This conclusion depends on how we define competition, however. Is it the traditional (1) price competition that static microeconomic analysis focuses on, or is it Schumpeter's (2) technological competition? These two types of competition are not necessarily complementary. In the Schumpeterian model the quest for profits drives technological competition. Aghion and Howitt (1998) refer to a Schumpeterian model of technological progress similar to the one we have presented to conclude that "product market competition is unambiguously bad for growth: the more competition, the lower the size of the monopoly rents that will be appropriated by successful innovators, and therefore the smaller the incentive to innovate."[84]

Figure 6-6 illustrates a case in which an integrated economy with a greater number of innovators increases price competition. Suppose, as we did earlier in Section 6.1, that international trade integrates two separate economies into one single world economy in which new technology becomes immediately available to everyone. Suppose, however, that trade increases price

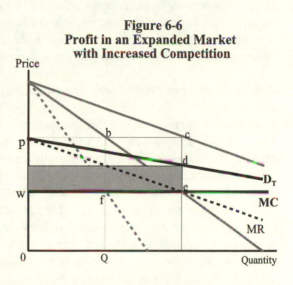

Figure 6-6
Profit in an Expanded Market
with Increased Competition

competition and product demand becomes more elastic. In Figure 6-6, the two-country model from Figure 6-1 is shown in thin gray lines. A new, more competitive world economy is shown in bold black lines. In the case illustrated here, the increased competition in the large world economy exactly offsets the potential gain from selling in a larger world market. Hence, globalization no longer seems to provide an incentive to expand innovative activity. The idea that greater competition reduces profit and, therefore, discourages innovation had been noted earlier by Rodrik (1992).

The empirical evidence discussed in Chapter 2 strongly suggests that open economies grow faster than closed ones. More specific evidence suggests that it may be specifically trade's effect on competition that increases innovation and growth. For example, Nickell (1996) and Blundell, Griffith, and Van Reenen (1995) provide empirical support that

---

[84] Aghion and Howitt (1998), p. 58.

price competition in general is good for innovation. Also, MacDonald (1994) found a close correlation between import penetration and productivity growth in U.S. manufacturing industries over the fifteen year period 1972-1987. Galdón-Sánchez and Schmitz (2003) found that increased foreign competition in the iron ore mining industry greatly increased productivity in U.S. iron ore mines. And Levinsohn (1993) found strong support for the hypothesis that trade enhances innovation using data that spanned the dramatic market opening in Turkey in 1984. Thus, it appears that in practice the positive effects of increased economic integration outweigh the negative effect of foreign competition. Despite the obvious conclusion of the simple Schumpeterian model, there are several reasons why, even in a Schumpeterian world, international trade's effect on price competition may actually enhance economic growth.

6.4.2 Maintaining Profit Margins in a Global Economy

First of all, foreign price competition may not be as strong as suggested in Figure 5-14. Innovators have various tools at their disposal to maintain profit margins despite the increased number of potential competitors. First of all, intellectual property rights, such as patents and copyrights, can make *nonrival* goods like knowledge and ideas *excludable;* international enforcement of patents and copyrights can, therefore, potentially enable innovators to protect themselves, at least temporarily, against foreign competition as well as domestic competition. Excludability is a double-edged sword, however. Patents stimulate the creation of new knowledge by enabling the creators of knowledge to charge for the knowledge, but, the price can stifle the creation of further knowledge.

Plant (1934) and Nordhaus (1969) have confirmed that theoretically intellectual property rights can increase or decrease the rate of innovation. Empirical studies have shed some light on the issue. Mansfield (1986) found evidence that intellectual property rights increased innovation in the United States. Gould and Gruben (1996) used data for 79 countries and found a strong positive statistical relationship between patent protection and growth, and the relationship was larger and stronger in open economies than it was in closed economies. Also supporting the hypothesis of a positive relationship between intellectual property rights and economic growth is the evidence that patents and copyrights are likely to be less restrictive for the dissemination of ideas than the traditional alternative to patents, which is secrecy. The formal recognition of intellectual property rights can *accelerate* the spread of technology because owners of intellectual property gain the ability to market their rights to others and thus stop them from opting to keep ideas and knowledge secret. Lamoreaux and Sokoloff (1999, 2002) have found that in 19th century United States, "the expansion of opportunities to trade in patent rights was closely associated with increases in specialization at invention, as well as advances in the rates of invention more generally."[85] Thus, patent rights permit inventors to concentrate on what they do best, which is to invent, and they can sell their inventions to those who are better at producing and marketing.

Another way of maintaining profit margins in the international economy is for innovators to become multinational firms.[86] As described by Shatz and Venables (2000), much of the activity of multinational firms in the developed economies consists of establishing similar activities and producing similar products in different countries. Evidence presented by Hipple (1990), Zeile (1997), and Mataloni (2000) suggests nearly four-fifths of all goods traded across borders originate or terminate, or both, with a multinational firm. Also important is the establishment of international brands and reputations, as well as the centralization of marketing activities. The dominance of large multinational firms in the world economy and international trade suggests that (1) profits in open international markets may not be greatly lower than they would be in domestic markets, and (2) Schumpeterian competition through innovation is more likely than price competition. In either case, technological progress will be accelerated, not slowed, by globalization.

6.4.3 The Darwinian View of Competition

Leibenstein (1966) originated the concept of *x-efficiency* to account for managerial behavior he called "satisficing," which is the tendency for managers to reduce pressure on their employees when conditions permit. Specifically, Leibenstein hypothesized that the production function is a variable relationship, hence the term *x-efficiency*, that depends on competitive pressures. More recently, Porter (1990) similarly relaxed the assumption that firms always maximize profit. According to Porter, when managers are more concerned with preserving their private benefits than with maximizing the long-run profit of the firm they are likely to opt for less innovation, which is inherently disruptive and costly. Threatened with the potential loss of their position of control in the firm, managers will react

---

[85] Lamoreaux and Sokoloff (1999), abstract.

[86] For a detailed discussion of the incentives that led to the formation of multinational firms see Caves (1996).

to increased competition by speeding up the development and adoption of new technologies. Aghion, Dewatripont, and Rey (1999) present a variation on the Schumpeterian growth model that logically shows how increased competition increases innovation when there is "slack" in firms. Nickell, Nicolitsas, and Dryden (1997) examined productivity data and found that competition has a positive effect on firm performance only for firms without dominant shareholders. They interpret this result as confirming trade's positive effect on efficiency under the assumption that the latter firms give managers greater slack to satisfice.

6.4.4 Step-by-Step Innovation in Place of Leapfrogging

Aghion, Harris, and Vickers (1997) arrived at the theoretical conclusion that competition is good for growth using an alternative Schumpeterian model of technological progress in which new innovators do not destroy (replace) earlier innovators in a leapfrogging pattern, but rather innovators take a step-by-step approach to catching up or moving further ahead of their competitors. In such a model, current market leaders simply enjoy a bit more profit than their lagging competitors. Current leaders are therefore stimulated to continue innovating in order to raise profits by increasing their lead over competitors, and competitors are continually stimulated to innovate in order to catch up and reduce their profit disadvantage. This view of competition has been referred to as the *Darwinian view* because it resembles a survival of the fittest competition.

A characteristic of this alternative step-by-step Schumpeterian model is that innovation rises in industries where competitors are *neck-to-neck* in terms of their levels of technology, but technological progress slows in industries where competitors are technologically far apart. Overall technological progress then depends on how many industries are characterized by neck-to-neck competition and how many industries have a clear technological leader. International trade has a potential role to play in this case: integrating the national economies into a single world economy through trade increases the number of firms that are similar in terms of technology, which means more industries will be characterized by neck-to-neck innovative competition. Thus, if past innovative competition in each small national economy gradually slowed because single leaders emerged in each industry, the opening of these economies to free trade can restore neck-to-neck competition and accelerate innovation. Baily (1993) and Baily and Gersbach (1995) analyzed the role of competition on innovation, and they concluded that global competition among best-practice firms is especially good in stimulating innovation.

Aghion and Griffith (2005) integrate the above ideas into a coherent theory of competition and growth. They distinguish between competition *in* markets and competition *for* markets. Competition *for* markets increases innovation, provided enough firms are close to the technology frontier and there is neck-to-neck competition. Competition *in* markets is likely to reduce innovation, although cases can be found where even competition *in* markets increases innovation. To understand how that can occur, Aghion and Griffith also distinguish between *pre-innovation* rents and *post-innovation* rents. A large difference between pre-innovation rents and post-innovation rents stimulates competition *for* markets by making it more lucrative to innovate and thus escape the current market for a higher-profit new market. An increase in competition *in* markets reduces pre-innovation rents and thus makes competition *for* new markets more attractive. Aghion and Griffith conclude that "stimulating competition in the market, especially in sectors that are close to the corresponding world frontier and/or where incumbent innovators are neck-and-neck, can also foster competition for the market through the escape competition effect."[87] The simple Schumpeterian model that we have used earlier in this chapter may, therefore, not be entirely accurate. Post-innovation profit must clearly be available if innovation is to occur, but traditional market competition can actually stimulate innovation provided it reduces only pre-innovation profit.

Another conclusion reached by Aghion and Griffith is that continued innovation requires that there be free entry into new markets. If firms cannot escape pre-innovation competition by innovating and entering high profit post-innovation markets, then innovation will suffer. This conclusion matches findings by several noted economic historians, as detailed in the next section.

6.5 Protectionism and Creative Destruction

For the process of *creative destruction* to work, there must be *destruction* as well as *creation*. If an initial creation is not followed by a second creation, which implies the destruction of the first creation's advantage, then there will be no permanent growth. Lee and McKenzie (1993) point out that innovators have a strong incentive to try to prevent others from *destroying* their temporary advantage in the market. In many societies the political environment permits them to slow the creative destruction process.

---

[87] Aghion and Griffith (2005), p. 86.

Rajan and Zingales (2003) described this situation very well:

> Instead of viewing destruction as the inevitable counterpart of creation, it is far easier for the politician to give in to the capitalist, who ostensibly champions the distressed by demanding that competition be shackled and markets suppressed.[88]

In short, vested interests often use the political system to gain protection from competition.

6.5.1 Protectionism to Maintain the Status Quo

The conflict between vested interests and society's long-run gain from continued innovation has been modeled by Holmes and Schmitz (1995, 1998), Mokyr (1990, 2002), and Parente and Prescott (2000), among others. Klapper, Laeven, and Rajan (2004) and Morck, Wolfenzon, and Young (2004) provide empirical evidence supporting these models. They show that vested interests do in fact reduce innovation. The World Bank's *World Development Report 2005* (2004) discusses the barriers to economic growth across all countries of the world in great detail. The latter study also provides comparison data on which countries are best at preventing vested interests from slowing creative destruction.

The negative relationship between protecting vested interests and technological progress is discussed very thoroughly by Mokyr (1990):

> the enemies of technological progress were not the lack of useful new ideas, but social forces that for one reason or another tried to preserve the status quo.[89]

Mokyr (2002) elaborates on precisely how institutions and policies affect a nation's rate of technological progress. Parente and Prescott (2000) attribute the large differences in levels of technology across countries to the variations in institutions and political structures that permitted vested interests to maintain the status quo. Parente and Prescott therefore propose that policy makers who are truly interested in promoting economic growth should promote competition, especially the Schumpeterian kind that brings rapid technological progress.

---

[88] Rajan and Zingales (2003), p. 2.

[89] Mokyr (1990), p. 301.

Parente and Prescott also conclude that: "To promote competition, governments should foster free trade."[90] In an earlier work, Mokyr (1990) appealed to the growth of international competition in an increasingly globalized economy to conclude that technological progress will continue in the future:

> As long as some segment of the world economy is creative, the human race will not sink into the technological stasis that could eventually put an end to economic growth.[91]

The importance of international competition in maintaining the creative destruction process helps to explain why vested interests often oppose the globalization. Baldwin (1992b) and Holmes and Schmitz (1995, 1998) show how international trade limits vested interests' ability to block continued innovation and thus promotes long-run growth.

6.5.2 The Holmes and Schmitz Model

In the Schumpeterian tradition, Holmes and Schmitz (1995) hypothesize that a certain country has two imperfectly competitive manufacturers who engage in Schumpeterian competition, each trying to establish technological superiority. Technological leadership enables a firm to earn a monopoly profit from production after effectively *destroying* its competition with its *creativity*. The *technological follower*, unable to profitably produce its obsolete product, then devotes all available resources to research and development in order to recapture technological leadership. The leading firm, on the other hand, must decide how many resources to allocate to the production that generates the profit with which to recoup its past investment in creating new technology and how much to allocate to research to create further innovations that will generate new profits after its current innovation is creatively destroyed.

Holmes and Schmitz add an important wrinkle to the standard Schumpeterian model, however. They permit the technological leader to allocate resources to a *third* activity: *obstructing* the efforts of the technological follower to regain leadership. The decision to produce, research, or obstruct depends on the potential payoffs from each form of activity. Resources are allocated to R&D so long as the expected payoff is

---

[90] Parente and Prescott (2000), p. 143.

[91] Mokyr (1990), p. 304.

at least as great as the opportunity cost, the rate of interest on loans or alternative investments. Obviously, the more resources that are devoted to R&D, the faster is the rate of technological progress. If resources are used to obstruct the follower, then technological progress slows.

Holmes and Schmitz model an economy in which foreign suppliers of manufactured goods can be subject to import tariffs. Consumers are assumed have specific preferences over domestic manufactured goods, foreign manufactured goods, and domestic services provided. The latter are provided by a competitive domestic service sector, the manufactured goods are provided by a single leading producer who has most recently innovated successfully. Only one manufactured product is supplied by a domestic firm, depending on which firm has most recently innovated and has the leading product all consumers prefer. Holmes and Schmitz assume a positive elasticity of substitution between domestic and foreign manufactures, which means that demand for domestic manufactures will be higher if foreign products are denied entry into the domestic market or if the foreign products are highly taxed.

In the Holmes and Schmitz model, the degree to which domestic manufacturers engage in research or obstruction of each others' research depends on the relative payoffs to each form of activity. Holmes and Schmitz show that there will be less obstruction under free trade than under restricted trade. The intuition for this conclusion is straightforward. In a protected domestic economy, the technological leader enjoys greater returns to innovation when it only has to compete with the domestic service sector for consumer dollars, and, hence, the payoff to obstructing other domestic manufacturers' research efforts is higher. In an open economy, when the manufacturer also has to compete with foreign firms, obstructing domestic competition has little effect on future profits. Worldwide competition would have to be obstructed, and that is much more difficult and costly. Hence, it becomes more useful to innovate than to expend resources obstructing the domestic competitor, and the domestic economy gains a more rapid rate of technological progress under free trade.

In a Schumpeterian framework, protectionism has very different consequences that the traditional deadweight losses detailed in the traditional models of international trade. Protection is a dynamic concept, driven by the interest of earlier innovators to prevent future innovators from creatively destroying their profits. It is worthwhile noting that Joseph Schumpeter's writing suggest that he was not always very optimistic about governments' ability to resist protectionism even in his dynamic creative destruction framework. Among other things, past innovators currently enjoy the profits of their past accomplishments, and this gives them a real advantage to obstruct future innovators. Potential future innovators do not yet know whether they will be profitable in the future; they have enough trouble raising resources to innovate much less raising resources to defend themselves against obstructionists. Vested interests are quite aware of their vested interests, and they enjoy the profits with which to obstruct. Foreign innovative competition indeed can play a very important role in maintaining the momentum of the creative destruction process. Is the active cross-border merger and acquisition (M&A) activity of the past decade, at least in part, the response of vested interests to obstruct global competition?

6.6 Conclusions and Further Issues

This chapter showed why international trade can enhance technological progress when it is the result of intentional and costly innovative activity. In the last section of this chapter, however, we signaled some potential difficulties when the simplifying assumptions about the relative capabilities of economies and the ease with which ideas transfer from one economy to another do not hold. Especially troublesome is the issue of whether it matters *where* innovation takes place. When innovation is concentrated in some countries, the long-run levels of per capita income across countries depend on how quickly technology spreads across borders from the technology leaders to the followers. There has always been the perception that the advantage that the most developed economies have in creating new knowledge serves to perpetuate the huge income differences that exist among the countries of the world. This chapter has discussed many studies that suggest international inequities are not permanent. There are many reasons why followers can grow faster and catch up to technology leaders. However, the common fear that the rich get richer because they have the resources to innovate, and that the poor stay poor because they do not have the resources to innovate, is not entirely unwarranted either.

The next two chapters will address the issue of how trade can influence the relative rates of growth of economies that trade. Neither evidence nor theoretical reasoning provides very strong support for the often-voiced fear that international trade will perpetuate or worsen the inequality in per capita incomes across countries in the future. However, neither does it put the controversy to rest. When innovation is concentrated in some countries, the distribution of the gains from innovation are very dependent on how technology spreads across borders. Also, there is ample evidence that distance and political borders are barriers to the flow of knowledge and ideas. Therefore, the relationship between trade and growth hinges on whether international trade facilitates or retards the flow of knowledge across borders. Until we clear up this controversy, we cannot be comfortable with the statistical evidence of a positive relationship between international trade and economic growth.

The next chapter examines models in which trade affects the accumulation of knowledge disproportionately across countries. The subsequent chapter specifically examines the available evidence on technology diffusion across countries.

Chapter Seven

Multi-Sector Models
and International Trade

It is not infant industries that get protection but senile industries–American auto, shoe, and steel producers.
(David Friedman)[92]

Chapters 3 through 6 presented a historical sequence of growth models. It is clear that by introducing international trade into these models, logical and consistent explanations for the positive relationship between trade and economic growth found in statistical studies can be pieced together. The combination of dynamic theoretical arguments and the large amount of empirical evidence greatly strengthens the case for free trade, compared to the traditional static theoretical arguments economists have always employed to make their case for free trade. We cannot yet feel fully confident in our dynamic theoretical and empirical case for free trade, however. The previous chapter pointed out some exceptions to the theoretical conclusions. Chapter 2 explained some doubts about the empirical results supporting the pro-growth role of free trade. Recall, for example, the theoretical discussion of the effect of international competition on innovation and Dani Rodrik's criticism of the empirical results of studies linking trade and growth. This chapter extends our analysis of the growth models by examining the explicit and implicit assumptions on which they are based. Are there plausible changes in these assumptions that would result in the conclusion that international trade slows long-run economic growth?

---

[92] David Friedman (1996), *The Hidden Order*, New York: HarperBusiness, p. 289.

There are weaknesses in the dynamic models presented in the last four chapters that can be exploited to construct logical arguments that refute the claim that free trade is the optimal long-run growth strategy. One potential weakness of the growth models presented so far is that they represent the economy with an aggregate production function that effectively lumps together all sectors of the economy into a single industry producing a uniform product called output or GDP. Such aggregate growth models are useful for analyzing many aspects of economic growth, but they are incapable of showing how international trade's disproportionate effects on different sectors of the economy translate into the economy's overall rate of economic growth.

A shift to free trade from a protectionist policy regime generally changes the set of products produced in the economy, as comparative advantage causes some industries to expand and others to contract, all other things equal. In a dynamic setting, a shift to free trade causes industries to grow at different rates, some of which may be negative. These changes in the relative sizes of industries can have various effects, not all of which are necessarily favorable to long-run human welfare within a country. For example, a country's overall growth rate could fall if its comparative advantage increases the relative size of industries that generate relatively few technology spillovers to the rest of the domestic economy. Or, comparative advantage could result in an expansion of industries that face declining world demand, thus making the country more likely to suffer terms of trade declines. This chapter introduces multi-sector models with which we can analyze the impacts of international trade on different sectors of the economy.

7.1 A Two-Sector Learning-by-Doing Model

Grossman and Helpman (1990, 1991a,b) built a simple two-sector learning-by-doing model that permits variations in the rate of learning across two industries. This model shows that, under certain circumstances, the dynamic relationship between trade and growth can be a negative one. In this model, trade's growth effect depends critically on how easily technology transfers across industries and from one country to another.

7.1.1 Industry-Specific Technology Transfers

Suppose that each industry uses a single input, say "productive factor" P, to produce its product, Y, under constant returns to scale. Suppose also that the amount of P necessary to produce output in each industry depends on the accumulated experience from past production in each specific industry. Suppose the production function for producing the ith good, Y_i, is:

(7-1) $$Y_i = A_i(P_i/a_i).$$

The variable A_i represents the accumulated technological know-how for producing the ith good, and the constant a_i represents the productive factor's initial level of productivity in producing the ith good before learning began.

Grossman and Helpman first examine the case where technology is *industry specific*. That is, they assume knowledge accumulated through learning is unique to each industry, of use to other firms in the same industry but of no use at all to firms in other industries. In the tradition of the learning-by-doing model of growth, perfect competition is preserved because the learning is assumed to be external. That is, a single firm does not notice any gain in knowledge from its own accumulated production, but the accumulated production of the entire industry does noticeably affect the level of labor productivity in that industry. The assumption of perfect competition is convenient because it means, among other things, that product prices can be assumed to accurately reflect the costs of the resources used in production. In this first case, Grossman and Helpman also assume that knowledge spills over into all countries without delay or costs. That is, knowledge is not *country specific*. Thus, the model assumes that accumulated experience in one industry does not increase productivity in another industry, but any knowledge gained in an industry in one country becomes immediately available to that same industry in all countries. Finally, this model assumes that learning-by-doing occurs at a different rate in each industry.

Suppose that there are two countries in the world, Home and Foreign. Accumulated knowledge in each industry i in the two countries is thus represented as

(7-2) $$A_i = A_i^* = \gamma_i(Q_i + Q_i^*)$$

where Q_i is defined as the cumulative output of industry i in Home, γ_i is the constant that defines how much knowledge is created from learning that has occurred in industry i as a result of total accumulated production in that industry. The variables with "*" are the Foreign equivalents of A, Q, etc. The factor requirements for producing a unit of output of good i depends only on the productivity of the factor in Home's (Foreign's) industry i, or

a_i (a_i*).   The relative factor requirements in Home and Foreign are determined by a_i/a_i* because, according to equation (7-2), productivity improves at the same rate in both countries.

Suppose, for simplicity, that there are two industries, and that Home enjoys a comparative advantage in industry 1 and Foreign enjoys a comparative advantage in industry 2. In this case:

(7-3) a_1/a_1* $< a_2/a_2$*

Suppose, also, that learning is faster in industry 1 than in industry 2, or that $\gamma_1 > \gamma_2$. In this case, a switch to free trade increases economic growth in Home because comparative advantage causes the faster-growing industry 1 to expand and the slower-growing industry 2 to contract. Economic growth in the Foreign economy slows as trade causes that country to specialize in producing 2, the industry that learns at a slower rate. This hypothetical case seems to suggest that Foreign would be better off not trading and thus preventing its "high tech" industry from shrinking.

Grossman and Helpman show that the differences in growth rates will eventually tend to disappear, however. Note that national growth rates are weighted averages of the growth rates of the two industries, weighted by each industry's share of of combined output. If markets are competitive, the price of good 1 falls relative to the price of good 2 as output becomes ever more efficient in industry 1 relative to production in industry 2. Then, under a rather broad range of plausible consumer preference functions, consumers substitute one good for another in response to relative price changes. Specifically, consumers switch more and more toward good 1, and ultimately the Foreign economy, which at first specialized in the production of 2, begins to produce more and more of product 1 as well. Because technology is assumed to spill over within industries, when both countries specialize in the production of 1, both experience identical rates of growth.

Graphically, Grossman and Helpman's model is shown in Figures 7-1 and 7-2. The first diagram shows the *growth rates* of the Home and Foreign economies, labeled A and B, respectively.   With identical preference functions, identical production functions, and the same accumulated knowledge, both countries initially grow at the same rate of learning by doing. Then, at time t both countries begin trading according to their comparative advantages. Economic growth thus rises in Home, and it falls in Foreign. But, as the price of product 1 falls in proportion to that industry's relatively fast growth in productivity, production abroad gradually includes greater shares of product 1 output in total output and, hence, the rate of growth gradually increases. The exact trajectory of total output in Foreign depends on the specific consumption function and the rate at which consumers substitute the cheaper product 1 for the relatively more expensive product 2. Figure 7-2 illustrates Grossman and

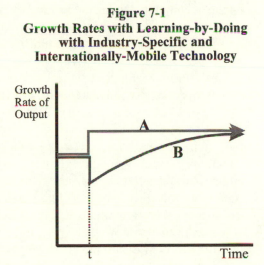

Figure 7-1
Growth Rates with Learning-by-Doing
with Industry-Specific and
Internationally-Mobile Technology

Helpman's conclusions about the *levels* of per capita output. It shows two isolated economies that start out at the same levels of per capita output and grow at the same rate because they produce the same mix of goods 1 and 2. Then at time t they shift to free trade, and their growth rates change because the Foreign country specializes in the production of y, which stimulates less learning. There is a divergence of the *levels* of per capita output. Eventually, however, both economies will grow at the same faster post-trade rate of economic growth, but economy B permanently lags behind in terms of its *level* of per capita output.

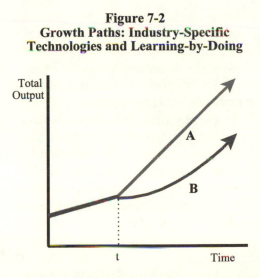

Figure 7-2
Growth Paths: Industry-Specific
Technologies and Learning-by-Doing

7.1.2 When There Are No Technology Transfers

Grossman and Helpman also examine the case in which there are no international spillovers of technology. That is, technology is assumed to be both *industry specific* and *country specific*. With no technology transfers, the level of accumulated knowledge in each industry in Home (Abroad), A_i (A_i^*), depends exclusively on the initial levels of technology and the accumulated domestic production in that industry, Q_i (Q_i^*):

(7-4) $A_i = \gamma_i(Q_i)$ and $A_i^* = \gamma_i(Q_i^*)$

Suppose, furthermore, that γ_1 > γ_2. In this case, the country that specializes in the production of product 1 will enjoy a more rapid rate of technology growth than the country that specializes in the production of product 2. Grossman and Helpman show that in this case where there are no international technology transfers, even if consumers prefer the cheaper good to the more expensive good, prices will not fall as fast as in the case of full

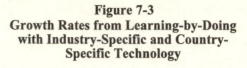

Figure 7-3
Growth Rates from Learning-by-Doing with Industry-Specific and Country-Specific Technology

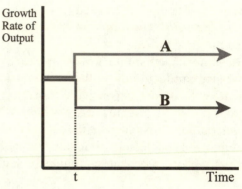

technology transfers because the country that initially specializes in the production of the product with the lower technology product will accumulate experience in the production of 1 more slowly than the country with the initial comparative advantage in 2. As illustrated in Figure 7-3, the two countries experience permanently different rates of technological progress. As shown in Figure 7-4, the growth paths permanently diverge.

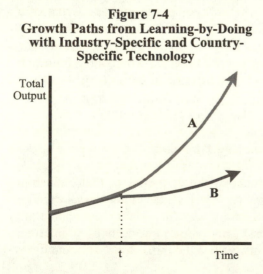

Figure 7-4
Growth Paths from Learning-by-Doing with Industry-Specific and Country-Specific Technology

This latter case of country specific technology clearly suggests that it would be advantageous for some countries to restrict international trade and avoid specializing in slow-growth industries. By protecting the faster-learning industries, knowledge could be accumulated more rapidly and the economy could grow more rapidly than if free trade locked the economy into producing goods for which the learning process is relatively slow. Perhaps subsidies, tariffs, quotas, or other measures to promote exports or restrict imports could increase the output of the higher learning industries and reduce relative output of the slower learning industries, thereby increasing the overall rate of technological progress. Such policies are often referred to as *strategic trade policies*. Note that the above model that justifies a strategic trade policy depends critically on the assumption that learning is *country-specific* and *industry-specific*.

7.1.3 Innovation as a Source of Comparative Advantage

The learning-by-doing model above also shows that accumulated knowledge is not only influenced by comparative advantage, but it can actually determine comparative advantage. For example, if technology is *country-specific*, then in the case where $A_1 / A_1^* > A_2 / A_2^*$, Home will have a comparative advantage in the production of product 1. But the values of A_1, A_1^*, A_2, and A_2^* are the result of past learning, as for example specified in equation 7-2 in the case of industry-specific learning.

The idea that a country's comparative advantage is related to accumulated technology is as old as comparative advantage itself. David Ricardo's original 1817 example of comparative advantage linked the gains from trade directly to comparative advantages created by technology differences across countries. More recently, Archibugi and Michie (1998) pointed out that, because innovation creates new comparative advantages, the welfare effects of technological innovation show up, in part, in gains from trade. One important implication of this observation is that the full gains from innovation depend on whether a country is open to international trade or not. Samuelson (2004) showed that, because innovation affects countries' comparative advantages and, hence, the gains from trade, the returns to innovation clearly extend beyond a country's borders. Samuelson thus suggested that free trade might not be optimal for a country that is a leader in technology.

Protection can be justified if it raises a country's accumulation of knowledge and thereby shifts the country's comparative advantage to products that will give the country more favorable terms of trade. The more general implication of the learning-by-doing model is that industrial targeting and protectionist trade policies *can* increase national welfare. The idea that technological progress can change a country's comparative advantage lies behind the so-called infant industry argument for protection. This argument is discussed below in Section 7.4. The exact welfare effects of protection depend on a very complex set of circumstances, however. One of the most difficult conditions to satisfy is that policy makers must be able to accurately predict the future performance of the industries they protect or subsidize. Will the protected or subsidized industries really learn more quickly than other industries?

7.2 Other Sectoral Models of Trade and Economic Growth

The Grossman and Helpman (1990) model introduced at the beginning of this chapter was not the first or only model that linked international trade and differences across sectors of the economy. Grossman and Helpman's conclusions depend on their specific sets of assumptions about the production function, the growth process, and the spread of technology across sectors and countries. An obvious question is whether the conclusions we reached using Grossman and Helpman's simple two-sector learning-by-doing model above remain intact in other sectoral models of economic growth. Others have made different assumptions and reached somewhat different conclusions about how international trade impacts economic growth. The brief survey of alternative models that follows suggests that the rates at which technologies transfer between countries and industries play the critical role in whether international trade enhances economic growth.

7.2.1 More Complex Models of Learning

Young (1991) reached conclusions similar to those of Grossman and Helpman (1990) with a model in which he assumes that newer industries generate more learning than older industries, and therefore, countries that "lead" in developing new industries experience more learning-by-doing than countries that are technological "followers." Young argues that leader countries are those countries that are relatively well endowed with resources appropriate for innovation. Those countries have a comparative advantage in innovation and are able to generate faster technological progress. However, Young also shows that if technology gradually diffuses across countries, then all countries eventually grow at similar rates albeit from different levels of technology. Like the Grossman and Helpman model, Young's model suggests that income differences across countries can exist indefinitely even though rates of growth converge.

Another variation on Grossman and Helpman (1990) is the three-sector model developed by Chong and Zanforlin (2000). In addition to the faster-learning and slower-learning sectors included in Grossman and Helpman's model, Chong and Zanforlin add a third sector that learns from the fast-learning sector. They set up a Heckscher-Ohlin model in which the fast-learning industry flourishes in the country with a relative abundance of human capital. They also directly introduce technology transfers into their three-sector model. They then show that within a Heckscher-Ohlin framework, a human capital-scarce country can still achieve economic growth even though it enjoys a comparative advantage in the slow-learning industry because it can use its relatively scarce human capital to copy from other countries' high-tech sector. This can be more efficient than using its scarce human capital directly in its fast-learning sector. They also find that the country that is poorly endowed with innovative factors eventually grows at the same rate as the better-endowed country, but the relative levels of income will differ.

7.2.2 Demand Driven Technological Progress

In contrast to Young (1991) and Chong and Zanforlin (2000), who model comparative advantage as being the result of supply-side differences in the endowments of resources needed for technological innovation, Linder (1961) hypothesized that home market demand determines what products are developed by local producers. The demand for output determines which industries produce the most and, therefore, enjoy the most learning. Linder argued that this demand-driven learning is the basis for a country's comparative advantage. Porter (1990) further justified Linder's hypothesis.

Fagerberg (1998) empirically tested the Linder-Porter hypothesis. He found strong support for the hypothesis that domestic market conditions determine the competitiveness of specific industries. An interesting illustration of the Linder-Porter hypothesis is the case study by Owen (2001), which compares the performances of wool textile firms in Biella, Italy and the West Riding of Yorkshire. The Italian wool textile industry surpassed its British counterpart during the post World War II period, and Owen attributes the different performances to differences in the domestic markets for wool textiles. The British wool textile producers catered to the concentrated British retailing sector that required long runs of standard fabrics that were used to produce traditional garments, such as men's suits, marketed under the names of traditional retailers like Marks & Spencer. The Italian wool textile producers sold to the Italian fashion houses such as Gucci, Prada, and Armani, which required constantly changing styles to satisfy demand in the volatile fashion industry. The Italian industry wool textile industry thus became much more flexible than its British counterpart, and the Italian fashion industry became more successful in international fashion markets. The Linder-Porter hypothesis is often interpreted as suggesting that a country will gain more from international trade if its domestic market shaped the learning process to where its production matched international market trends. On the other hand, if the domestic market drives domestic producers in a direction that diverges from global market trends, then exporting becomes more difficult and the country will enjoy fewer gains from trade.

To the extent that country-specific learning is driven by a country's internal market, differences in income levels and cultures will cause country growth rates to permanently differ. A country could find itself in a virtuous cycle of having learned to do things that the world market values highly, in which case it will gain from trade and continue to learn more. Or, it could find itself in a vicious cycle whereby a country's exports and terms of trade stagnate and deteriorate, its gains from trade shrink, and the learning process remains slow. The vicious or virtuous cycles that countries find themselves in can be broken only if technology crosses borders and overwhelms the Linder-Porter demand effects on learning. International trade's role is somewhat ambiguous. A country may end up simply reinforcing its comparative advantage gained from learning according to its domestic demand. On the other hand, trade can also serve to impose international demand on a domestic market, thereby altering the country's rate of learning and technological progress. Intentional policies to force or motivate domestic producers to enter export markets could be seen as an attempt to impose international product demand on domestic producers and thus direct the domestic learning process to take advantage of trends in world demand.

7.3 Terms of Trade Arguments for Protection

Sectoral models capture the effects of changing *terms of trade*, the rate at which it exchanges its real exports into real imports. The terms of trade are crucial for determining a country's gains from trade. When an economy is open to trade, shifts in world demand and supply can substantially increase or decrease a country's welfare gains from trade. The potential for a country's terms of trade to shift adversely has often been used as a justification for protectionist policies. This section examines whether such terms-of-trade arguments for protection are logically sound.

7.3.1 Immizerizing Growth

Traditional models of international trade show that, in the case of a "large" country, the gains from increased international trade are likely to be tempered by adverse price movements. Under certain circumstances, economic growth that increases an economy's capacity to export can trigger a worsening terms of trade that completely eliminates the welfare gains from the increased output and trade. One such case, detailed by Bhagwati (1958) and known as *immizerizing growth*, effectively refutes the generally accepted hypothesis that economic growth and international trade are always welfare enhancing.

Figure 7-5 illustrates how economic growth that expands a country's capacity to export can actually cause national welfare to decline. Suppose the economy's productive capacity is initially represented by the production possibilities frontier PPF_1. If the world's terms of trade are given by the line ToT_1, then the country can specialize by producing at the point P_1 and trading to consume at the consumption point A, thus reaching the indifference curve I_4. The country exports food in exchange for clothing at the terms of trade given by the slope of the line ToT_1. Then, suppose the economy grows and the production possibilities frontier shifts out to PPF_2. The diagram suggests that the economy's growth seems to have been concentrated in the economy's export sector, the food industry. According to the Rybczinsky theorem of the Heckscher-Ohlin model, this will be the case when there is an increase in the stock of the factors of production used intensively by the export industry.[93] If, furthermore, the country is a major supplier of food to the world economy the price of food will decline. In Figure 7-5, the country's terms of trade decline from ToT_1 to ToT_2 as exports of food increase. The diagram shows that this decline in the terms of trade is large enough to more than offset the increase in welfare inherent in the increase in productive capacity. After the growth in capacity and the increase in exports, the country consumes at the point B, which lies on a lower indifference curve! If the country had not been open to trade, then the growth of production would have unequivocally provided a gain in welfare. But because the country was already fully engaged in trade, it was vulnerable to terms of trade movements. Figure 7-5 makes it clear that it is not trade per se that is the problem. Comparing the consumption points A and B with C and D shows that a closed economy does not suffer

---

[93] The Rybczynski theorem is discussed in advanced international economics textbooks, such as Chacholiades (1990) or Yarbrough and Yarbrough (2000).

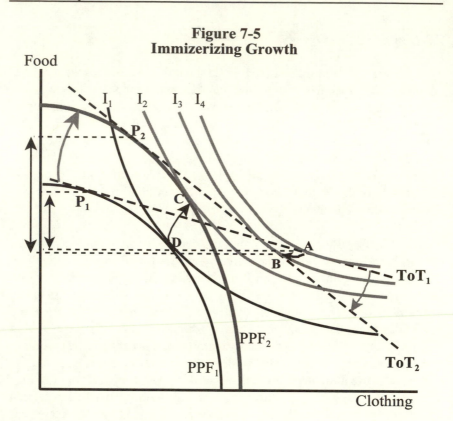

Figure 7-5
Immizerizing Growth

immizerizing growth, but it never attains the levels of welfare achieved by an open economy either before or after the immizerizing growth. However, the rate of (immizerizing) growth in an open economy is negative and the rate of growth resulting from only the shift of the production possibilities frontier in a closed economy is positive.

Even though Figure 7-5 shows that growth and increased trade can, theoretically, be immizerizing, how likely is such an outcome? Chacholiades (1990) lists the conditions that make immizerizing growth possible: (1) the exporting country's growth in productive capacity is concentrated in the sectors of the economy that export, (2) the price elasticity of demand for the export product is inelastic, (3) exports account for a large share of the country's GDP, (4) technological progress is minimal, (5) the export country supplies a large portion of total world output, and (6) the export country does not restrict trade. Not all six of these conditions have to be satisfied for growth to be immizerizing, however. Bhagwati (1958) showed that even if demand is elastic, the other five conditions may still be strong enough to cause immizerizing growth.

Brazil in the very early 20th century is often suggested as an example of immizerizing growth. Brazil was at that time the dominant supplier of coffee to the world, demand for coffee is somewhat price inelastic, coffee accounted for a very large percentage of Brazilian GDP, and the sector's growth was based mostly on factor accumulation, not technological progress. Other than Brazil a century ago, there have been few other clear cases of immizerizing growth. The reason why immizerizing growth is rare is that its occurrence requires that one other critical condition be met: investment in the factors of production used intensively in the export industry must continue to occur even as the terms of trade deteriorate and, hence, the returns to those factors decline. Normally, as factor returns decline investment tends to diminish or cease altogether. In the case of Brazil, investment in coffee plantations may have been especially vulnerable because it takes 6-8 years before a newly planted coffee tree produces its first harvest of coffee beans. Hence, the feedback from coffee prices to investment is delayed in the coffee sector, and this lag between investment and the eventual decline in prices may have caused a misdirection of investment in early 20th century Brazil.

7.3.2 The Terms of Trade Effect of Foreign Growth

Hymans and Stafford (1995) present an interesting model that illustrates how, under free trade, economic growth in a poor country can cause a decline in a rich country's welfare. They use the Heckscher-Ohlin model to show how economic growth in a poor country can have an adverse effect on a wealthy country's terms of trade.

Suppose that there are two economies in the world, Richland and Poorland, which have production-possibilities frontiers (PPFs) as illustrated in Figure 7-6. Suppose also that both Richland and Poorland have the same number of residents, so that Poorland's much lower PPF implies it has a much lower per capita income than Richland. Poorland's lower PPF, and thus its relative poverty, may be due to (1) a lower stock of physical and human capital and/or (2) a lower level of technology. Notice that Richland's PPF is not only much larger than Poorland's, but Richland is also much better endowed with productive resources and technology appropriate for producing high-tech goods. Thus, Richland's PPF is skewed toward high-tech goods and Poorland's PPF is skewed toward production of low-tech products.

Figure 7-7 shows that when free international trade equalizes prices in Richland and Poorland, the terms of trade are reflected in a common

Figure 7-6
Equilibrium in Poorland and Richland before Trade

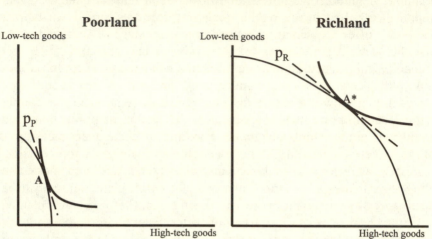

international price line p_1, at which Poorland's exports of low-tech goods to Richland is exactly equal to the value of Richland's exports of high-tech goods to Poorland. Each country attains a higher level of welfare with free trade than they would under self-sufficiency, but the assumption that both countries have identical populations implies that the higher indifference curve reached by Richland's economy provides a higher per capita level of income than Poorland attains.

Figure 7-7
The Welfare-Maximizing Free Trade Equilibrium

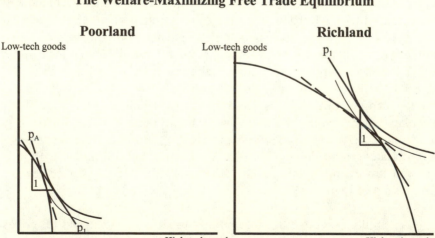

Now, suppose that Poorland saves a large portion of its low per capita income and invests to expand physical and human capital. Suppose, also, that Richland saves only enough to maintain its capital stocks. Also, suppose that a deteriorating education system and low savings levels in Richland hinder research and development activity, and there is no accumulation of new knowledge. Richland's PPF therefore remains exactly the same, but in Poorland there is economic growth and its PPF shifts outward. Because the accumulation of physical and human capital, as well as the assimilation of knowledge from Richland, improves Poorland's ability to produce high-tech goods, Poorland's PPF becomes more similar in shape to Richland's PPF. The change in Poorland's PPF causes its comparative advantage to change, and therefore the pattern of international trade must change.

Figure 7-8 illustrates an interesting result: Even though absolutely nothing has changed in Richland, its per capita real income declines. This decline in welfare is caused by Poorland's improved ability to produce high-tech goods, which causes the relative price of high-tech goods to fall in the world market. This deterioration in Richland's terms of trade, as illustrated by the change in the international price line from p_1 to p_2, *reduces* Richland's per capita welfare.

Figure 7-8
Free Trade Equilibrium after Growth in Poorland Trade

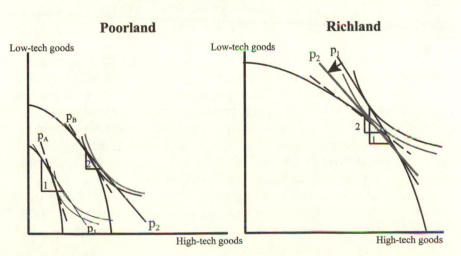

Both the previous case of immizerizing growth and this case of foreign growth have a common lesson: even though international trade seems to be the source of a decline in income, cutting off trade altogether does not improve welfare. In the case of foreign growth, Poorland's economic growth has not eliminated Richland's gains from trade, it has only reduced them. Richland still consumes a bundle of goods that lies outside of its PPF on a higher indifference curve than it could reach without trade. Also, the entire world's welfare would be lower if Richland combats the deterioration in its terms of trade by restricting international trade. Not only would Richland's residents experience lower standards of living, but Poorland would lose the gains in welfare from trade under gradually improving terms of trade. Krugman (1994a) discusses this issue further.

7.3.3 An Alternative Scenario: Trade Itself Diffuses Technology

Samuelson (2004) looks at the static welfare effects in a rich country when its poorer trading partner improves its technology. He suggests that, all other things equal, as the economy with less technology acquires more technology and "catches up" to the high tech economy the two economies become more similar. Hence, the gains from trade are reduced. This case is similar to the previous case where saving and investment in the poor economy makes the PPF of the poor country more similar to the PPF of the rich country, only now the PPF is transformed by technological progress. Samuelson goes one step further, however, by linking international trade directly to the transfer of technology from the technology leader to the technology follower. Samuelson suggests that because international trade effectively transfers technology, international trade is directly the cause of the loss of welfare in a high income economy.

Samuelson's argument is relevant to the recent discussions about outsourcing of production to low wage countries. Critics of outsourcing have often claimed that the shift in production stimulates movements of capital and technology. Technology transfers appear to be especially likely when the shift in production abroad also involves foreign direct investment. By shifting production to take advantage of low wages and manufacture the products demanded in the high income economies, multinational enterprises supply the capital and the technology that effectively makes the poorer economies more similar to high income economies. Samuelson describes how this foreign direct investment and transfer of technology by U.S. firms to China "gives to China some of the comparative advantage that had belonged to the United States."[94] Furthermore, he warns that this loss of comparative advantage can result in "permanent lost per capita real income" in the U.S.:

> Historically, U.S. workers used to have kind of a *de facto* monopoly access to the superlative capitals and know-hows (scientific, engineering and managerial) of the United States. All of us Yankees, so to speak, were born with silver spoons in our mouths–and that importantly explained the historically high U.S. market-clearing real wage rates for (among others) janitors, house helpers, small business owners and so forth.[95]

In short, the equalization of factor ratios and technologies will equalize factor returns to the detriment of the abundant factors in the high tech economy.

7.3.4 The Long-Run Dynamics of Knowledge Transfers

The Hymans and Stafford model, in which a poor country catches up through rapid investment, and the Samuelson model, in which the poor country catches up by acquiring technology, assume that things stay the same in the rich economy. In his critique of Samuelson, the international economist Jagdish Bhagwati points out that "we can change the terms of trade by moving up the technology ladder."[96] That is, if the high technology economy continues to develop new technology when old technology is transferred to the poor economy, then it can maintain enough of a difference between the two countries to keep the terms of trade gains from trade from systematically changing. This is like the dynamic process that Vernon (1966) described in his product cycle model of trade discussed in the previous chapter. Samuelson suggests, however, Vernon's model may not be correct. For one thing, in an increasingly global, integrated world economy, technology will tend to flow more quickly and, therefore, reduce the period during which the technology leaders can exploit their technologies. The quickening of the pace at which technology spreads may reduce the benefits from innovation, and this may reduce the rate of innovation, and hence income, in the wealthy country.

---

[94] Samuelson (2004), p. 137.

[95] Samuelson (2004), p. 144.

[96] Quoted in Steve Lohr (2004), "An Elder Challenges Outsourcing's Orthodoxy," *New York Times*, September 9, 2004.

7.3.5 Some Additional Points

The special cases presented in this section show that, under certain circumstances, the deterioration in a country's terms of trade cause international trade to be statistically correlated with a decline in per capita real income. These special cases do not necessarily constitute a strong case against international trade, however. In most circumstances, poor countries' ability to invest, adopt technology, and even create new technology does not necessarily threaten wealthy countries' standards of living. In fact, the logic of the Schumpeterian model of technological progress suggests that the accumulation of physical capital, human capital, and knowledge in poor countries will increase their ability to adopt foreign technologies more quickly and eventually to participate in creating new, cutting edge technologies. As more people in more countries attempt to create new knowledge, the higher will be the rate of technological progress. Today's rich countries will increasingly benefit from other countries' knowledge, just like other countries currently benefit from the technologies developed in the rich countries. Japan, Taiwan, and Finland, among many others, are recent examples of countries that at one time lagged in terms of technology but have become important developers of new knowledge and technology. It would be difficult to argue that the United States is worse off because Japan, Taiwan, and Finland are advanced economies now.

Most likely, international trade will have a very beneficial effect on long-run welfare in both rich and poor economies precisely because it increases global competition. The threat of immizerizing growth will push developing economies to improve their allocation of resources and the flexibility with which they adjust to the many changes that inevitably accompany economic growth. At the same time, rich countries will not be able to rest on their laurels, reaping the benefits of past innovation forever. Rich countries will have to focus on maintaining the institutions that favor further innovation. The increased competition and the potential terms of trade costs will underscore the need for better education, incentives for saving and investment, resources for research and development, protection of property rights and human rights, maintaining peace, etc. This global innovative competition may not be appreciated by those workers and industries who have to compete with the foreign innovators, but future generations will no doubt be thankful for the increase in technological progress and economic growth caused by the growing worldwide competition and innovation.

7.4 Protectionism to Promote Technological Progress

One of the oldest and still popular arguments for protection, the *infant industry* argument, is based on the idea that, in the long run, it is beneficial to protect certain industries in an economy because they are likely to generate technological progress and gain a comparative advantage in the future. The recent strategic trade arguments for trade protection or other government support are in many ways just modern versions of the centuries-old infant industry argument for protection.

7.4.1 The Infant Industry Argument for Protection

The infant industry argument is one of the oldest arguments for protection, and references to it can be found as far back as the seventeenth century Europe. One of the first complete presentations of the infant industry argument was made in 1791 by Alexander Hamilton, the first U.S. Secretary of the Treasury, in his *Report on Manufactures*. In the mid-1800s John Stuart Mill's best-selling economics text stated:

> The only case in which, on mere principles of political economy, protecting duties can be defensible, is when they are imposed temporarily (especially in a young and rising nation) in hopes of naturalizing a foreign industry, in itself perfectly suitable to the circumstance of the country. The superiority of one country over another in a branch of production often arises only from having begun it sooner. There may be no inherent advantage on one part, or disadvantage on the other, but only a present superiority of acquired skill and experience. A country which has this skill and experience yet to acquire, may in other respects be better adapted to the production than those which were earlier in the field....A protecting duty, continued for a reasonable time, will sometimes be the least inconvenient mode in which the nation can tax itself for the support of such an experiment. But the protection should be confined to cases in which there is good ground of assurance that the industry it fosters will after a time be able to dispense with it; nor should the domestic producers ever be allowed to expect that it will be continued to them beyond the time necessary for a fair trial of what they are capable of accomplishing.[97]

---

[97] Mill (1848), p. 922.

Mill's endorsement of the infant industry argument gave it intellectual credibility. Mill also detailed the assumptions on which the infant industry argument was based, however. These assumptions are not easily satisfied.

7.4.2 The Argument's Many Implicit Assumptions

The infant industry argument effectively makes several strong assumptions: (1) there is a *learning-by-doing* process that relates production costs to accumulated output, (2) only domestic production experience can help the learning process because technology and know-how cannot be acquired from abroad (technology is country-specific), and (3) know-how and technology are industry-specific, so that they cannot be acquired from other sectors of the economy. With industry-specific technology, the infant industry argument concludes that technology in a specific industry can be improved only by accumulating experience in that industry. Therefore, a country can only achieve a new comparative advantage if it "protects" an industry long enough for accumulated production experience to bring costs down to where it can compete in world markets. The argument does not deny the validity of comparative advantage. In fact, the protection of an "infant industry" is justified precisely because that industry will gain a comparative advantage if it is given *temporary* protection. Of course, a correct phrasing of the infant industry argument recognizes that the true infant industry must eventually become competitive (what has come to be known as the *Mill criterion*, in honor of John Stuart Mill), but it must eventually generate enough welfare gains from trade and growth to more than cover the initial costs of protection, properly discounted (this is called the *Bastable criterion*).

Baldwin (1969) pointed out that the infant industry argument also depends on several other assumptions that its proponents seldom explicitly mention. For example, if certain industries do not enjoy a comparative advantage because they lack experience, then instead of "protecting" these industries from foreign competition, it would in most cases be less costly to have the government use tax revenue to subsidize them until they mature. Bhagwati's (1971) well-known comparison of policy tools showed that, in this case where learning-by-doing lowers costs, production subsidies are likely to be less costly than import protection. Thus, before protection of some alleged infant industry is justified, it must be the case that more direct types of support during the industry's maturation period are not available. Nor is it clear why the consumer of imports must pay for the "growing up" of an industry by being forced to consume more expensive domestic goods. Why cannot an industry that needs time to mature simply borrow in the financial markets in order to tide it over its learning period? After all, virtually all investments require some time before they generate profit. The financial markets normally finance investment projects, but, of course, in this case the owners of the project must cover the costs of the financing. The infant industry argument for protection therefore implicitly assumes that normal financial channels are not available. In many cases, calls for infant industry protection are likely to be driven by special interests seeking to transfer industry start-up costs to consumers.

Like all policies that target specific industries, the infant industry argument also assumes that policy makers can accurately predict future comparative advantage. Krueger and Tuncer (1982) tested the infant industry argument using data on India and Turkey, and they found no evidence that protection was in any way systematically related to firms that ultimately became competitive in international markets. Infant industry protection also raises the potential for foreign retaliation, especially by countries who have industries that currently enjoy the comparative advantage. World Trade Organization (WTO) rules do not permit government subsidies or protection to help domestic industries compete and gain world market share. If countries take a complaint to the WTO, it is likely to authorize countries to retaliate by restricting the import of products from the offending country.

Despite all of the qualifications, however, it is nevertheless possible that there are individual firms or even whole sectors of an economy that qualify as *infant industries*. In developing economies the financial sector is often not well developed and unable to provide financing for long-term or large projects. Or, there may be external benefits from new industries that cannot be captured by the individual owners or the financial sector. Finally, governments may not have well-run tax systems that can cover the costs of direct subsidies to an infant industry; the indirect method of having consumers of imports effectively pay for the temporary cost of protection may be the most efficient way to bring a potentially profitable infant industry into existence. It should be clear, however, that the assumptions underlying the logic of the infant industry argument are not general. The infant industry argument applies to very special circumstances.

7.5 Import Substitution Policies

After World War II, many countries in Latin America, Africa, and Asia actively restricted international trade as part of what have come to be called *import substitution* (IS) policies. IS policies consisted of a broad range of trade bans, quotas, and high tariffs on imports, all intended to "protect" domestic industries so that they could effectively defy comparative advantage and "substitute" domestic production of goods for formerly-imported goods. IS policies were based on the perception that economic growth could be accelerated by actively directing economic activity away from the traditional agricultural and resource sectors of the economy and toward manufacturing. Few proponents of import substitution based their support for such policies on rigorous two-sector growth models, but their thinking reflected the belief that expansion of manufacturing would lead to a more rapid growth of technology and technology spillovers in developing economies than would the traditional specialization in raw materials such as foods and minerals. Developing countries usually enjoyed a comparative advantage in primary goods, and it was feared that free trade would make permanent their specialization in such "slow-growth industries" and, therefore, permanently slower economic growth.

7.5.1 Why Import Substitution Policies Were Popular

Bruton (1998), in his thorough survey of import substitution, details the fascination with industrialization among leaders and policy makers in the developing world after Word War II. Most development economists focused on the "dual" nature of developing economies, which was the coexistence of large "traditional" agricultural sectors and smaller "modern" sectors that looked more like those sectors in developed countries. Hence, development was viewed as a process of shrinking the traditional sector and all of the institutions that guided it, and promoting the growth of the modern sector. In time, developing economies would become fully developed economies by completing this shift from the traditional activities to modern economic activities. Import substitution was seen as a way to stimulate more "modern" activities like manufacturing. Important intellectual contributors supporting IS policies were the noted development economists Arthur Lewis (1954), Gunnar Myrdal (1956), and John Fei and Gustav Ranis (1964).

7.5.2 The Favorable Political Environment

Also contributing to the popularity of import substitution policies was the intellectual support of the United Nations Economic Commission for Latin America, or ECLA. The director of ECLA was the Argentinean economist, Raúl Prebisch (1950, 1959), who presented thorough arguments justifying import substitution policies in Latin America and other developing regions of the world. Prebisch began by pointing out that developing economies usually had comparative advantages in producing primary products. Furthermore, he argued that the income elasticity of demand for primary products was less than one, which meant that the terms of trade of primary product exporters would gradually deteriorate in the long run as demand for the industrial products of the wealthier countries increased more rapidly as world income rose. He further stated that, because less developed economies were structurally rigid and unable to respond to price changes, less developed countries would remain saddled with economies whose productive capacity was concentrated in slow-growth, declining-price sectors. As a result, investment would be low in developing economies, there would be less effort to innovate, and, hence, overall economic growth would be slow relative to the rest of the world.

Many authors contested Prebisch's prediction of declining primary product prices, but for most of the 20th century, commodity prices indeed trended downward, the occasional oil price spike notwithstanding. However, a recent statistical study on the determinants of economic growth by Hadass and Williamson (2001) argues that "the terms of trade debate was about an event which was pretty minor for most participants in the center [developed countries] and the periphery [developing economies]."[98] Thus, Prebisch was correct on the trend in commodity prices, but the effect of the declines may not have been very important. Perhaps the aspect of commodity prices that Prebisch should have emphasized is their year-to-year volatility rather than their persistent decline. According to Blattman, Hwang, and Williamson (2004), statistically it is the volatility of export prices, not persistent price declines, that significantly depresses economic growth in developing countries. In general, economies can much more easily deal with gradual changes than sudden, unpredictable changes. Prebisch's other assumptions have proved to be much less accurate, however.

Prebisch's argument that economies in Latin America and other less developed regions of the world could not adjust to changing prices is not supported by the evidence. Furtado (1963) and Baer (1995) have described the rapid shift in resources from export-oriented agriculture to domestically-oriented industry in Brazil in response to the collapse of world commodity prices in the 1930s. This experience shows that a developing economy could and did reallocate resources very quickly when the price incentives were clear. Even though Prebisch was aware of the Brazilian experience,

---

[98] Hadass and Williamson (2001), p. 33.

he opted to ignore that evidence. He instead embraced the arguments of the *structuralist school*, a popular Latin American school of economic thought after World War II. The *structuralists* rejected the neoclassical approach to modeling the economy. Where neoclassicals assumed smooth functions that implied continuous marginal adjustments to price signals, the structuralists modeled developing economies as plagued by structural rigidities that prevented such smooth adjustments. The structuralists were convinced that developing countries' current comparative advantage would lock them into exporting primary products forever, regardless of falling commodity prices and deteriorating terms of trade. They therefore called for intentional government action to change the "structure" of developing economies, increasing the manufacturing sector by drawing resources away from traditional primary economic activities like agriculture and mining. Import substitution policies that closed a country's borders and intentionally defied its current comparative advantage were seen as a "necessary short-run cost" to force a long-run structural change in an economy. The structuralists and Prebisch claimed that the forced structural change would more than pay for itself in the form of higher rates of economic growth in the long run.

An important factor behind the spread of IS policies throughout the developing world, especially Latin America, was their political viability. For example, in most Latin American developing countries the national government was supported by an implicit coalition of urban businesses and workers. Under IS policies, it was they who would gain from the trade protection at the expense of consumers and farmers in general. Also lurking behind the scenes was a popular ideology shared by many Latin American intellectuals called *dependency theory*, which asserted that international trade is the channel through which rich countries "exploit" poor countries and effectively perpetuate the unequal distribution of world income. Dependency theory was convincingly presented by Frank (1967), who argued that a developing country could escape its fate as a "peripheral" economy only by isolating itself from the global economy. Dependency theorists in Latin America's universities were enthusiastic supporters of import substitution because it would result in less international trade and, they believed, less exploitation by the rich countries. With organized labor, left-wing intellectuals, government bureaucrats, and the urban business classes sympathetic, import substitution enjoyed a supportive political environment in many developing countries throughout the world.

7.5.3 An Assessment of IS Policies

Table 7-1 shows that while international trade grew as a percentage of overall economic activity in most of the world between 1950 and 1973, it declined as a percentage of GDP for Latin America and South Asian countries such as India that actively embraced import substitution. On the other hand, in East Asian economies such as Taiwan and South Korea, which abandoned protectionism in the 1950s and early 1960s, respectively, trade grew very rapidly relative to these countries' rapidly growing GDPs.

Table 7-1
Merchandise Exports as Percentage of GDP

	1929	*1950*	*1973*	*1992*
Western Europe	13.3	9.4	20.9	29.7
Canada	15.8	13.0	19.9	27.2
U.S.	3.6	3.0	5.0	8.2
Argentina	6.1	2.4	2.1	4.3
Brazil	7.1	4.0	2.6	4.7
Mexico	14.8	3.5	2.2	6.4
Total Lat. America	9.7	6.2	4.6	6.2
China	1.7	1.9	1.1	2.3
India	3.7	2.6	2.0	1.7
Indonesia	3.6	3.3	5.0	7.4
Japan	3.5	2.3	7.9	12.4
Korea	4.5	1.0	8.2	17.8
Taiwan	5.2	2.5	10.2	34.4
Thailand	6.6	7.0	4.5	11.4

Source: Angus Maddison (1995), *Monitoring the World Economy 1820-1992*, Paris: OECD,Table 2-4, p. 38.

Most developing countries abandoned strict import substitution after the 1970s, although the remnants of the tariff and quota barriers erected during the 1950s and 1960s linger on in various forms. Table 7-1 shows that during the period 1973-1992, only India saw trade as a share of its GDP shrink further as India continued to pursue IS policies into the

1990s. The success of the Asian tigers and their "outward-looking" policies seems to have swung policy makers in many other developing economies toward favoring policies that encourage international trade.

Also causing import substitution policies to lose favor is the evidence showing that import substitution policies brought only temporary spurts of growth followed by a gradual slowdown and, in the case of quite a few countries, macroeconomic imbalances that caused severe economic crises. This initial spurt of growth followed by stagnation was the opposite of the outcome predicted by the proponents of import substitution, which was that initial sacrifices in the form of tariffs and other trade barriers would eventually bring faster growth and technological progress.

Table 7-2
Economic Growth in Latin America: 1940-1985

Years	Argentina	Brazil	Chile	Mexico	Peru
Total Factor Productivity Growth (annual % rate):					
1940-50	3.1	n.a.	1.9	4.4	0.5
1950-60	0.8	3.6	0.7	1.0	*-2.6*
1960-70	0.2	1.4	1.3	1.2	1.0
1970-80	*-0.3*	1.1	1.0	0.1	*-0.5*
1980-85	*-2.9*	*-1.0*	*-2.7*	*-2.4*	*-2.6*
Growth of Per Capita GDP (annual % rate):					
1950-73	2.1	3.7	1.3	3.2	2.5
1973-98	0.6	1.4	2.6	1.3	*-0.3*

Source: Victor J. Elías (1992), *Sources of Growth: A Study of Seven Latin American Countries*, San Francisco: ICS Press.; Angus Maddison (2001), *The World Economy: A Millennial Perspective*, Paris: OECD.

Table 7-2 presents Elías' (1992) estimates of total factor productivity (TFP) for five Latin American economies, Argentina, Brazil, Chile, Mexico, and Peru, between 1940 and 1985. Recall from Chapter 2 that TFP is the difference between the growth of real GDP and the weighted average of the growth of real inputs such as labor, capital, human capital, and natural resources. During the decades 1940-1950, 1950-1960, and 1960-1970, TFP growth was positive in all cases but one for Argentina, Brazil, Chile, Mexico, and Peru. TFP growth tended to slow in each successive decade. During 1970-1980 and the first half of the 1980s, TFP growth turned negative in all five Latin American countries shown. As also shown in Table 7-2, the slowdown in TFP growth in the 1970s and 1980s resulted in a sharp slowdown in economic growth through the end of the century in four of the five countries. Only Chile actually grew faster in the last quarter of the twentieth century, its growth fueled by sharply increased savings and, eventually in the 1990s, rapid productivity growth. Of the five countries, Chile was the first of the five countries to abandon import substitution; Chile opened its economy wide to trade in the mid-1970s.

There are several possible reasons why IS policies did not cause economic growth to increase in the long run. First of all, the high static costs of protection lowered income below what it could have been in the case of higher per capita incomes based on exploiting comparative advantage. Secondly, investment was usually not well allocated among the most productive sectors of the economy because the broad protection under IS policies promoted all industries indiscriminately, regardless of whether they generated technology externalities or their prospects for achieving competitive costs. Thirdly, IS policies often led to substituting imports of intermediate goods and capital goods as well as final consumer products. For example, the Indian Second Plan (1956-1961) specifically targeted the heavy capital goods sector, a course advocated by the influential director of the Indian Statistical Institute, P. C. Mahalanobis (1955). Protection of a domestic capital goods industry implied higher costs of capital equipment, and more importantly, the protected economies lost the opportunity to import technology embodied in equipment and machinery.

Joseph Schumpeter's model of creative destruction describes the failure of import substitution quite accurately: The sudden increase in protection when import substitution policies are first instituted provides new profit opportunities for entrepreneurs, often foreign multinational firms who are cut off from the market and therefore set up manufacturing behind the tariff wall. This leads to an initial spurt of innovation and economic growth, which can surprise even the most avid proponents of import substitution policies. However, the high levels of protection from foreign competition tend to inspire collusion among the protected producers to reduce costly innovation and lobbying for government-regulated limits on innovation. According to Bruton (1998), "The principal reason for the failure of import substitution was that, as practiced, it created an environment that discouraged learning."[99] Recall the discussion that price competition can stimulate innovation because it raises the difference between pre-innovation profit and post-innovation profit. Also very relevant here is the discussions of dynamic protectionism in Section 6.5 of Chapter 6 and the references cited there, especially Holmes and Schmitz (1995, 1998), Mokyr (1990, 2002), and Parente and Prescott (2000).

7.5.4 How Well Do Governments Pick Winners?

Strategic trade arguments for protection, the infant industry argument, and import substitution all effectively assume that policy makers can correctly predict the future performance of specific industries and sectors of the economy. Government policy makers have seldom been very god at picking the "winners" from among the many industries clamoring for protection. Pack (2000) reviewed various studies on how protectionism affects economic growth and concluded that even in the cases of Japan and South Korea, two countries that have been held up by some as examples of successful targeted trade intervention, the benefits were at best very small. Svensson (1998) examined detailed data on 24 manufacturing sectors in 13 developed economies and found that government subsidies for R&D activity were allocated for political reasons as well as economic reasons. Svensson found that sometimes subsidies indeed went to the industries with highest levels of technology, but just as often the subsidies went to industries that were declining or were highly labor-intensive, clearly not *strategic industries* deserving of special assistance in developed economies. This finding is in accord with Baldwin and Robert-Nicoud (2002), who use political science models to predict that indeed dying industries are more likely to lobby for, and gain, protection than new, growing industries.

Japan's Ministry of Finance recently issued a report showing that its predecessor, the well-known Ministry of International Trade and Industry (MITI), actually hindered Japanese economic growth.[100] MITI often has been held up as an example of successful industrial planning and protection to promote key industries in which Japan came to dominate world markets, especially by industries in other countries seeking support from their governments. However, the report claims that the industries supported by MITI failed more often than they succeeded. For example,

---

[99] Bruton (1998), p. 903.

[100] As reported in Issei Morita (2002), "Japanese Explode the Myth of MITI," *Financial Times*, June 27.

MITI was heavily involved in financing the Japanese textile, chemical, and aircraft industries, all of which have failed to become competitive in the world market. However, MITI provided no assistance for the automobile industry because, back in the 1950s and 1960s, it saw little prospect for that industry to become internationally competitive.

Equally damaging to industrial targeting is the finding by Martin and Mitra (2001) that in both developed and developing countries, productivity grew faster in agriculture than in manufacturing in the latter part of the twentieth century. This result, of course, runs counter to the conventional wisdom that led so many developing countries in the 1950s and 1960s to follow policies designed to promote the growth of industry at the expense of agriculture.

Anne Krueger (1980), who studied import substitution policies in a number of developing countries, points out that, in contrast to free trade, import substitution policies and their inherent need for heavy governmental involvement in economic decisions often lead to political influence peddling, costly paperwork, bureaucratic bottlenecks, wasteful rent-seeking activities, and corruption. Furthermore, it is simply politically difficult for governments to favor one sector over another purely on objective economic criteria. Even if it were possible to predict the future with some degree of accuracy, political systems are just not well set up to make such choices objectively and accurately. This does not imply that there are no circumstances under which governments can be successful in carrying out strategic trade policies or assisting an infant industry. But it is clear that skepticism is in order when arguments for protection demand that politicians make difficult choices among industries and sectors of the economy. Recall David Friedman's words about U.S. industrial protection at the start of this chapter: "It is not infant industries that get protection but senile industries–American auto, shoe, and steel producers."[101]

7.6 Conclusions

The case for selective protection from imports depends on how easily ideas, knowledge, and techniques flow between countries and industries. If new technology moves promptly to all countries and industries, either in pure form or embodied in products and capital, then international trade generally

---

[101] Friedman (1996), p. 289.

will be welfare enhancing. However, when technology does not flow between countries and industries, special cases can be constructed in which protectionist trade policies can raise an economy's rate of growth.

In this chapter, we addressed some of the most common arguments used to justify trade restrictions. In terms of their influence in shaping trade policy in developing economies, the most powerful arguments for protection have been (1) the so-called strategic trade arguments for protection, (2) the infant industry argument for temporary protection, and (3) the structuralist arguments for import substitution (IS) policies. This is not to say that trade restrictions are not also, or even predominantly, driven by simple self-interest and political maneuvering by special interest groups. But, clearly, these three arguments for protection have had an influence in shaping trade policies. The strategic trade arguments have been especially popular among supporters of protectionist policies in developed economies. The infant industry argument for protection has been used for over two centuries in nearly all countries. And import substitution policies have been popular in developing economies for over 50 years.

The special cases where protection may be preferable to free trade in the eyes of people on one side of the border depend on a complex set of assumptions being satisfied, however. Especially devastating for the pro-protection arguments are the assumptions that unbiased information about the future is available and that government uses information objectively to apply protectionist measures. Strategic trade policies generally require government to correctly assess the economic conditions at hand and those likely in the future in order to pick the firms and industries that qualify for protection. The assumption of no foreign retaliation is also critical because strategic trade policies only bring welfare increases to a country if foreign countries do not retaliate with their own protectionist policies. These assumptions are unlikely to be satisfied in the real world, and therefore the case for industrial planning and protection is not nearly as strong as the proponents of protectionist trade policies claim. The world's extensive experience with import substitution policies provides further evidence that protection is not likely to be successful in generating increases in economic growth in the long run, although some short-run success may be attained.

An interesting implication of the sectoral model discussed in this chapter is that there may be more than one equilibrium growth rate in an economy. The models showed that international trade's effect on a country's rate of economic growth depends critically on how technology moves between countries. If international trade causes technology to move across borders more quickly, then trade's potentially damaging effect of pushing a country into specializing in what are currently viewed as slow-growth industries may not matter much in the long run. Thus, a policy of open trade will generate the needed technology flows to make trade generate positive long-run economic growth. That is, the prediction that open trade is positively correlated with economic growth will be self-fulfilling. On the other hand, if policy makers restrict trade to promote certain sectors of the economy, the lower level of trade will result in weaker technology transfers. These weaker technology transfers can then be held up as evidence to justify the strategic trade policies in the first place. Protectionism motivated by political concerns can be economically justified after the fact by taking low technology flows as a given and pointing to the relative gains from having protected alleged fast-growth industries. Of course, while the political implications of each of the two policies may be similar, from a welfare perspective the two choices have very different effects. The second option of free trade gives the economy a greater total value of goods and services to distribute among its residents.

It also appears that the special cases where protection might spur an economy to grow faster may not be of much practical importance. Remember, in the long run, economic growth depends on technological progress. This technological progress will have to be achieved through domestic innovation if knowledge and ideas do not arrive from outside the country. Reinventing the wheel is a lot more difficult and costly than copying the design or importing the wheels.

Despite this obvious conclusion, the special cases continue to dominate policy discussions. The legitimacy of the special cases depends on how well technology moves across borders. The next chapter details what recent research tells us about how readily technology diffuses across countries and what role trade plays in facilitating technology transfers.

Chapter Eight

Trade and Technology Transfers

The sea brought Greeks the vine from India, from Greece transmitted the use of grain across the sea, from Phoenicia imported letters as a memorial against forgetfulness, thus preventing the greater part of mankind from being wineless, grainless, and unlettered.
      (Plutarch, 100 A.D.)[102]

As discussed in the previous chapter, when technology does not move readily between countries then there are circumstances under which trade restrictions can enhance economic growth. There are many reasons why knowledge may not instantaneously or costlessly transfer from one economy to another. The evidence that the adoption of new ideas and knowledge follows the pattern of an S-curve even within a single country suggests that knowledge, ideas, techniques, and methods are unlikely to move instantaneously between countries. On the other hand, the quote by Plutarch reminds us that ideas and technology has often moved between countries. The quote further suggests that ideas and technology can move right along with goods and services. If ideas indeed move along with goods, then those special cases in which trade restrictions actually promote technological progress and economic growth are unlikely to occur. The Schumpeterian model in Chapter 6 suggested that if international trade causes knowledge to move more easily between countries, then trade would reduce the cost of innovation. And, if trade makes it easier to innovate, then open economies will tend to grow faster than closed economies.

---

[102] Quoted from "On Whether Water or Fire Is More Useful," in *Plutarch's Morelia*, Vol. 12, Loeb Classical Library, 1927, p. 299.

The models and possible outcomes remain nothing more than conjectures, however, in the absence of evidence on how knowledge moves between countries. Fortunately, we have a large amount of useful evidence on how knowledge and ideas move between firms, industries, and countries. Sarkar (1998) and Ruttan (2001) provide thorough surveys of the literature on the diffusion of technology in general, and Saggi (2000) and Navaretti and Tarr (2000) specifically survey the literature on international technology transfers. The evidence is still not fully convincing, however, and many questions remain. This chapter summarizes what economists know about the international spread of technology and the role that international trade plays in spreading ideas and knowledge.

8.1 Domestic Technology vs. Adopted Technology

The level of technology in an economy is the result of past original research performed in the economy and the acquisition of knowledge from abroad. Foreign technology indirectly plays a role in original research as well, however, because original research builds on previous knowledge, some of which came from abroad. Foreign technology is, therefore, a source of prior knowledge that can be combined to create new knowledge as well as a direct source of new knowledge.

8.1.1 Direct and Indirect Technology Transfers

If the cost of new foreign technology to produce a new product, reduce costs, improve quality, etc., is obtained at less than the original cost to the inventor, then there is said to be an international *spillover* of technology. And, if international trade facilitates such international spillovers, then the value of such net gains in technological progress must be added to the other gains from trade.

When ideas and knowledge are transferred in the form of designs, directions, instructions, blueprints, or diagrams that can be used directly by people to learn, understand, and apply the ideas and knowledge, the international transfers of technology are usually referred to as *direct transfers* of technology. International trade induces such direct transfers by creating contacts and increasing communication between buyers and sellers of products and services or by raising the level of competition between firms that forces producers to improve products and lower costs. International trade also *indirectly* motivates people and firms to transfer technology across borders by increasing the awareness of foreign technology incorporated in products and services. The exposure to foreign products may induce firms to reverse-engineer products, to copy general designs and ideas, and to improve on the foreign products. Finally, international trade also transfers technology *embodied* in the products that are traded. For example, a domestic firm can improve its production line by copying all aspects of the systems used overseas, or it can import all of the assembly line equipment and install in its own factory. The domestic firm can also "import" technology by outsourcing the design of its factory to a foreign firm. In our global economy, an increasing amount of technology is transferred between countries embodied in imported products and services.

8.1.2 Technology Moves Slowly

The very large differences in technology observed across countries mean that technology does not move quickly between countries and industries. In the case of direct transfers of technology, the process depends on others' ability to understand and apply the blueprints that are available. It also depends on the willingness of people and firms to pay for and apply the blueprints. The indirect influence of trade through observation of products, reverse engineering, and initiating new combinatoric processes of technological progress is also dependent on costly activities and time for learning and experimenting. Hence, trade's contribution to technology transfers is necessarily still somewhat restricted by the costs of learning, adopting, and applying new technologies. There is also a large body of evidence suggesting that new technologies are slow to spread geographically. The concentration of information technology firms in Silicon Valley, financial firms in London, and the automobile industry in Detroit are often interpreted as suggesting that knowledge tends to *agglomerate* close to where it was initially developed. If new ideas spread slowly within an economy, they are likely to spread even more slowly across borders.

Keller (2001a) has made the interesting suggestion that, because international trade is more costly and smaller the farther away from each other countries are, technology will disseminate to neighboring countries more quickly than to distant countries. There is ample evidence that indeed technology differs greatly across countries; the extent of these technology differences have been theoretically outlined by Lucas (1990) and empirically estimated by Hall and Jones (1999).

8.1.3 The Costs of Adopting New Technology

Researchers have often found widespread evidence of the cost of introducing new technologies in new locations. Teece (1977) estimated the costs of technology transfers across countries in the chemicals, petroleum refining, and machinery industries. He found that, on average, the cost of adopting foreign technologies was equal to 19 percent of total project costs. Mansfield, Schwartz, and Wagner (1981) also found the costs of adopting existing technologies to be substantial; for 48 product introductions in the chemical, drug, electronics, and machinery industries in the U.S., the estimated cost of imitation was equal to about 65 percent of the total cost of innovation. Von Hippel (1994) detailed the cost of adapting technology as a major business management problem.

Teece (1977) and David (1992) emphasized that most technology transfers between industrial plants require person-to-person contacts, follow-up information, training sessions, and many other repeated communications. Recall, also, Polanyi's (1958) description of most knowledge as "tacit" and thus requiring that it be passed on "by example from master to apprentice."[103] Technology transfers do not normally occur in the form of precise blueprints that are readily understood and copied. This means that the transfer of technology will tend to follow the patterns of international economic transactions, such as international trade and investment. The lack of easy instructions for applying foreign technologies also means that countries must have the resources necessary to learn, adopt, and apply technologies from other countries. Recent research has, therefore, increasingly focused on human capital and institutions as the critical elements for technology adoption.

8.1.4 The Costs of Adopting Foreign Technology

Abramovitz (1986) concluded that "differences among countries in the productivity levels create a strong potentiality for subsequent convergence of levels, provided that countries have a 'social capability' adequate to absorb more advanced technologies....the institutional and human capital components of social capability develop only slowly as education and organization respond to the requirements of technological opportunity and to experience in exploiting it."[104] Skinner and Staiger (2005) revisited the

---

[103] Polanyi (1958), p. 53.

[104] Abramovitz (1986), p. 405.

spread of hybrid corn, first studied in the pioneering studies of technology diffusion by Gross (1942), Ryan and Gross (1943), and Griliches (1957, 1958), as well as the spread of tractors, heart attack treatments, and computers. They found large differences in the spread of this knowledge across states of the U.S., and the differences were significantly associated with social capital and high school graduation rates. Thus, the international diffusion of technology may be slow because people in many countries lack the skills necessary to absorb foreign technologies. Keller (1996) used Abramovitz' ideas to develop a model of technology in which the rate at which technology is imported approaches the rate of growth of human capital in the importing country, not the rate at which technology grows overseas. He found evidence supporting his model.

Also hampering the spread of technology are the intentional barriers to the international flow of ideas and goods, such as tariffs, quotas, limits on immigration, restrictions on foreign investment, and many other forms of protectionism. Language differences and other cultural incompatibilities often hinder communications and prevent the spread of useful technology. When all of these other barriers to the flow of knowledge are added to the costs of adaptation and the scarcity of resources needed to adopt foreign technologies, there is clearly a realistic possibility that technology may not diffuse rapidly enough to rule out special cases that would make trade harmful to economic growth. A survey of the evidence on international technology diffusion is in order.

8.2 The Empirical Evidence on Technology Diffusion

Krugman (1991) called for economists to pay more attention to the geography of economic activity, but he also pointed out how difficult it is to research the geographic spread of technology. He suggested that there may not be much that economists can say about technology flows because "they leave no paper trail by which they may be measured and tracked, and there is nothing to prevent the theorist from assuming anything about them that she likes."[105] Krugman was a bit too pessimistic, however. Innovative researchers *have* found some paper trails.

One strategy for uncovering the flow of technology and ideas has been to examine patent data. Patents applications require an explicit listing

---

[105] Krugman (1991), p. 53.

of prior ideas and discoveries on which the new idea is based, and in many countries patent applications require that the country of origin of the prior patents and ideas be listed as well. Hence, patent applications provide a paper trail of where knowledge came from. For example, if a new patent application for some product or process in one country lists as a previous influence a patent first granted in another country, there has presumably been an international transfer of knowledge. Patent data has also been used as a proxy for overall innovative activity, which can be used in standard statistical analyses to find correlations between knowledge flows and international trade.

A shortcoming of patent data is that it captures only a small portion of all innovative activity that occurs in an economy. Most new knowledge is not patented. Also, some patented knowledge moves only after patents have run out; hence, there is a long lag between the creation of an idea and the time it spills over to other industries and countries. Finally, patents do not accurately reflect the importance of each innovation. Patents are awarded for all types of innovations, including those that turn out to have no practical applications and those that turn out to be major breakthroughs. To correct for this deficiency, Jaffe and Trajtenberg (2002) weighed patents by the number of citations in subsequent patents.

Many researchers have sought other data that more accurately capture the actual creation of what we broadly define as technology. Many researchers have used measures of R&D activity. Most OECD countries collect data on R&D activity within their borders, and a few developing countries also compile such data. These measures can be used to estimate international technology flows. A common approach has been to statistically test the relationship between measured R&D activity in one country and measures of productivity growth in other countries. Standard national accounts data can be used to calculate total factor productivity or the productivity of individual factors of production. In some countries, data has been compiled that permits researchers to calculate R&D activity and productivity in individual manufacturing sectors. Such detailed information permits the analysis of technology spillovers between sectors of the economy, between firms within sectors, and across borders.

However, published data on R&D activity probably does not accurately capture all innovative activity in a country either. Keller (2004) points out that this data captures "primarily resources spent towards innovation, and not those resources spent on imitation and technology adoption. Technology investment of middle income and poor countries can therefore typically not be analyzed using R&D data."[106] This data reflects the formal organization of firms into R&D departments and productive activities. The learning-by-doing process implies that there is innovation in production. Marketing departments and financial departments of firms can also make important contributions to innovation. The R&D data also attempts to measure innovative activity in universities, research institutions, the military, and other government organizations, but the split between innovative activity and other functions in such organizations is equally difficult to determine. For example, when a professor prepares a new lecture, how many new ideas are developed and how much of the lecture is a repetition of existing knowledge?

Estimates of productivity growth depend critically on the accuracy of national income accounts and estimates of factor supplies. The growth of total factor productivity is the simple difference between the growth of total output and the weighted average rate of growth of inputs. In practice, we use real GDP growth to represent output growth. We normally use labor force data to measure labor inputs, sometimes augmented by proxies for human capital, such as education levels, work experience, and other human characteristics. Labor force data in most countries captures only the labor supplied in the economy's formal labor markets, which means it ignores household production and production in informal sectors of the economy. Informal economic activity comprises a very large proportion of total economic activity in developing economies. Furthermore, capital stocks are normally derived from investment data in the national accounts, which is calculated according to the perpetual inventory method. This method simply assumes a rate of depreciation because we really have no idea what the true depreciations rate of capital is. Finally, total factor productivity requires that the contributions of the various categories of inputs be weighed according to their income shares.

Clearly, we need to gather primary data on the value of innovation and the exact inputs into the innovative process across industries and countries. The case study by Larrain, Lopez-Calva, and Rodriguez-Claré (2000) on Intel's foreign investment in Costa Rica is a good example of such a detailed analysis. But, such studies have been very rare because they are very costly and difficult to carry out. In the meantime, researchers have worked with the data available to them. Despite the serious measurement difficulties, however, researchers have been able to reach some useful, albeit tentative, conclusions about R&D activity and productivity gains.

---

[106] Keller (2004), p. 757.

8.2.1 Tracing Patent Citations

Jaffe, Trajtenberg, and Henderson (1993) compared the locations of the owners of patents with citations of those patents in later patent applications. They found that citations to domestic patents tend to also be domestic. In fact, Jaffe, Trajtenberg, and Henderson found that citations are even more regionally concentrated than the location of industries. They do find that "[l]ocalization fades over time, but only very slowly."[107] In a study of phamaceutical patents, Furman et al. (2005) find that pharmaceutical firms with research activities in many different locations gain more patents than firms theat restrict research to fewer geographic locations. They explain this finding by examining patent information, which reveals that, while firms do gain from global technology spillovers, "local knowledge is more likely to spill over than distant knowledge."[108] Similarly, Jaffe and Trajtenberg (1998) examine patent data for the U.S., the U.K., France, Germany, and Japan and find that patents are much more likely to cite earlier patents issued within the same industry and the same country than they are to cite patents from other industries and countries. The conclusion of these, and many similar studies, is that, all other things equal, technology moves much less *between* industries and countries than *within* industries and countries.

Foreign technology is nevertheless very important for a country's economic growth. Eaton and Kortum (1996) used patent data to examine the spread of technology among OECD countries. They report that, outside of the United States, every country obtains over 50 percent of its productivity growth from technological progress originating in other countries. For all countries other than the U.S., Japan, Germany, France, and the U.K., the percentage is over 90 percent. Three countries, the U.S., Japan, and Germany, together drive more than half of the technological progress of every country in the OECD. Connolly (1997) uses patent information for a different sample of countries over a different time period, and she similarly finds that for most countries technology imports from abroad are much more important than domestically-created technology. Overall, patent evidence suggests that even though it is easier to absorb other domestic technology than foreign technology, foreign technology is more important than domestically created technology for all but the very largest economies. Apparently, there is so much more new technology

---

[107] Jaffe, Trajtenberg, and Henderson (1993), p. 577.

[108] Furman, Kyle, Cockburn, and Henderson (2005), p. 25.

created abroad than at home that, despite the difficulties to absorb it, it is quantitatively more important than domestic technology.

Not all small countries benefit to the same extent from technological progress in the technological leaders, however. As suggested by Rosenberg (1972), a country's capacity to absorb foreign technology plays an important role as well, a conclusion that is confirmed in recent studies by Eaton and Kortum (1997, 1999). And there are often substantial differences even between seemingly similarly endowed countries. For example, Hu and Jaffe (2001) examine patent citations in Korea and Taiwan, and they find a very sharp difference in the sources of these two countries' technologies. Taiwanese patents were equally likely to cite U.S. and Japanese patents while Korean patents cited mostly Japanese patents. Thus, Korea's technology seems to have come mostly from Japan, while Taiwan imported technology eclectically.

The patent data has also been used to explicitly test the relationship between trade and technology flows. The patent evidence suggests that international trade plays a role in facilitating the flow of technology between countries. Sjöholm (1996) used information from the Swedish patent office on the origins of each patent to trace the international flow of ideas, and he related these technology flows to Sweden's international trade flows. Sjöholm found that the geographic distance from Sweden cannot robustly explain the flows of ideas as measured by patent information, but the flow of ideas into Sweden did closely parallel the flows of goods and services into and out of Sweden.

8.2.2 Statistical Analysis of R&D Activity

Coe and Helpman (1995) gathered data on R&D activity for 22 countries and then examined how accumulated R&D activity in each country affected total factor productivity (TFP) in the home country and the other 21 OECD countries. Coe and Helpman used national accounts data and labor force data to estimate TFP. The 22 developed economies, which were selected for the simple reason that data on R&D activity was available, are believed to account for much of the world's intentional R&D activity. Their results show that in large countries TFP is influenced more by domestic R&D activity than by foreign R&D activity. For the group of small countries, foreign R&D had the greater effect on TFP growth. Belgium, one of the most "open" economies in terms of the ratio of foreign trade to domestic output, enjoyed the greatest benefit from foreign R&D: for every 1 percent change in the stock of foreign R&D, Belgium's TFP went up by 0.26

percent. In a related study, Coe, Helpman, and Hoffmaister (1997) found that developing economies also gain from developed country R&D activity. But in line with previously mentioned findings that local institutions and absorption capacity determine whether foreign technology benefits an economy, their estimates varied greatly across countries. Overall, the influence of foreign technology was much smaller in developing countries than what Coe and Helpman (1995) found for 22 developed economies.

The estimated size of technology spillovers from the Coe and Helpman (1995) and Coe, Helpman, and Hoffmaister (1997) studies were used by Bayoumi, Coe, and Helpman (1999) to perform a simulation exercise to estimate hypothetical national growth effects of increases in R&D expenditures in other countries. Bayoumi, Coe, and Helpman first assumed an increase in R&D expenditures in individual countries, and then they assumed an increase in R&D activity in all developed economies simultaneously. Among other results, Bayoumi, Coe, and Helpman estimated that if the United States were to increase R&D activity by one-half of one percent of its GDP, the U.S. economy would grow an additional 9 percent after 80 years, other developed economies would grow an additional 3 percent and developing economies an additional 4 percent. Bayoumi, Coe, and Helpman also estimated that if *all* developed countries increase their R&D expenditures by an amount equal to one-half of one percent of their GDPs, all industrial countries would raise their output after 80 years by nearly 20 percent and developing countries by almost 15 percent. Bayoumi, Coe, and Helpman also estimated that if developing countries were to increase international trade by five percentage points of GDP, they would grow by another 9 percentage points after 80 years, a greater increase than the developed economies would achieve with a similar increase in trade.

Lichtenberg and van Pottelsberghe de la Potterie (1996) build on Coe and Helpman's (1995) study by incorporating alternative potential channels of technological transfers into their regression equations. Specifically, they incorporate explicit variables for exports, imports, and flows of foreign direct investment, and they concluded that imports still matter for a country's level of technology. Keller (1998) used different statistical methods to examine technology transfers among the same countries that Coe and Helpman (1995) included in their sample, and he found that international trade lost its significance as a determinant of technology transfers. However, when Lumenga-Neso, Olarreaga, and Schiff (2000) used Keller's (1998) methods to explicitly account for indirect trade flows between the trade partners of their trade partners as well as trade in intermediate products, trade again regained its significance as the major channel through which technology moves between countries. Keller (2002a) himself conducted further tests using other data and statistical methods, and he again found a statistically significant relationship between one country's R&D activities and other countries' gains in total factor productivity.

Bernstein (1996) examined R&D and TFP across a broad sample of individual Canadian and U.S. industries. Among other things, his estimates show that in Canada, the influence of U.S. R&D activity on TFP was greater than the influence of domestic R&D. On the other hand, as other studies of technology diffusion have suggested, in the U.S. domestic R&D activity accounts for nearly all productivity gains. Evenson and Singh (1997) tested for technology spillovers in 11 Asian economies, and they conclude that a country's productivity growth clearly depended on the R&D expenditures of its trade partners. Their statistical results also confirmed once again that domestic institutions and education are significant determinants of technology inflows. Technology spillovers have been small in the South Asian economies of Bangladesh, India, Nepal, Pakistan, and Sri Lanka compared to the fast-growing East Asian economies. The latter group of countries, of course, invested more in education, improved their institutions so that they were more favorable to investment and innovation, and opened their economies more widely to trade.

Bernstein and Mohnen (1998) found that U.S. R&D activity accounted for 60 percent of Japan's total factor productivity growth, while Japanese R&D activity contributed 20 percent of the U.S.'s productivity gains. Frantzen (2000) specifically applied data on R&D expenditures and estimates of industry total factor productivity to the same sample of OECD countries included in Eaton and Kortum's (1996) patent study, and, like Eaton and Kortum, he concludes that small countries' TFP was more influenced by R&D in the rest of the world while large countries' TFP depended mostly on their own R&D expenditures. Park (1995) estimates that for 10 OECD countries, foreign R&D activity accounts for about two-thirds of the average country's productivity growth, a slightly higher percentage than that found by Eaton and Kortum using patent data.

Some other studies of specific industries include Gisselquist and Pray (1999), who investigated agricultural technology in Turkey and found that new technology came mostly from abroad after imports of agricultural inputs were liberalized.[109] Caselli and Coleman (2001) examined the spread of computer technology across a large sample of countries between 1970 and 1990, and they found that openness to trade has had a strongly positive effect on the diffusion of computer technology.

Several authors have examined whether inflows of foreign technology depend on who the country's trade partners are. Vamvakidis (1998) concluded that developing countries that trade freely with larger, more developed neighbors grow faster, all other things equal, than countries that trade more with other developing countries. Specifically, he notes that countries that joined regional trade blocs consisting only of other developing economies do not, on average, experience any acceleration of economic growth as a result of their regional economic integration. Vamvakidis' finding supports Connolly and Gunther (1999) prediction that Mercosur, the common market recently formed by Argentina, Brazil, Paraguay, and Uruguay, would not have very strong growth effects for its member economies because it is likely to divert trade from developed countries to its fellow developing country members. Their analysis concludes that trade with developed countries is "especially important for the diffusion of technology to developing countries."[110] Schiff and Wang (2003) found that Mexico achieved a permanent rise in its total factor productivity after joining Canada and the United States in the North American Free Trade Area. Keller (2000a, 2000b), Schiff, Wang, and Olarreaga (2002), and Venables (2003) provide further evidence that developing countries gain more technology inflows by trading with developed countries than they do through trade with other developing countries.

Schiff, Wang, and Olarreaga's study also noted that some traditional low-technology industries in developing countries may benefit more from technology in other developing economies. Basu and Weil (1998) and Acemoglu and Zilibotti (2001) have investigated the "appropriateness" of developed country technology for developing countries, and they also concluded that in some cases developing countries would be better off importing technology from other developing countries. In general, however, other developing countries have relatively little technology that a developing country does not already have, and thus there is little technology to be gained from fellow developing economies.

---

[109] See also Gisselquist and Grether (2000).

[110] Connolly and Gunther (1999), p. 5.

It has been hypothesized that technology diffusion depends on a country's capacity to absorb foreign technology. Dosi, Pavitt, and Soete (1990), Evenson and Singh (1997), and Coe, Helpman, and Hoffmaister (1997) have reported specific statistical evidence to support this hypothesis. Also relevant is the study by Benhabib and Spiegel (2002), who tested models of technology diffusion that can distinguish whether a follower country is catching up to the technology leader. They found that developing countries with low levels of human capital were not achieving the relatively faster rates of technological progress necessary to catch up. Also relevant is Mayer's (2001) interpretation of the strong statistical relationship between economic growth, the importation of machinery, and the growth of human capital as suggesting that "the main role of human capital in economic growth is to facilitate the adoption of technology from abroad, rather than to act as an independent factor of production."[111] Caselli and Coleman (2001) used imports of office equipment, computers, and accounting machinery to proxy the flow of foreign technology to developing countries, and they found that imports were closely correlated with human capital, which was measured by education levels. Finally, in their study of technology diffusion of 20 specific technologies across 23 industrial countries, Comin and Hobijn (2003) found that a country's endowment of human capital is a statistically significant determinant of the speed at which technology diffuses.

8.2.3 International and Inter-Sectoral Transfers

Recall from Chapter 7 that Grossman and Helpman's (1991b) sectoral model of learning-by-doing showed that international trade affected countries' relative rates of growth differently depending on how readily technology transferred across industries and across borders. There have been a number of empirical studies that examined the differences in technology transfers across industrial sectors and across countries. For example, Bernstein and Yan (1997) examined detailed Canadian and Japanese industry data and found that domestic technology transfers between manufacturing sectors were greater than transfers between foreign and domestic manufacturing sectors. Keller (2002b) used data covering 13 industrial sectors and 8 countries to examine technology spillovers across industries and borders. He confirmed that technology spills over both borders and industry boundaries. Frantzen (2002) used a panel of industries and countries and applied cointegration analysis to arrive at a similar conclusion as Keller's.

---

[111] Mayer's (2001) quote is from the Abstract of the paper.

Irwin and Klenow (1994) examined how learning-by-doing spills across industries and borders. Specifically, they calculated the correlation between accumulated production in one semiconductor firm and cost reductions at other domestic and foreign firms. They found that in the semiconductor industry, learning spills over just as much to firms in other countries as to other firms in the same country. Of course, international spillovers may be less prevalent in industries not as internationally integrated through trade and investment as the semiconductor industry, but this evidence does suggest that when international trade is high, national borders may not be as big a barrier to the transfer of technology. Irwin and Klenow also found that there were only weak spillovers from one generation of semiconductors to another. This finding, combined with the other finding that foreign firms are at no disadvantage to domestic firms in their ability to acquire technology, means that the production of successive generations of products will tend to move around the world in accordance with the traditional sources of comparative advantage, such as resource costs, increasing returns to scale, and human capital and entrepreneurial skills. This evidence effectively undermines the arguments of proponents of industrial planning and strategic trade policies, who insist that governments should protect specific high-tech industries in order to "lock up" the gains from technological progress so that domestic firms can continue to exploit past innovations in the long run.

Park (2004) split R&D and productivity data for 14 OECD countries and three East Asian economies into manufacturing and non-manufacturing activities and estimated regressions relating TFP and R&D activity. He found that R&D activity in the manufacturing sector significantly increased productivity in non-manufacturing activity, but R&D in non-manufacturing sectors of the economy had no effect on productivity in manufacturing. He also found that, on average, foreign manufacturing R&D contributes to productivity in countries' manufacturing and non-manufacturing sectors. Interestingly, manufacturing R&D in the three east Asian economies, Korea, Singapore, and Taiwan, does not appear to have spilled over to 14 other OECD economies during the 1980-1995 period, although manufacturing R&D in each of the other OECD countries generated strongly positive international technology spillovers. These latter results are compatible with the hypothesis that differences in countries' absorptive capacities affect technology transfers. They are also compatible with the hypothesis that countries gain more from interacting with countries that have more advanced technologies than they do interacting with countries with the same or less advanced technologies.

Also relevant are the results from Hakura and Jaumotte (1999), who related TFP directly to inter-industry and intra-industry trade flows in 87 countries. They found that over the period 1970-1993, total factor productivity growth was influenced more by intra-industry trade than by inter-industry trade. Their result further confirms that there are indeed barriers to technology transfers between industries.

It is difficult to distinguish international trade from other hypothesized influences on technology transfers across borders. Caves (1996), Balasubramanyam, Salisu, and Sapsford (1996), and Moran (1999), for example, tout foreign direct investment as the major driving force of technology diffusion. However, Keller (2001b, 2002a) provides evidence that trade patterns statistically explain over half of the variation in technology diffusion between countries, whereas foreign direct investment explains only about 15 percent of the bilateral variation.

8.3 Summary and Conclusions

The studies surveyed in this chapter are fairly consistent in their conclusions about how technology moves between countries. The conclusions of the many studies of technology diffusion can be summarized as follows:

■ Foreign countries are the principal source of new technologies for all but the very largest economies (Eaton and Kortum [1996], Connolly [1997], Coe and Helpman [1995], Coe, Helpman, and Hoffmaister [1997], Bernstein [1996]).

■ Small developed economies and all developing economies depend on foreign sources for most of their technological progress (Coe and Helpman [1995], Eaton and Kortum [1996], Frantzen [2000, 2002]).

■ International flows of technology are far from instantaneous, and in general it takes longer for technology to move across borders than within countries (Jaffe and Trajtenberg [1998a,b]).

■ Developed economies absorb more foreign technology than developing economies, which is compatible with many authors' suggestion that technology diffusion depends critically on a country's absorptive capacity (Evenson and Singh [1997], Coe, Helpman, and Hoffmaister [1997], and Benhabib and Spiegel [2002]).

■ The volume of bilateral trade is able to explain a large part of the variation in bilateral technology flows (Sjöholm [1996], Evenson and Singh [1997], Vamvakidis [1998], Bayoumi, Coe, and Helpman [1999], Gisselquist and Pray [1999], Lumenga-Neso, Olarreaga, and Schiff [2000], Keller [2001b], Caselli and Coleman [2001]).

■ Developing countries gain more technology from trade links with developed economies than they do from trade links with other developing economies (Vamvakidis [1998], Connolly and Gunther [1999], Keller [2000a]).

The conclusions above are fully compatible with Comin and Hobijn's (2003) summary of their ambitious study analyzing the diffusion of 20 specific technologies across 23 of the world's largest economies:

Our results suggest a pattern of trickle-down diffusion that is remarkably robust across technologies. Most of the technologies that we consider originate in advanced economies and are adopted there first. Subsequently, they trickle down to countries that lag economically. Our panel data analysis indicates that the most important determinants of the speed at which a country adopts technologies are the country's *human capital endowment*, type of government, degree of openness to trade, and adoption of predecessor technologies. We also find that the overall rate of diffusion has increased markedly since World War II because of the convergence in these variables across countries.[112]

From the perspective of this book, the most important conclusion is that the available evidence largely supports the hypothesis that international trade helps to spread technology across borders. Several studies that use patent data or specific measures of R&D activity have found that the volume of bilateral trade explains a large part of the variation in bilateral technology flows between countries. Also interesting is the observation that developing countries gain more technology from trade links with developed economies than they do from trade links with other developing economies. The apparent increase in the speed at which technology moved across borders in recent decades therefore appears to be a direct result of the rapid expansion of international trade in the post World War II period.

---

[112] Comin and Hobijn (2003), abstract.

The available evidence showing that technology does move between countries is useful for judging the accuracy of the assumptions made in the models that generate exceptions to the general conclusion that international trade increases the rate of economic growth, which were discussed in the previous chapter. The special cases where trade could slow technological progress and economic growth, as discussed in the previous chapter, are not generally applicable. At the same time, the evidence showing that technology still moves slowly to developing economies suggests that more needs to be done to improve these countries' capacity to adopt technology. And for those countries that do improve their capacity to absorb foreign technology, international trade is likely to enhance technological progress and economic growth.

All of the above conclusions must be viewed as still somewhat tentative, however. The studies are severely hampered by the lack of accurate data. It is very difficult to quantify technological progress and to track its movements. Using patents and patent citations as measures of innovation and technology diffusion is of questionable value since most new ideas are not patented. Using total factor productivity as a proxy for technology, as most studies have done, is also problematic: total factor productivity is imperfectly measured as a residual using the sources of growth equation discussed in Chapter 2. It would be useful to perform more studies of technology transfers in specific industries where technological advances can be more accurately measured in the form of specific product characteristics. Also useful would be studies that monitor the spread across borders of specific scientific ideas, specific products and services, management techniques, production methods, and institutional changes. Such studies would require the gathering of original data, and that is necessarily a difficult and costly process. On the bright side, economists still have many opportunities to add to our understanding of how international trade and globalization contribute to human welfare.

Chapter Nine

Restating the Case for Free Trade

The doctrine of free trade has been subject to deep and searching scrutiny for many decades. The debate over the economic merits of free trade is an ongoing and never ending one that exhibits the richness and subtlety that can occur in the course of evolution of economic analysis. The doctrine of free trade will continue to experience changes as new theories and new ideas confront and challenge our understanding of the theory of commercial policy.
    (Douglas A. Irwin)[113]

This book was motivated in large part by Douglas Irwin's book, *Against the Tide.* Irwin argues that economists' case for free trade has held up very well against the many attempts by critics of free trade to undermine the case over the past several centuries. Irwin claims that economists have achieved an *intellectual victory.* In this book, we have taken a skeptical view of this claim of victory. Free trade still remains controversial in the eyes of many people, and policy makers in all countries routinely restrict international trade. The intellectual victories of economists have, clearly, not been powerful enough to convince the average citizen of the merits of free trade. And, with their constituents not convinced, politically motivated policy makers have enjoyed ample leeway to pursue policies that hinder international trade and undermine globalization.

---

[113] Irwin (1996a), p. 230.

We argue that economists' failure to convince the public of the merits of free trade is partly due to their focus on the traditional *static* models of comparative advantage. These models' conclusions about international trade are logically sound, many would say irrefutable, and they make it clear that free trade generates net gains in real income for all countries. However, the models also clearly show that the net gains are not uniformly shared throughout the populations of all countries. And, the net static gains from trade are not very large. Estimates of the static gains from trade are very small, on the order of 1 to 2 percent of GDP. Such small gains suggest that free trade is just not very important. Why should policy makers risk controversy and the ire of specific groups who fear they will suffer substantial losses for economy-wide welfare gains equal to less than one year's normal economic growth?

This book brings together theory and evidence that strongly suggest there are in fact very large gains from free trade, but these gains are not the static gains from comparative advantage shown in the traditional models of international trade. The largest gains from trade are the long-term dynamic gains derived from international trade's positive effect on economic growth. Both evidence and theory suggest that, all other things equal, open economies grow faster than closed economies. More important, the *power of compounding* implies that these growth effects are very important for human welfare. The mathematics of compounding shows that small improvements in growth rates can eliminate the huge income differences between rich and poor countries within a couple of generations. Equally important to the case for free trade, in comparison to the unequally distributed welfare gains described by the static models of comparative advantage, persistent economic growth over long periods of time provides substantial welfare gains to everyone. In short, trade's growth effects are not only very real, they are very important for human welfare.

To gain a true intellectual victory, economists must convince the public and their policy makers to embrace the cause of free trade. Economists are likely to be more successful in convincing people to embrace free trade if they supplement their static arguments for free trade with a consistent *dynamic* case for free trade. Economists must redirect their research and clarify the dynamic arguments for free trade in order to direct the public's attention to the really big potential gains from free trade. The key to finding the true intellectual victory of free trade over protectionism lies in the complex process of economic growth that has over the past two centuries globalized economic activity and increased average real per capita income ten-fold.

9.1 Dynamic Arguments for Free Trade

While economists embraced their static models of comparative advantage, critics of free trade have never been afraid to make dynamic arguments. The infant industry argument, the import substitution model, and strategic trade arguments are very much dynamic in nature. These arguments effectively suggest that long-run technological progress and economic growth would be greater in an economy protected from foreign competition than an economy open to foreign competition. They usually argue that different industries generate different rates of technological progress, often with different spillovers to other sectors of the economy, and that free trade's unequal effects on different sectors will prove to harm industries important for growth. Economists' static arguments for free trade appear weak when faced with calls to protect important industrial sectors such as steel, autos, microchips, air transport, or any number of other industries.

The previous chapters of this book show that these dynamic arguments for protectionism can be countered by logically sound, empirically supported, and convincing dynamic arguments for expanding international trade. Fundamentally, models of economic growth show that continued growth in human welfare requires technological progress. Technological progress does not flourish in a closed economy, however. With free trade and foreign technology transfers, technology will improve most in those countries whose levels of technology lag the furthest behind the technology leaders. The post World War II "growth miracles" in Europe and Japan were possible precisely because those countries integrated their economies into the global economy. And the recent surges in economic growth in East Asia and China were the result of technology flows and resource allocation shaped by global competition.

Especially important for establishing a logical explanation for the observed correlation between trade and economic growth are the conclusions reached when international trade is introduced into a Schumpeterian model of technological progress. Within the framework of the Schumpeterian model it is difficult to arrive logically at the conclusion that technological progress could be accelerated by restricting international trade. While special cases that show that free trade does not maximize a country's rate of economic growth can be constructed, the relevance of such hypothetical cases is very limited for several reasons. First of all, the special circumstances under which trade restrictions can be shown to raise welfare are not often satisfied in the real world. Second, even if the predicted circumstances indeed call for trade restrictions, politics normally prevents policy makers from restricting trade exactly as required by the predicted case. Third, foreign retaliation is likely to prevent a welfare-increasing outcome even when the circumstances call for protection and politics do not distort the required intervention.

Interestingly, these three critiques of dynamic arguments for protection are very similar to Irwin's (1996a) assessment of traditional protectionist arguments:

> the three lines of defense economists have developed against proposals for import protection, all of which implicitly admit that an economic case for protection exists in principle are: circumstances, politics, and retaliation.[114]

The importance of Irwin's warning is much greater in a dynamic setting than it is in the traditional static setting because the cost of protection is so much greater in a dynamic setting. Closed borders make it easier for vested interests to not only gain in the short run, but with less foreign competition they can slow down the creative destruction process or stop it altogether. Also, the high likelihood of making mistakes in exploiting the special cases under which protection could be welfare enhancing implies enormous long-term welfare losses.

A broader look at the dynamic relationship between international trade and economic growth reveals two additional reasons why the special cases favoring protectionism are unrealistic. First of all, in the dynamic case it is not only necessary to correctly identify the special circumstances required, it is necessary to identify future circumstances. International trade affects economic growth over a long period of time, which implies that policy makers would have to fine-tune their policies over a long series of circumstances that must be *predicted*, not just *observed*. Until someone invents a crystal ball that really works, accurate predictions of the future will have to be derived from evaluating wide distributions of plausible outcomes. Without accurate information on the precise circumstances under which protection may enhance welfare, we simply cannot accurately decide whether trade restrictions are even called for, much less set precise levels of trade restrictions or pick the industries that should be protected.

Second, international trade's positive influence on economic growth has the characteristics of a self-fulfilling prophecy, and that results

---

[114] Irwin (1996a), p. 228.

in multiple dynamic equilibria. Because the dynamic growth effects of international trade are dependent on how well technology spreads across borders and the mobility of technology is itself dependent on the volume of international trade, the establishment of free trade is likely to create the technology flows necessary to avoid the special negative cases described in Chapter 7. On the other hand, if policy makers opt to restrict international trade, they may be able to justify their choice by pointing to the reduced transfers of technology and, thus, the satisfaction of the assumptions underlying the sectoral arguments for protecting certain industries.

The difficulty of predicting the future and the possibility of multiple equilibria imply that we have to choose our trade policy carefully. Frédéric Bastiat wrote two centuries ago:

> Between a good and a bad economist this constitutes the whole difference–the one takes account of the visible effect; the other takes account of both of the effects which are seen, and also of those which it is necessary to foresee.[115]

Our models of economic growth and technological progress can help us foresee some of the long-run consequences of trade policy. Those models show that the special cases outlined under the infant industry, import substitution, and strategic trade arguments for protection require very delicate policy responses to guarantee welfare improvements. Such delicate responses are unlikely in realistic political environments. There is, therefore, a high likelihood of large welfare losses from attempts to apply strategic protectionism that is valid only in very special cases. The case for sophisticated trade controls is therefore not as proponents have suggested.

In summary, the dynamic case for free trade is potentially a strong one. The empirical evidence suggests that the long-run relationship between trade and growth is economically important. The power of compounding implies that the likely positive effects of trade on growth will translate into very large improvements in human welfare. Therefore, combining trade theory and growth theory potentially leads to a strong case for free trade. Economists' work is not yet done, however. The special cases and exceptions to our models' conclusions remind us that economic growth is a complex process that must be fully understood before economists can present the dynamic case for free trade to the public. We

---

[115] Frédéric Bastiat, "That Which Is Seen, and That Which Is Not Seen," available on www.freedomsnest.com/bastiat.html.

are confident that further research will indeed lead to a consistent dynamic case for free trade because, as the next section describes, trade among nations is actually part of the much broader and long-running process by which we humans have improved our lives by expanding the number of people we interact with.

9.2 A Much More General View of Trade and Growth

The rapid growth of international trade over the past 50 years covers but a brief episode in human history. The growth of trade and other international economic activities is not really as new a phenomenon as many dramatically inclined proponents and critics of globalization would have us believe. Specialization and exchange have been growing, off and on, since the origins of humanity several hundred thousand years ago. It is true that the expansion of human interaction among ever larger groups of people has been especially rapid over the past 10,000 years.

The spread of agriculture and animal husbandry transformed human societies from bands of hunters and gatherers into more complex societies consisting of much larger groups of people living in permanent settlements. First villages, then towns, cities, and, eventually, nations have come to characterize our social organization. In small hunter and gatherer societies, permanent personal relationships governed human interaction. Beginning 10,000 years ago, however, humans began to find ways to interact with much larger and dispersed groups of people. This growth in the size of human communities was a slow process because dealing with strangers is not easy. Engaging in transactions with unfamiliar people on a one-time basis is much more difficult than dealing repeatedly with the same small group of relatives and fellow clan members. There have been many failures and disasters, and human history provides an endless set of examples of exploitation, theft, slavery, rape, murder, war, and other destructive behaviors among people. Still today, people remain fearful of foreigners, people from different ethnic backgrounds, and just "strangers."

In his insightful book, *The Company of Strangers*, Paul Seabright (2004) refers to the transition from traditional small hunting and gathering communities to the increasing dependence on strangers over the past ten thousand years as a "great experiment." Despite the inherent dangers, we slowly figured out how to deal constructively with people beyond our immediate families and clans. We were motivated to do this by the many gains from dealing with strangers.

9.2.1 The Gains from Dealing with Strangers

There are three fundamental advantages from expanding the number of people we interact with. By dealing with others, we achieve:

- Gains from specialization.

- Reductions in risks from unpredictable adverse outcomes.

- Faster expansion of knowledge.

Today's high standards of living would be impossible without extensive trade and other forms of economic cooperation among large numbers of people who did not know each other prior to their encounter, may not even meet face to face when they deal with each other, and do not expect to ever meet again or deal with each other in the future.

The gain from specialization was detailed by Adam Smith (1776) over two centuries ago. In *An Inquiry into the Nature and Causes of the Wealth of Nations*, Smith wrote:

> The greatest improvements in the productive powers of labour, and the greater part of the skill, dexterity, and judgement with which it is any where directed, or applied, seem to have been the effects of the division of labour.[116]

That is, economic growth is a function of increased specialization. Of course, the division of labor requires people to exchange their production. In the words of Adam Smith, the division of labor depends critically on people's "propensity to truck, barter, and exchange one thing for another."[117] Specialization can obviously be exploited to a greater degree if exchange can occur among a greater number of people:

> As it is the power of exchanging that gives occasion to the division of labour, so the extent of this division must always be limited by the extent of the power, or, in other words, by the extent of the market.[118]

---

[116] Adam Smith (1776 [1976]), Vol. 1, p. 7.

[117] Adam Smith (1776 [1976]), Vol. 1, p. 17.

[118] Adam Smith (1776 [1976]), Vol. 1, p. 21.

In sum, because specialization, exchange, and economic growth are interrelated, Smith effectively concluded that international trade positively influences economic growth. More generally, dealing with more people, many of whom will be strangers, raises our standard of living.

The second advantage of expanding economic activities to include more people beyond our immediate families and clans is that such broader interaction creates opportunities to reduce the various risks that threaten our lives and our well being. To the extent that people face risks that are, at least in part, specific to them rather than to all of society, cooperation among people can reduce individual risks. For example, when one isolated community's crops fail, it starves. If communities can devise a mechanism whereby they provide each other with food in such emergencies, people are likely to survive longer together than they would on their own. Modern societies have developed a whole range of institutions, markets, and organizations that effectively enable distrustful individuals and complete strangers to effectively help each other deal with unfortunate events and outcomes.   The insurance industry, bond markets, private charities, international banking, foreign trade, the protection of property and assets, enforcement of contracts, and various government transfer programs are modern institutions that enable individuals and communities to deal with unexpected catastrophes and thus reduce the risks they face.

The third advantage of living in larger societies is that the advancement of knowledge becomes easier and more efficient. The fundamental source of knowledge is, of course, the human ability to think. Humans have evolved to become a species that has an extraordinary ability to think abstractly, reason logically, and expand knowledge. We humans have used our extraordinary intelligence to enhance our tools of knowledge creation; we have developed language, writing, record keeping, formal systems of logic, and the scientific method.   With our ability to communicate abstract knowledge, one person's discovery becomes available to all of us. The widespread embrace of the scientific method has made the advancement of knowledge more efficient and much less likely to falter. Most important for the creation of knowledge, however, has been our ability to deal with more people. Knowledge and technology are nonrival goods in that they can be used by many people at the same time. If everyone lives in isolation, then every person has to effectively "reinvent the wheel" if they want to enjoy the benefits of the wheel. But if people communicate and observe, the wheel need only be invented once. It is no coincidence that throughout history the most advanced societies were those that had the most contact with other societies. The more people linked themselves together by exploiting language, writing, and newer forms of communication, the more rapid innovation becomes. Recall the words of the 17th century intellectual William Petty, quoted during our discussion of technology in Chapter 5: "it is more likely that one ingenious curious man may rather be found among 4 million than among 400 persons."[119]

9.2.2 Dependence on Strangers Is Inherently Problematic

As already noted, interaction with strangers can be dangerous. Despite the good reasons for cooperating with others, individuals also have strong incentives to exploit, steal from, enslave, and kill others. We also have an incentive to renege on agreements and misrepresent our side of the bargain. It is really much easier to let someone else work to grow a field of grain and then steal it just when it is ready. It is often more convenient to force others to do the hard work rather than doing it ourselves. What Seabright called the "great experiment" has not progressed smoothly. Effectively, human evolution over the extended period of hunters and gatherers and their earlier ancestors has not fully prepared us for dealing with strangers.

Ridley (1996) detailed how the evolutionary process over the past several million years has given selfish humans practical instincts for cooperating within small groups of individuals. Such cooperation appears to be altruistic, in the same way that game theory describes how a "tit-for-tat" strategy in repeated games by completely self-interested individuals ends up looking like cooperative behavior. But "tit-for-tat" strategies work only in a repeated game, such as interaction between members of the same family or clan, not in a one-time game, as when complete strangers interact. Hence the fear of strangers that people instinctively demonstrate.

The globalization of economic activity over the past centuries shows that humans have somehow found ways to deal with strangers despite their evolved instincts. Deepak Lal (1998) writes:

> The cooperative gains that result from the increasing division of labor in a more complex civilization would not have been available without some mechanism for dealing with the increased potential for defection when social interactions became anonymous and sporadic.[120]

---

[119] Petty (1682), p. 474.

[120] Lal (1998), p. 10.

But what is this "mechanism" for dealing with strangers that has allowed humans to overcome their instinctive fears and to enable them to reap the benefits of ever more extensive human interactions? Part of the answer to the question of how humans have been able to accomplish today's extraordinary cooperation among strangers is provided by Seabright:

> It is only in the last ten thousand years that human beings have had to come to terms on a significant scale with the impact of strangers, and it is only in the last two hundred or so that this impact has become a dominant fact of everyday life. To manage the hazards imposed on us by the actions of strangers has required us to deploy a different skill bequeathed to us by evolution for quite different purposes, the capacity for abstract symbolic thought.[121]

That is, humans have used their intelligence and capacity for abstract thought to design institutions and incentives that effectively induce people, who are to some extent hard-wired by evolution to fear strangers, to cooperate and deal with strangers. The evolution of human intelligence means that people do not just instinctively react to circumstances, but they understand enough about their social environment to shape it and change it to their advantage.

9.2.3 Getting the Institutions Right

Douglass North (2005) reminds us, however, that the creation of institutions and the shaping of incentives to stimulate cooperative behavior "has been a trial and error process of change with lots of errors, endless losers, and no guarantee that we will continue to get it right in spite of the enormous accretion of knowledge over those centuries."[122] To see how wrong humans have gotten their institutions, one need only look back at the 20th century and its two World Wars, the Great Depression, and the extreme poverty that persists in many parts of the world. According to North, the frequent inconsistencies between people's objectives and society's actual outcomes are caused by (1) the lack of accurate information on our physical, social, and economic environment, and (2) the resistance to change by certain people and groups of people because they prefer the status quo to further change. The latter cause is consistent with humans' evolutionary instinct to survive, which challenges our intelligence to devise ways to overcome

---

[121] Seabright (2004), p. 257.

[122] North (2005), p. 15.

it. The former cause of institutional failures, namely the lack of knowledge and understanding of our environment, is perhaps an even more daunting barrier to continued human progress.

Knowledge about our physical and social environments is woefully incomplete, and that means logical and abstract thinking also ends up being incomplete. According to North:

> Throughout human history there has always been a large residual that defied rational explanation—a residual to be explained partly by non-rational explanations embodied in witchcraft, magic, religions; but partly by more prosaic non-rational behavior characterized by dogmas, prejudices, "half-baked" theories. Indeed despite the...assertion by eminent theorists that it is not possible to theorize in the face of uncertainty, humans do it all the time; their efforts range from ad hoc assertions and loosely structured beliefs such as those encompassed in the labels "conservative" and "liberal" to elegant systematic ideologies such as Marxism or organized religions.[123]

We humans have clearly learned enough to greatly reduce the uncertainty of our physical environment, as evidenced by the impressive reductions in mortality and the rise in life expectancy over the past several centuries. But, much remains to be understood. Very few serious scientists feel that we have done much more than scratch the surface in any branch of science. More troubling is the fact that in the social sciences, we actually continue to create more complexity. As we have used our intelligence and understanding of our environment to expand our societies to include more and more strangers, we effectively create increasingly complex and uncertain social environments that we do not fully understand. We therefore have to draw on "ad hoc assertions and loosely structured beliefs" to make sense of both our physical and social environments.

The difficulty of catching up to the moving target that is our continually more complex society is described by Lal (1998). Lal argues that the ad hoc assertions and loosely structured beliefs, or what many sociologists would call culture, change slowly. Culture tends to lag behind the ever-changing realities of our environment; it also tends to lag behind our accumulation of rational knowledge and understanding of the realities of our environment. Change in our non-rational culture and beliefs only

---

[123] North (2005), pp. 15-16.

stays ahead of the evolution of our genetic behavioral systems. The differences in the rates of progress of reality, knowledge, culture, and human instinct imply that the faster our real economic and social environment changes, the further behind our non-rational beliefs and evolutionary hard-wired behavioral systems fall. The continuation of the great experiment and the increased interaction with strangers, of which globalization is just the latest phase, therefore tends to become increasingly tenuous as change in our physical and social environment speeds up. Lal concludes that, unless we somehow increase the rate at which we expand rational knowledge and our understanding of our environment by replacing non-rational beliefs with rational knowledge, the accelerating social and economic change brought by globalization will undermine globalization itself. The accelerating pace of social change is likely to outpace our capacity to accurately update the institutions and incentives necessary to keep globalization, Seabright's great experiment, alive and expanding.

Throughout human history, episodes of globalization were all eventually reversed, sometimes for extended periods of time. The Roman Empire and the late 19th century globalization were effectively reversed during, respectively, the Dark Ages and the political and economic turmoil following World War I. China after the Sung Dynasty provides another example. While China was the most advanced economy of the world in the year 1000, and it traded with other countries throughout the Far East and the Asian subcontinent, China stagnated for the remainder of the last millennium when its leaders opted to isolate the country from foreign influences. These reversals in the extent of dealing with strangers were the result of human reliance on "half-baked" theories and loosely structured beliefs to fill in where knowledge was lacking. Sometimes knowledge and culture caught up to and kept pace with changing reality, but it seems as though inevitably reality and knowledge leave culture far behind. Despite our intelligence and capacity for abstract reasoning, we humans have not consistently been able to accurately design and put in place institutions that accurately reflect the increasing complexity of our social and economic environments and permit the consistent growth of welfare-enhancing interaction among strangers.

This book should thus be seen as an attempt to speed the growth in understanding of our global economic environment. By developing a rational and compelling dynamic theory of international trade and economic growth, we economists will hopefully be able to not only improve our knowledge of our true environment, but also to bring our culture more closely in line with that reality by inducing the public and their policy makers to replace some of the "half-baked" theories and other non-rational explanations of our global economic environment with a more accurate and compelling explanation of the advantages of international trade. The gains from interacting with strangers across the globe are too great to ignore. Economists have much to contribute toward continuing the great experiment.

9.3 Final Comments

In the spirit of Douglas Irwin, whose words were quoted at the start of this chapter, this book has carried on the debate over the "economic merits of free trade." We have argued for extending the debate to the dynamic realm by examining the relationship between international trade and economic growth. We need dynamic models that relate trade and growth for the simple reason that the world economy is dynamic. Static analysis cannot accurately illustrate the full welfare gains from international trade. We are also convinced that we can make a much more powerful case for free trade by integrating growth theory into our analysis of international trade. Only within a growth context does international trade unequivocally raise everyone's welfare and are those welfare gains sufficiently large to overcome the inevitable resistance to short-term change and disruption that accompanies the growth of specialization and trade. We need a dynamic case for free trade if we are to be successful in convincing the public and our leaders that we are better off dealing with strangers than hiding behind protectionist barriers. It is our hope that this book has contributed to both the development of dynamic models of trade and the building of a more convincing case for free trade.

In closing, we must acknowledge our debt to Adam Smith. In his *Wealth of Nations* (1776), Smith presented international trade both from a static and a dynamic perspective by first providing the foundation for Ricardo's comparative advantage and then linking international trade to the division of labor, increasing returns to scale, and innovation. Why international trade theory became such a static affair over the past 150 years is really something of a mystery, especially because economic growth has become the unique distinguishing feature of the world economy during this same time. Most likely, international economists followed the "culture" of mainstream economics by adopting its static models developed to explain opportunity costs and resource allocation. Perhaps it was the failure to understand the dynamics that led to two world wars and a Depression that eventually stimulated economists to focus on the question of whether trade could serve as an "engine of growth." Recall D. H. Robertson's 1938 quote at the start of this book: "The specializations of the nineteenth century were not simply a device for using to the greatest effect the labours of a given number of human beings; they were above all an engine of growth."[124] It has only been in the latter half of the 20th century that mainstream economists again began to focus on economic growth. Solow's (1956) model still serves as the standard growth model that students are introduced to in beginning economics courses. Solow's model also made it clear that long-run growth is fundamentally linked to technological progress. It was Romer's (1990) Schumpeterian growth model that has provided the best insights into how an economy generates technological progress. With Romer's model, the economics profession has come full circle. For the first time since Adam Smith and the early 19th century classical economists, economic growth is again given prominence in economics textbooks.

It is time for international economics to follow suit. After all, if Smith could grasp the importance of the relationship between trade and growth back in the 18th century, when per capita incomes were just barely beginning to rise above the subsistence levels at which they had been stuck throughout human history, surely we can recognize the need to build economic growth into our models of international trade now that economic growth and globalization are the dominant features of our world.

---

[124] Robertson (1938), p.5.

Bibliography

Abramovitz, Moses (1986), "Catching Up, Forging Ahead, and Falling Behind," *Journal of Economic History*, Vol. 46(2), pp. 385-406.

Acemoglu, Daron, and Joshua Linn (2003), "Market Size and Innovation: Theory and Evidence from the Pharmaceutical Industry," MIT Department of Economics Working Paper 03-33, September.

Acemoglu, Daron, and Fabrizio Zilibotti (2001), "Productivity Differences," *Quarterly Journal of Economics*, Vol. 116(2), pp. 563-606.

Ades, Alberto F., and Edward L. Glaeser (1999), "Evidence on Growth, Increasing Returns, and the Extent of the Market," *Quarterly Journal of Economics*, Vol. 114(3), pp. 1025-1045.

Aghion, Philippe, M. Dewatripont, and P. Rey (1999), "Competition, Financial Discipline and Growth," *Review of Economic Studies*, Vol. 66, pp. 825-852.

Aghion, Philippe, and Rachel Griffith (2005), *Competition and Growth, Reconciling Theory and Evidence*, Cambridge, MA: MIT Press.

Aghion, Philippe, C. Harris, and J. Vickers (1997), "Competition and Growth with Step-by-Step Innovation: An Example," *European Economic Review*, Vol. 41, pp. 771-782.

Aghion, Philippe, and Peter Howitt (1992), "A Model of Growth through Creative Destruction," *Econometrica*, Vol. 60, pp. 323-351.

Aghion, Philippe, and Peter Howitt (1998), *Endogenous Growth Theory*, Cambridge: MIT Press.

Aghion, Philippe, and Jeffrey G. Williamson (1998), *Growth, Inequality and Globalization*, Cambridge, U.K.: Cambridge University Press.

Ahmad, Jaleel, and Somchai Harnhirun (1995), "Unit Root and Cointegration in Estimating Causality Between Exports and Economic Growth: Empirical Evidence from the ASEAN Countries," *Economic Letters*, Vol. 49, pp. 329-334.

Ahmad, Jaleel, and Andy C.C. Kwan (1991), "Causality Between Exports and Economic Growth: Empirical Evidence from Africa," *Economic Letters*, Vol. 37, pp. 243-248.

Alam, M. Shahid (1991), "Trade Orientation and Macroeconomic Performance in LDCs: An Empirical Study," *Economic Development and Cultural Change*, Vol. 39, pp. 839-848.

Alchian, Alan (1963), "Reliability of Progress Curves in Airframe Production," *Econometrica*, Vol. 31(1), pp. 87-97.

Alesina, Alberto, Enrico Spolaore, and Romain Wacziarg (2000), "Economic Integration and Political Disintegration," *American Economic Review*, Vol. 90(5), pp. 1276-1296.

Al-Yousif, Yousif K. (1997), "Exports and Economic Growth: Some Empirical Evidence from the Arab Gulf Countries," *Applied Economics*, Vol. 29, pp. 263-267.

Amin Gutierrez de Pineres, Sheila, and Michael Ferrantino (1999), "Export Sector Dynamics and Domestic Growth: The Case of Colombia," *Review of Development Economics*, Vol. 3(3), pp. 268-280.

Amirkhalkhali, Saleh and Atul A. Dar (1995), "A Varying-Coefficients Model of Export Expansion, Factor Accumulation and Economic Growth: Evidence from Cross-Country, Time Series Data," *Economic Modelling*, Vol. 12(4), pp. 435-441.

Anderson, James A. (1979), "A Theoretical Foundation for the Gravity Equation," *American Economic Review*, Vol. 69, pp. 178-190.

Archibugi, Daniele, and Jonathan Michie (1998), "Trade, Growth and Technical Change: What Are the Issues?" Chap. 1 in Daniele Archibugi and Jonathan Michie, eds., (1998), *Trade, Growth, and Technical Change*, Cambridge, U.K.: Cambridge University Press.

Atesoglu, H. Sonmez (1994), "An Application of a Kaldorain Export-Led Model of Growth to the United States," *Applied Economics*, Vol. 26, pp. 479-483.

Aw, Bee Yan, Sukkyun Chung, and Mark J. Roberts (2000), "Productivity and Turnover in the Export Market: Micro-Level Evidence from the Republic of Korea and Taiwan (China)," *The World Bank Economic Review*, Vol. 14(1), pp. 65-90.

Baer, Werner (1995), *The Brazilian Economy, Growth and Development*, Westport, CT: Praeger.

Bahk, Byong-Hong, and Michael Gort (1993), "Decomposing Learning by Doing in New Plants," *Journal of Political Economy*, Vol. 101(4), pp. 155-173.

Bahmani-Oskooee, Mohsen, and Janardhanan Alse (1993), "Export Growth and Economic Growth: An Application of Cointegration and Error Correction Modeling," *The Journal of Developing Areas*, Vol. 27, pp. 535-542.

Baily, M. N. (1993), "Competition, Regulation, and Efficiency in Service Industries," *Brooking Papers on Economic Activity: Microeconomics*, pp. 71-130.

Baily, M. N., and H. Gersbach (1995), "Efficiency in Manufacturing and the Need for Global Competition," *Brooking Papers on Economic Activity: Microeconomics*, pp. 307-358.

Balassa, Bela (1978), "Exports and Economic Growth: Further Evidence," *Journal of Development Economics*, Vol. 5, pp. 181-189.

Balassa, Bela (1985), "Exports, Policy Choices, and Economic Growth in Developing Countries After the 1973 Oil Shock," *Journal of Development Economics*, Vol. 18, pp. 23-35.

Balasubramanyam, V.N., M. Salisu, and David Sapsford (1996), "Foreign Direct Investment and Growth in EP and IS Countries," *The Economic Journal*, Vol. 26, pp. 92-105.

Baldwin, Richard E. (1989), "The Growth Effects of 1992," *Economic Policy: A European Forum,* Vol. 4(2), pp. 247-281.

Baldwin, Richard E. (1992a), "Measuring Dynamic Gains from Trade," *Journal of Political Economy,* Vol. 100(11), pp. 162-174.

Baldwin, Richard E. (1992b), "On the Growth Effects of Import Competition," NBER Working Paper No. 4045, April.

Baldwin, Richard E., and Rikard Forslid (1999), "The Core-Periphery Model and Endogenous Growth: Stabilizing and De-Stabilizing Integration," *NBER Working Paper* W6899, January.

Baldwin, Richard E., J. Francois, and Richard Portes (1997), "The Costs and Benefits of Eastern Enlargement: The Impact on the EU and Central Europe," *Economic Policy*, April, pp. 127-170.

Baldwin, Richard E., and Frédérc Robert-Nicoud (2002), "Entry and Asymmetric Lobbying: Why Governments Pick Losers," NBER Working Paper 8756, February.

Baldwin, Richard E. and Elena Seghezza (1996), "Testing for Trade-Induced Investment-Led Growth," *NBER Working Paper* No. 5416.

Baldwin, Robert E. (1969), "The Case Against Infant Industry Protection," *Journal of Political Economy*, Vol. 77(3), pp. 295-305.

Baldwin, Robert E. (2003), "Openness and Growth: What's the Empirical Relationship?" in Robert E. Baldwin and L. Alan Winters (eds.), *Challenges to Globalization*, Chicago: University of Chicago Press.

Barlow, Thomas (2001), "The Great Thing About Frivolous Research," *Financial Times*, August 4/5.

Barro, Robert J. (1997), *Determinants of Economic Growth*, Cambridge, MA: MIT Press.

Barro, Robert J., and Jong-Wha Lee (1993), "International Comparisons of Educational Attainment," *Journal of Monetary Economics*, Vol. 32(3), pp. 363-394.

Barro, Robert J., and Xavier Sala-i-Martin (2004), *Economic Growth,* 2nd ed, Cambridge, MA: MIT Press.

Basevi, Giorgio (1966), "The United States Tariff Structure: Estimates of Effective Rates of Protection of U.S. and Industrial Labor," *Review of Economics and Statistics*, Vol. 48(2), pp. 147-170.

Basu, Susanto, and David N. Weil (1998), "Appropriate Technology and Growth," *Quarterly Journal of Economics*, Vol. 108(4), pp. 1025-1054.

Baumol, William J. (2002), *The Free-Market Innovation Machine*, Princeton, NJ: Princeton University Press.

Baumol, William J., Sue Ann Batey Blackman, and Edward N. Wolff (1989), *Productivity and American Leadership*, Cambridge, MA: MIT Press.

Bayoumi, Tamin, David T. Coe, and Elhanan Helpman (1999), "R&D Spillovers and Global Growth," *Journal of International Economics*, Vol. 47, pp. 399-428.

Bayoumi, Tamin, and Markus Haacker (2002), "It's Not What You Make, It's How You Use IT: Measuring the Welfare Benefits of the IT Revolution Across Countries," IMF Working Paper WP/02/117, July.

Becker, Markus C., Hans Ulrich Esslinger, Ulrich Hedtke, and Thorbjørn Knudsen (2005), Introduction to Schumpeter's "Development," *Journal of Economic Literature*, Vol. 43(1), pp. 109-110.

Bell, R. M., and D. Scott-Kemmis (1990), "The Mythology of Learning-by-Doing in World War II Airframe and Ship Production," *Explorations in Economic History*, 27.

Ben-David, Dan (1993), "Equalizing Exchange: Trade Liberalization and Income Convergence," *Quarterly Journal of Economics*, Vol. 108(3), pp. 653-679.

Ben-David, Dan, and Michael B. Loewy (1998), "Free Trade, Growth, and Convergence," *Journal of Economic Growth*, Vol. 3, pp. 143-170.

Benhabib, Jesse, and Mark M. Spiegel (2002), "Human Capital and Technology Diffusion," Federal Reserve Bank of San Francisco Working Paper #2003-02.

Benkard, C. Lanier (1999), "Learning and Forgetting: The Dynamics of Aircraft Production," NBER Working Paper No. W7127, May.

Bergsman, Joel (1974), "Commercial Policy, Allocative Efficiency, and 'X-Efficiency,'" *Quarterly Journal of Economics*, Vol. 88(3), pp. 409-433.

Bernard, Andrew B., and J. Bradford Jensen (1999a), "Exporting and Productivity," *NBER Working Paper*, No. 7135.

Bernard, Andrew B., and J. Bradford Jensen (1999b), "Exceptional Exporter Performance: Cause, Effect, or Both?" *Journal of International Economics*, Vol. 47(1), pp. 1-25.

Bernhofen, Daniel M., and John C. Brown (2005), "An Empirical Assessment of the Comparative Advantage Gains from Trade: Evidence from Japan," *American Economic Review*, Vol. 95(1), pp. 208-225.

Bernstein, Jeffrey I. (1996), "International R&D Spillovers between Industries in Canada and the United States, Social Rates of Return and Productivity Growth," *Canadian Journal of Economics*, Vol. 29, pp. 463-467.

Bernstein, Jeffrey I., and Pierre Mohnen (1998), "International R&D Spillovers between U.S. and Japanese R&D Intensive Sectors," *Journal of International Economics*, Vol. 44(2), pp. 315-338.

Bernstein, Jeffrey I., and X. Yan (1997), "International R&D Spillovers between Canadian and Japanese Industries," *Canadian Journal Economics*, Vol. 30(2), pp. 276-315.

Bhagwati, Jagdish (1958), "Immizerizing Growth: A Geometrical Note," *Review of Economic Studies*, Vol. 25(2), pp. 201-205.

Bhagwati, Jagdish (1971), "The Generalized Theory of Distortions and Welfare," in Jagdish Bhagwati *et al.*, eds., *Trade, Balance of Payments, and Growth: Papers in*

International Economics in Honor of Charles P. Kindleberger, Amsterdam: North-Holland Publishing Company.

Bhagwati, Jagdish (1978), *Foreign Trade Regimes and Economic Development: Anatomy and Consequences of Exchange Control Regimes*, Cambridge, MA: Balinger and NBER.

Blalock, Garrick, and Paul J. Gertler (2004), "Learning from Exporting Revisited in a Less Developed Setting," *Journal of Development Economics*, Vol. 75(2), pp. 379-416.

Blattman, Christopher, Jason Hwang, and Jeffrey Williamson (2004), "The Impact of the Terms of Trade on Economic Development in the Periphery, 1870-1939: Volatility and Secular Change," NBER Working Paper 10600, July.

Blendon, Robert J., *et al.* (1997), "Bridging the Gap Between the Public's and Economists' View of the Economy," *Journal of Economic Perspectives*, Vol. 11(3), pp. 105-118.

Blinder, Alan S., and Alan B. Krueger (2004), "What Does the Public Know about Economic Policy, and How Does It Know It?" NBER Working Paper w10787, September.

Bloom, David E., David Canning, and Jaypees Sevilla (2002), "Technological Diffusion, Conditional Convergence, and Economic Growth," NBER Working Paper w8713, January.

Blundell, R., R. Griffith, and J. Van Reenen (1995), "Dynamic Count Data Models of Technological Innovation," *Economic Journal*, Vol. 105(429), pp. 333-344.

Brezis, Elise, Paul Krugman, and Daniel Tsiddon (1993), "Leapfrogging in International Competition: A Theory of Cycles in National Technological Leadership," *American Economic Review*, Vol. 83(5), pp. 1211-1219.

Broda, Christian, and David E. Weinstein (2004), "Globalization and the Gain from Variety," NBER Working Paper 10314, February.

Bruton, Henry J. (1998), "A Reconsideration of Import Substitution," *Journal of Economic Literature*, Vol. 31, pp. 903-936.

Burney, Nadeem A. (1996), "Exports and Economic Growth: Evidence from Cross Country Analysis," *Applied Economic Letters*, Vol. 3, pp. 369-373.

Carlino, Gerald, Satyajit Chatterjee, and Robert Hunt (2001), "Knowledge Spillovers and the New Economy of Cities," Working Paper No. 01-14, Federal Reserve Bank of Philadelphia, September.

Caselli, Francesco, and Wilbur John Coleman II (2001), "Cross-Country Technology Diffusion: The Case of Computers," *American Economic Review*, Vol. 91(2), pp. 328-335.

Caves, Richard E. (1996), *Multinational Enterprise and Economic Analysis*, Cambridge, U.K.: Cambridge University Press.

Chacholiades, Miltiades (1990), *International Economics*, New York: McGraw-Hill.

Chong, Alberto, and Luisa Zanforin (2000), "Technological Adaption, Trade, and Growth," *IMF Working Paper*, WP/00/161, October.

Chong, Alberto, and Luisa Zanforlin (2002), "Technology and Epidemics," IMF Staff Papers, Vol. 49(3), pp. 426-455.

Chow, Peter C.Y. (1987), "Causality Between Export Growth and Industrial Development: Empirical Evidence from NICs," *Journal of Development Economics*, Vol. 26, pp. 55-63.

Cipolla, Carlo M. (1978), *Clocks and Culture, 1300-1700*, New York: Norton.

Clausing, Kimberly A. (2000) "Does Multinational Activity Displace Trade?" *Economic Inquiry*, Vol. 38(2), pp. 190-205.

Clerides, Sofronis K., Saul Lach, and James Tybout (1998), "Is Learning by Exporting Important? Micro-Dynamic Evidence from Colombia, Mexico, and Morocco," *Quarterly Journal of Economics*, Vol. 113(3), pp. 903-947.

Coe, David T., and Elhana Helpman (1995), "International R&D Spillovers," *European Economic Review*, Vol. 39, pp. 859-87.

Coe, David T., Elhana Helpman, and Alexander W. Hoffmaister (1997), "North-South R&D Spillovers," *Economic Journal*, Vol. 107, pp. 134-149.

Cohen, Wesley, and Daniel Levinthal (1989), "Innovation and Learning: The Two Faces of R&D," *Economic Journal*, Vol. 99, pp. 569-596.

Collins, Susan M., and Barry P. Bosworth (1996), "Economic Growth in East Asia: Accumulation versus Assimilation," Brooking Papers on Economic Activity, No. 2, pp. 135-191.

Comin, Diego, and Bart Hobijn (2003), "Cross-Country Technology Adoption: Making the Theories Face the Facts," Federal Reserve Bank of New York Staff Reports, No. 169, June.

Connolly, Michelle (1997), "Technology, Trade and Growth: Some Empirical Findings," Federal Reserve Bank of New York Research Paper #9727.

Connolly, Michelle, and Jenessa Gunther (1999), "Mercosur: Implications for Growth in Member Countries," *Current Issues in Economics and Finance*, Federal Reserve Bank of New York, Vol. 5(7), pp. 1-6.

Coppin, Addington (1994), "Determinants of LDC Output Growth During the 1980s," *Journal of Developing Areas*, Vol. 28, pp. 219-228.

Darrat, Ali F. (1987), "Are Exports an Engine of Growth? Another Look at the Evidence," *Applied Economics*, Vol. 19, pp. 277-283.

David, Paul (1990), "The Dynamo and the Computer: An Historical Perspective on the Modern Productivity Paradox," *American Economic Review*, Vol. 80(2), pp. 355-361.

David, Paul (1992), "Knowledge, Property, and the Systems Dynamics of Technological Change," in Larry Summers and Anwar Shah, eds., *Proceedings of the World Bank Annual Conference on Development Economics 1992*, pp. 215-248.

David, Paul, and Gavin Wright (1999), "General Purpose Technologies and Surges in Productivity: Historical Reflections on the Future of the ICT Revolution," Stanford University Department of Economics Working Paper 99-026.

Davis, David R., and David E. Weinstein (2001), "Market Size, Linkages, and Productivity: A Study of Japanese Regions," NBER Working Paper w8518, October.

Deardorff, Alan V. (1998), "Determinants of Bilateral Trade: Does Gravity Work in a Neoclassical World?" in Jeffrey A. Frankel, ed., *The Regionalization of the World Economy*, Chicago: University of Chicago Press.

De Long, J. Bradford, and Laurence Summers (1991), "Equipment Investment and Economic Growth," *Quarterly Journal of Economics*, Vol. 106(2), pp. 445-502.

De Long, J. Bradford, and Laurence Summers (1992), "Equipment Investment and Economic Growth: How Strong Is the Nexus?" *Brookings Papers on Economic Activity*, No. 2, pp. 157-199.

De Long, J. Bradford, and Laurence Summers (1993), "How Strongly Do Developing Economies Benefit from Equipment Investment?" *Journal of Monetary Economics*, Vol. 32, pp. 395-415.

Dertouzos, Michael, Richard Lester, and Robert Solow (1990), *Made in America: Regaining the Competitive Edge*, Cambridge: MIT Press.

de Vries, Jan, and Ad van der Woude (1997), *The First Modern Economy*, Cambridge, U.K.: Cambridge University Press.

Dhananjayan, R.S., and N. Sasikala Devi (1997), "Exports and Economic Growth: A Study of Select Nations in Asia and Europe During 1980-81 to 1993-94," *Indian Journal of Applied Economics*, Vol. 6, pp. 41-63.

Dodaro, Santo (1993), "Exports and Growth: A Reconsideration of Causality," *Journal of Developing Areas*, Vol. 27, pp. 227-244.

Dollar, David (1992), "Outward-Oriented Developing Economies Really Do Grow More Rapidly: Evidence from 95 LDCs, 1976-1985," *Economic Development and Cultural Change*, Vol. 40(3), pp. 523-544.

Domar, Evsey D. (1946), "Capital Expansion, Rate of Growth, and Employment," *Econometrica*, Vol. 14, pp. 137-147.

Domar, Evsey D. (1957), *Essays in the Theory of Economic Growth*, Oxford: Oxford University Press.

Doppelhofer, Gernot, Ronald I. Miller, and Xavier Sala-i-Martin (2000), "Determinants of Long-Run Growth: A Bayesian Averaging of Classical Estimates (BACE) Approach," *NBER Working Paper*, No. 7750, June.

Dosi, G., K. Pavitt, and L. Soete (1990), *The Economics of Technical Change and International Trade*, New York: New York University Press.

Dougherty, John C. (1991), "A Comparison of Productivity and Economic Growth in the G-7 Countries," Ph.D. dissertation, Harvard University.

Easterly, William (1993), "How Much Do Distortions Affect Growth?" *Journal of Monetary Economics*, Vol. 32(2), pp. 187-212.

Easterly, William (1998), "The Quest for Growth," *World Bank Working Paper*, November.

Easterly, William (1999), "The Ghost of Financing Gap: How the Harrod-Domar Model Still Haunts Development Economics," *Journal of Development Economics*, Vol. 60(2), pp. 423-438.

Easterly, William (2001), *The Elusive Quest for Growth*, Cambridge, MA: MIT Press.

Easterly, William, and Ross Levine (2001), "It's Not Factor Accumulation: Stylized Facts and Growth Models," *The World Bank Economic Review*, Vol. 15(2), pp. 177-219.

Eaton, Jonathan, and Samuel Kortum (1996), "Trade in Ideas, Patenting and Productivity in the OECD," *Journal of International Economics*, Vol. 40(3), pp. 251-278.

Eaton, Jonathan, and Samuel Kortum (1997), "Engines of Growth: Domestic and Foreign Sources of Innovation," *Japan and the World Economy*, Vol. 9(2), pp. 235-259.

Eaton, Jonathan, and Samuel Kortum (1999), "International Patenting and Technology Diffusion: Theory and Measurement," *International Economic Review*, Vol. 40(3), pp. 537-570.

Eaton, Jonathan, and Samuel Kortum (2001), "Trade in Capital Goods," *European Economic Review*, Vol. 45, pp. 1195-1235.

The Economist (1994), "The Tyranny of Triangles," July 16.

The Economist (1999), "A Survey of the 20th Century, On the Yellow Brick Road," September 11.

Edwards, Sebastian (1992), "Trade Orientation, Distortions and Growth in Developing Countries," *Journal of Development Economics*, Vol. 39(1), pp. 31-57.

Edwards, Sebastian (1993), "Openness, Trade Liberalization, and Growth in Developing Countries," *Journal of Economic Literature*, Vol. 31, pp. 1358-1393.

Edwards, Sebastian (1998), "Openness, Productivity and Growth: What Do We Really Know?" *The Economic Journal*, Vol. 108, pp. 383-398.

Elías, Victor J. (1992), *Sources of Growth: A Study of Seven Latin American Economies*, San Francisco: ICS Press.

Emery, Robert F. (1967), "The Relation of Exports and Economic Growth," *Kyklos*, Vol. 20, pp. 470-486.

Esfahani, Hadi S. (1991), "Exports, Imports, and Economic Growth in Semi-Industrialized Countries," *Journal of Development Economics*, Vol. 35, pp. 93-116.

Evenson, Robert E., and Lakhwinder Singh (1997), "Economic Growth, International Technology Spillovers and Public Policy: Theory and Empirical Evidence from Asia," Economic Growth Center, Yale University, *Discussion Paper* No. 777.

Fagerberg, Jan (1998), "User-Producer Interaction, Learning and Comparative Advantage," in Daniele Archibugi and Jonathan Michie, eds., *Trade, Growth, and Technical Change*, Cambridge, U.K.: Cambridge University Press, pp. 208-225.

Feder, Gershon (1982), "On Exports and Economic Growth," *Journal of Development Economics*, Vol. 12, pp. 59-72.

Feenstra, Robert C. (1992), "How Costly is Protectionism?" *Journal of Economic Perspectives*, Vol. 6, pp. 159-178.

Feenstra, Robert C. (1994), "New Product Varieties and the Measurement of International Prices," *American Economic Review*, Vol. 84, pp. 157-177.

Feenstra, Robert C., James A. Markusen, and Andrew Rose (2001), "Using the Gravity Equation to Differentiate Among Alternative Theories of Trade," *Canadian Journal of Economics*, Vol. 34(2), pp. 430-447.

Fei, John C. H., and Gustav Ranis (1964), *Development of the Labor Surplus Economy*, Homewood, IL: Richard Irwin.

Fernandes, Ana Margarida, and Alberto Isgut (2005), "Learning-by-Doing, Learning-by-Exporting, and Productivity: Evidence from Colombia," World Bank Policy Research Paper 3544, March.

Findlay, Ronald (1996), "Modeling Global Interdependence: Centers, Peripheries, and Frontiers," *American Economic Review*, Vol. 86(2), pp. 47-51.

Florax, Raymond J.G.M., Henri L.F. de Groot, and Reinout Heijungs (2002), "The Empirical Economic Growth Literature," Tinbergen Institute Discussion Paper TI 2002-040/3.

Formani, Robert L. (2001), "The Engine of Capitalist Process: Entrepreneurs in Economic Theory," *Economic and Financial Review*, Federal Reserve Bank of Dallas, Fourth Quarter, pp. 1-11.

Fosu, Augustin K. (1990), "Exports and Economic Growth: The African Case," *World Development*, Vol. 18, pp. 831-835.

Fosu, Augustin K. (1996), "Primary Exports and Economic Growth in Developing Countries," *World Economy*, Vol. 19, pp. 465-475.

Frank, Andre Gunder (1967), *Dependent Accumulation and Under-Development*, London: MacMillan.

Frankel, Jeffrey A., and David Romer (1999), "Does Trade Cause Growth?" *American Economic Review*, Vol. 89(3), pp. 379-399.

Frantzen, Dirk (2000), "Innovation, International Technological Diffusion and the Changing Influence of R&D on Productivity," *Cambridge Journal of Economics*, Vol. 24(2), pp. 193-210.

Frantzen, Dirk (2002), "Intersectoral and International R&D Knowledge Spillovers and Total Factor Productivity," *Scottish Journal of Political Economy*, Vol. 49(3), pp. 280-303.

Frederick, Shane, George Lowenstein, and Ted O'Donoghue (2002), "Time Discounting and Time Preference: A Critical Review," *Journal of Economic Literature*, Vol. 40(2), pp. 351-401.

Friedman, David (1996), *The Hidden Order*, New York: HarperBusiness.

Fujita, Masahisa, Paul Krugman, and Anthony Venables (1999), *The Spatial Economy: Cities, Regions, and International Trade*, Cambridge, MA: MIT Press.

Furman, Jeffrey L., Margeret.K. Kyle, Iain Cockburn, and Rebecca. Henderson (2005), "Public and Private Spillovers, Location, and the Productivity of Pharmaceutical Research," Boston University Department of Economics Working Paper, January.

Furtado, Celso (1963), *The Economic Growth of Brazil: A Survey from Colonial Times to Modern Times*, Berkeley: University of California Press.

Galdón-Sánchez, José E., and James A. Schmitz, Jr. (2003), "Competitive Pressure and Labor Productivity: World Iron Ore Markets in the 1980s," Federal Reserve Bank of Minneapolis *Quarterly Review*, Vol. 27(2), pp. 9-23.

Gisselquist, David, and Jean-Marie Grether (2000), "An Argument for Deregulating the Transfer of Agricultural Technologies to Developing Countries," *World Bank Economic Review*, Vol. 14(1), pp. 111-127.

Gisselquist, David, and Carl Pray (1999), "Deregulating Technology Transfer in Agriculture: Reform's Impact on Turkey in the 1980s," *World Bank Policy Research Working Paper*, No. 2086, March.

Glaeser, Edward, H.D. Kallal, José A. Scheinkman, and Andre Schleifer (1991), "Growth in Cities," NBER Working Paper 3787, July.

Goncalves, R., and J. Richtering (1987), "Intercountry Comparison of Export Performance and Output Growth," *The Developing Economies*, Vol. 25, pp. 3-18.

Gordon, Robert J. (1990), *The Measurement of Durable Goods Prices*, Chicago: University of Chicago Press.

Gort, Michael, Jeremy Greenwood, and Peter Rupert (1999), "How Much of Economic Growth Is Fueled by Investment-Specific Technological Progress?" *Federal Reserve Bank of Cleveland Economic Commentary*, No. 9806.

Gort, Michael, and Richard Wall (1998), "Obsolescence, Input Augmentation, and Growth Accounting," *European Economic Review*, Vol. 42, pp. 1653-1665.

Gould, David M., and William C. Gruben (1996), "The Role of Intellectual Property Rights in Economic Growth," *Journal of Development Economics*, Vol. 48(3), pp. 323-350.

Grabowsky, R. (1988), "Early Japanese Development: The Role of Trade, 1885-1940," *Quarterly Journal of Business and Economics*, Vol. 27, pp. 104-129.

Granger, Clive, and P. Newbold (1974), "Spurious Regressions in Econometrics," *Journal of Econometrics*, Vol. 2, pp. 111-120.

Greenaway, David, Wyn Morgan, and Peter Wright (1997), "Trade Liberalization and Growth in Developing Countries: Some New Evidence," *World Development*, Vol. 25(11), pp. 1885-1892.

Greenaway, David, and David Sapsford (1994a), "What Does Liberalization Do for Exports and Growth?" *Weltwirtschaftliches Archiv*, Vol. 129(2), pp. 153-173.

Greenaway, David, and David Sapsford (1994b), "Exports, Growth, and Liberalization: An Evaluation," *Journal of Policy Modeling*, Vol. 16, pp. 165-186.

Greenwood, Jeremy, and Gokce Uysal (2004), "New Goods and the Transition to a New Economy," NBER Working Paper w10793, September.

Griliches, Zvi (1957), "Hybrid Corn: An Exploration of the Economics of Technical Change," *Econometrica*, Vol. 25(4), pp. 501-522.

Griliches, Zvi (1958), "Research Costs and Social Returns: Hybrid Corn and Related Innovations," *Journal of Political Economy*, Vol. 66(5), pp. 419-431.

Griliches, Zvi (1990), "Patent Statistics as Economic Indicators: A Survey," *Journal of Economic Literature*, Vol. 28(4), pp. 1681-1707.

Griliches, Zvi (1994), "Productivity, R&D, and the Data Constraint," *American Economic Journal*, Vol. 84(1), pp. 1-23.

Gross, Neal C. (1942), *The Diffusion of a CultureTrait in Two Iowa Townships*, M.S. Thesis, Ames, Iowa State College.

Grossman, Gene M., and Elhanan Helpman (1990), "The 'New' Growth Theory: Trade, Innovation, and Growth," *American Economic Review*, Vol. 80(2), pp. 86-91.

Grossman, Gene M., and Elhanan Helpman (1991a), *Innovation and Growth in the Global Economy*, Cambridge, MA: MIT Press.

Grossman, Gene M., and Elhanan Helpman (1991b), "Trade, Knowledge Spillovers, and Growth," *European Economic Review*, Vol. 35, pp. 517-526.

Guellec, D., and B. Van Pottelberghe de la Potterie (2001), "R&D and Productivity Growth: Panel data Analysis of 16 OECD Countries," *OECD Economic Studies*.

Hadass, Yael S., and Jeffrey Williamson (2001), "Terms of Trade Shocks and Economics Performance 1870-1940: Prebisch and Singer Revisited," NBER Working Paper 8188, March.

Hahn, Chin Hee (2003), "Exporting and Performance of Plants: Evidence on Korea," paper presented at the 14th NBER East Asia Seminar on Economics, Taipei, Taiwan.

Hakura, Dalia, and Florence Jaumotte (1999), "The Role of Inter- and Intraindustry Trade in Technology Diffusion," *International Monetary Fund Working Paper*, WP/99/85, April.

Hall, Robert E., and Charles I. Jones (1999), "Why Do Some Countries Produce so Much More Output per Worker than Others?" *Quarterly Journal of Economics*, Vol. 114(1), pp. 83-116.

Hansen, P. (1994), "The Government Exporters and Economic Growth in New Zealand," *New Zealand Economic Papers*, Vol. 28, pp. 133-142.

Harris, Richard (1984), "Applied General Equilibrium Analysis of Small Open Economies with Scale Economies and Imperfect Competition," *American Economic Review*, Vol. 74(5), pp. 1016-1032.

Harrison, Ann (1996), "Openness and Growth: A Time-Series, Cross-Country Analysis for Developing Countries," *Journal of Development Economics*, Vol. 48(2), pp. 419-447.

Harrison, Ann, and Gordon Hanson (1999), "Who Gains from Trade Reform? Some Remaining Puzzles," *Journal of Development Economics*, Vol. 59, pp. 125-154.

Harrison, G. W., T. F. Rutherford, and David G. Tarr (1996), "Trade Reform in the Partially Liberalized Economy of Turkey," *World Bank Economic Review*, Vol. 7(2), pp. 191-217.

Harrod, Roy F. (1939), "An Essay in Dynamic Theory," *The Economic Journal*, Vol. 49, pp. 14-33.

Heitger, Bernhard (1987), "Import Protection and Export Performance: Their Impact on Economic Growth," *Weltwirtschaftliches Archiv*, Vol. 123(2), pp. 249-261.

Helpman, Elhanan (1999), "The Structure of Foreign Trade," *Journal of Economic Perspectives*, Vol. 13, pp. 121-144.

Hendricks, Lutz (2000), "Equipment Investment and Growth in Developing Countries," *Journal of Development Economics*, Vol. 61, pp. 335-364.

Hicks, John (1969), *A Theory of Economic History*, Oxford, U.K.: Clarendon Press.

Higgins, Benjamin (1968), *Economic Development*, New York: W.W. Norton & Company.

Hipple, F. Steb (1990), "The Measurement of International Trade Related to Multinational Companies," *American Economic Review*, Vol. 80(5), pp. 1263-1270.

Hobijn, Bart (2001), "Embodiment in U.S. Manufacturing," Working Paper, New York Federal Reserve Bank, March.

Holman, J.A., and P. E. Graves (1995), "Korean Exports Economic Growth: An Econometric Reassessment," *Journal of Economic Development*, Vol. 20, pp. 45-56.

Holmes, Thomas J., and James A. Schmitz (1995), "Resistence to New Technology and Trade Between Areas," *Federal Reserve Bank of Minneapolis Quarterly Review*, Vol. 19(1), pp. 2-17.

Holmes, Thomas J., and James A. Schmitz (1998), "A Gain from Trade: More Research, Less Obstruction," Federal Reserve Bank of Minneapolis Staff Report No. 245.

Hoover, Edgar M., and Frank Giarratani (1984), *An Introduction to Regional Economics*, New York: Alfred A. Knopf.

Hornstein, Andreas, and Per Krusell (1996), "Can Technology Improvements Cause Productivity Slowdowns?" In Julio J. Rotemberg and Ben S. Bernanke, eds., *NBER Macroeconomics Annual 1996*, Cambridge, MA: MIT Press.

Hotchkiss, J.L., R.E. Moore, and M. Rockel (1994), "Export Expansion and Growth at Different Stages of Development," *Journal of Economic Development*, Vol. 19, pp. 87-105.

Hou, Chi-Ming, and San Gee (1995), "National Systems Supporting Technical Advance in Industry: The Case of Taiwan," in Richard R. Nelson, ed., *National Innovation Systems: A Comparative Analysis*, New York: Oxford University Press.

Hsiao, Mei-chu W. (1987), "Tests of Causality and Exogeneity Between Exports and Economic Growth: The Case of Asian NICs," *Journal of Economic Development*, Vol. 6, pp. 79-94.

Hu, Albert G. Z., and Adam Jaffe (2001), "Patent Citations and International Knowledge Flow: The Causes of Korea and Taiwan," *NBER Working Paper*, No. w8528, October.

Huber, J. Richard (1971), "Effect on Prices of Japan's Entry into World Commerce after 1858," *Journal of Political Economy*, Vol. 79(3), pp. 614-628.

Hufbauer, Clyde, and Kimberly Elliott (1994), *Measuring the Costs of Protection in the United States*, Washington D.C.: Institute for International Economics.

Hymans, Saul H., and Frank P. Stafford (1995), "Divergence, Convergence, and the Gains from Trade," *Review of International Economics*, Vol. 3(1), pp. 118-123.

Ibrahim, Izani, and Craig R. MacPhee (1997), "Export Externalities and Economic Growth," University of Nebraska-Lincoln, Working Paper.

Irwin, Douglas A. (1996a), *Against the Tide: An Intellectual History of Free Trade*, Princeton, NJ: Princeton University Press.

Irwin, Douglas A. (1996b), *Three Simple Principles of Trade Policy*, Washington, DC: AEI Press.

Irwin, Douglas A., and Peter J. Klenow (1994), "Learning-by-Doing Spillovers in the Semiconductor Industry," *Journal of Political Economy*, Vol. 102(6), pp. 1200-1227.

Isard, Walter (1975), *Introduction to Regional Science*, Englewood Cliffs, NJ: Prentice-Hall.

Iwata, Shigeru, Moshin S. Khan, and Hiroshi Murao (2002), "Source of Economic Growth in East Asia: A Nonparametric Assessment," IMF Working Paper WP/02/13, January.

Jaffe, Adam B., and Manuel Trajtenberg (1998), "International Knowledge Flows: Evidence from Patent Citations," *NBER Working Paper*, No. w6507, April.

Jaffe, Adam B., and Manuel Trajtenberg (2002), *Patents, Citations and Innovations: A Window on the Knowledge Economy*, Cambridge, MA: MIT Press.

Jaffe, Adam B., Manuel Trajtenberg, and Rebecca Henderson (1993), "Geographic Localization of Knowledge Spillovers as Evidenced by Patent Citations," *The Quarterly Journal of Economics*, Vol. 117(3), pp. 577-598.

Jenkins, Mauricio, Gerardo Esquivel, and Felipe Larrain B. (1998), "Exporting Processing Zones in Central America," Harvard Institute for International Development Discussion Paper No. 4, July.

Johnson, Harry G. (1971), *Aspects of the Theory of Tariffs*, Cambridge, MA: Harvard University Press.

Jung, Woo S., and Peyton J. Marshall (1985), "Exports, Growth and Causality in Developing Countries," *Journal of Development Economics*, Vol. 18, pp. 1-12.

Kavoussi, Rostam M. (1984), "Export Expansion and Economic Growth: Further Empirical Evidence," *Journal of Development Economics*, Vol. 14, pp. 241-250.

Keller, Wolfgang (1996), "Absorptive Capacity: On the Creation and Acquisition of Technology in Development," *Journal of Development Economics*, Vol. 49(1), pp. 199-227.

Keller, Wolfgang (1998), "Are International R&D Spillovers Trade-Related? Analyzing Spillovers Among Randomly Matched Trade Partners," *European Economic Journal*, Vol. 42(8), pp. 1469-1481.

Keller, Wolfgang (2000a), "Do Trade Patterns and Technology Flows Affect Productivity Growth?" *The World Bank Economic Review*, Vol. 14(1), pp. 17-47.

Keller, Wolfgang (2000b), "Geographic Localization of International Technology Diffusion," *NBER Working Paper*, No. 7509.

Keller, Wolfgang (2001a), "International Technology Diffusion," *NBER Working Paper*, No. 8573, October.

Keller, Wolfgang (2001b), "The Geography and Channels of Diffusion at the World's Technology Frontier," *NBER Working Paper*, No. 8150, March.

Keller, Wolfgang (2002a), "Geographic Localization of International Technology Diffusion," *American Economic Review*, Vol. 92(1), pp. 120-142.

Keller, Wolfgang (2002b), "Trade and the Transmission of Technology," *Journal of Economic Growth*, Vol. 7(1), pp. 5-25.

Keller, Wolfgang (2004), "International Technology Diffusion," *Journal of Economic Literature*, Vol. 42(3), pp. 752-782.

Kelly, Morgan (1997), "The Dynamics of Smithian Growth," *Quarterly Journal of Economics*, August, pp. 939-964.

Keuschnigg, Christian, and Wilhelm Kohler (1996), "Commercial Policy and Dynamic Adjustment Under Monopolistic Competition," *Journal of International Economics*, Vol. 40, pp. 373-409.

Khan, A., Ashfaque H., and Najam Saqib (1993), "Exports and Economic Growth: The Pakistan Experience," *International Economic Journal*, Vol. 7(3), pp. 53-64.

Klapper, Leora, Luc Laeven, and Raghuram Rajan (2004), "Business Environment and Firm Entry: Evidence from International Data," NBER Working Paper 10380, March.

Klenow, Peter, and Andres Rodriguez-Clare (1997), "The Neoclassical Revival in Growth Economics: Has It Gone Too Far?" in Ben S. Bernanke and Julio J. Rotemberg, eds., *NBER Macroeconomics Annual 1997*, Cambridge, MA: MIT Press, pp. 73-103.

Kohli, Inderjit, and Nirvikar Singh (1989), "Exports and Growth: Critical Minimum Effort and Diminishing Returns," *Journal of Monetary Economics*, Vol. 30, pp. 391-400.

Kravis, Irving B. (1970), "Trade as a Handmaiden of Growth: Similarities between the Nineteenth and Twentieth Centuries," *Economic Journal*, Vol. 80(32), pp. 850-872.

Kremer, Michael (1993), "Population Growth and Technological Change: One Million B.C. to 1990," *Quarterly Journal of Economics*, Vol. 108(3), pp. 681-716.

Krueger, Anne O. (1974), "The Political Economy of the Rent-Seeking Society," *American Economic Review*, Vol. 69, pp. 291-303.

Krueger, Anne O. (1978), *Foreign Trade Regimes and Economic Development: Liberalization Attempts and Consequences*, Cambridge, MA: Ballinger Publishing Company.

Krueger, Anne O. (1980), "Trade Policy as an Input to Development," *American Economic Review*, Vol. 70(2), pp. 288-292.

Krueger, Anne O. (1983), *Trade and Employment in Developing Countries: Synthesis and Conclusions*, Chicago: University of Chicago Press.

Krueger, Anne O. (1997), "Trade Policy and Economic Development: How We Learn," *American Economic Review*, Vol. 87(1), pp. 1-22.

Krueger, Anne O., and Barab Tuncer (1982), "An Empirical Test of the Infant Industry Argument," *American Economic Review*, Vol. 72(5), pp. 1142-1152.

Krugman, Paul R. (1979), "Increasing Returns, Monopolistic Competition, and International Trade," *Journal of International Economics*, Vol. 9(4), pp. 469-479.

Krugman, Paul R. (1987), "Is Free Trade Passé?," *Journal of Economic Perspectives*, Vol. 1(2), pp. 131-144.

Krugman, Paul R. (1991), *Geography and Trade*, Cambridge, MA: MIT Press.

Krugman, Paul R. (1994a), "Does Third World Growth Hurt First World Prosperity?" *Harvard Business Review*, July-August, pp. 113-121.

Krugman, Paul R. (1994b), "The Myth of Asia's Miracle," *Foreign Affairs*, Vol. 73(6), pp. 62-78.

Krugman, Paul R., and Anthony Venables (1995), "Globalization and the Inequality of Nations," *Quarterly Journal of Economics*, Vol. 110(4), pp. 857-880.

Kwan, A.C.C., J. A. Cotsomitis, and B. Kwok (1996), "Exports, Economic Growth and Exogeneity: Taiwan 1953-88," *Applied Economics*, Vol. 28, pp. 467-471.

Lal, Deepak (1998), *Unintended Consequences: The Impact of Factor Endowments, Culture, and Politics on Long-Run Economic Development*, Cambridge, MA: MIT Press.

Lamoreaux, Naomi R., and Kenneth L. Sokoloff (1999), "Inventive Activity and the Market for Technology in the United States, 1840-1920," NBER Working Paper w7107.

Lamoreaux, Naomi R., and Kenneth L. Sokoloff (2002), "Intermediaries in the U.S. Market for Technology, 1870-1920," NBER Working Paper No. w9017, June.

Larrain, Felipe, Luis Lopez-Calva, and Adrea Rodriguez-Claré (2000), "Intel: A Case Study of Foreign Direct Investment in Central America," Working Paper 58, Center for International Development, Harvard University.

Lawrence, Robert Z., and David E. Weinstein (1999), "Trade and Growth: Import-Led or Export-Led? Evidence from Japan and Korea," *NBER Working Paper*, No. 7264.

Leamer, Edward E. (1983), "Let's Take the Con Out of Econometrics," *American Economic Review*, Vol. 73(1), pp. 31-41.

Leamer, Edward E. (1985a), "Vector Autoregressions for Causal Inference," in Karl Brunner and Allan H. Meltzer, eds., *Carnegie-Rochester Conference Series on Public Policy: Understanding Monetary Regimes*, Vol. 22. New York: McGrawHill, pp. 255-304.

Leamer, Edward E. (1985b), "Sensitivity Analyses Would Help," *American Economic Review*, Vol. 75(3), 308-313.

Lee, Dwight R., and Richard B. McKenzie (1993), *Failure and Progress, The Bright Side of the Dismal Science*, Washington, DC: The Cato Institute.

Lee, Ha Yan, Luca Antonio Ricci, and Roberto Rigobon (2005), "Once Again, Is Account Openness Good for Growth?" *Journal of Development Economics*, Vol. 75(2), pp. 451-472.

Lee, Jong-Wha (1993), "International Trade, Distortions, and Long-Run Economic Growth," *IMF Staff Papers*, Vol. 40(2), pp. 299-328.

Lee, Jong-Wha (1995), "Capital Goods Imports and Long-Run Growth," *Journal of Development Economics*," Vol. 48, pp. 91-110.

Leibenstein, Harvey (1966), "Allocative Efficiency vs. 'X-Efficiency,'" *American Economic Review*, Vol. 56(3), pp. 392-415.

Lerner, Abba P. (1934), "The Symmetry Between Import and Export Taxes," *Economica*, August, pp. 306-313.

Levine, Ross, and David Renelt (1992), "A Sensitivity Analysis of Cross-Country Growth," *American Economic Review*, Vol. 82(4), pp. 942-963.

Levinsohn, J. (1993), "Testing the Imports-As-Market-Discipline Hypothesis," *Journal of International Economics*, Vol. 35(1-2), pp. 1-22.

Lewer, Joshua J. (2002), "International Trade Composition and Medium-Run Growth: Evidence of a Causal Relationship," *International Trade Journal*, Vol. 16(3), pp. 295-317.

Lewer, Joshua J. and Neil Terry (2003) "Capital Account and Foreign Direct Investment Policies in the Late Nineties: What Effect on Trade?" *ASEAN Economic Bulletin*, Vol. 20(3), pp. 256-271.

Lewer, Joshua, and Hendrik Van den Berg (2001), "Do Capital-Importing Countries Really Grow Faster? An Empirical Test Using Panel Data for 27 Countries," *Global Economy Quarterly*, Vol. 2(1), pp. 1-36.

Lewer, Joshua, and Hendrik Van den Berg (2003a),"Does Trade Composition Matter for Medium-Run Growth? Time Series Evidence for 28 Countries", *Journal of International Trade and Economic Growth*, Vol. 12(1), pp. 39-96.

Lewer, Joshua J., and Hendrik Van den Berg (2003b), "How Large Is International Trade's Effect on Economic Growth?" *Journal of Economic Surveys*, Vol. 17(3), pp. 363-396.

Lewis, W. Arthur (1954), "Economic Development with Unlimited Supplies of Labor," *Manchester School*, Vol. 22(2), pp. 139-191.

Lewis, W. Arthur (1955), *The Theory of Economic Growth*, London: Allen and Unwin.

Lichtenberg, Frank, and Bruno van Pottelsberghe de la Potterie (1996), "International R&D Spillovers: A Re-Examination," NBER Working Paper 5668, July.

Lin, Shuanglin (2000), "Foreign Trade and China's Economic Development: A Time-Series Analysis," *Journal of Economic Development*, Vol. 25(1), pp. 145-153.

Linder, Steffan B. (1961), *An Essay on Trade and Transformation*, Uppsala: Almquist & Wicksell.

Linnemann, Hans (1966), *An Econometric Study of International Trade Flows*, Amsterdam: North-Holland.

Lubitz, Raymond (1973), "Export-Led Growth in Industrialized Economies," *Kyklos*, Vol. 26, pp. 307-320.

Lucas, Robert E., Jr. (1988), "On the Mechanics of Economic Development," *Journal of Monetary Economics,* Vol. 22(3), pp. 3-42.

Lucas, Robert E., Jr. (1990), "Why Doesn't Capital Flow from Rich to Poor Countries?" *American Economic Review*, Vol. 80(2), pp. 92-96.

Lucas, Robert E., Jr. (2000), "Some Macroeconomics for the 21st Century," *Journal of Economic Perspectives*, Vol. 14(1), pp. 159-168.

Lumenga-Neso, Oliver, Marcelo Olarreaga, and Maurice Schiff (2000), "On 'Indirect' Trade-Related R&D Spillovers," *World Bank Working Paper*.

MacDonald, James M. (1994), "Does Import Competition Force Efficient Production?" *The Review of Economics and Statistics*, Vol. 74, pp. 721-727.

Macfarlane, Alan, and Gerry Martin (2002), *Glass: A World History*, Chicago: University of Chicago Press.

Madani, Dorsati (2000), "A Review of the Role and Impact of Export Processing Zones," *World Bank Working Paper*.

Maddison, Angus (1991), *Dynamic Forces of Capitalist Development*, Oxford: Oxford University Press.

Maddison, Angus (1995), *Monitoring the World Economy 1820-1992*, Paris: OECD.

Maddison, Angus (2001), *The World Economy: A Millennial Perspective*, Paris: OECD.

Maddison, Angus (2003), *The World Economy: Historical Statistics*, Paris: OECD.

Mahalanobis, P. C. (1955), "The Approach of Operational Research to Planning in India," *Sankahya*, Vol. 16(1,2), pp. 3-120.

Malthus, Thomas (1798), *An Essay on the Principle of Population*, London: W. Pickering.

Mankiw, N. Gregory (1995), "The Growth of Nations," *Brookings Papers on Economic Activity*, No. 1, pp. 275-326.

Mankiw, N. Gregory, David Romer, and David N. Weil (1992), "A Contribution to the Empirics of Economic Growth," *Quarterly Journal of Economics*, Vol. 107(2), pp. 407-437.

Mansfield, Edwin (1961), "Technical Change and the Rate of Imitation," *Econometrica*, Vol. 29(4), pp. 741-766.

Mansfield, Edwin (1986), "Patents and Innovation: An Empirical Study," *Management Science*, February, pp. 173-181.

Mansfield, Edwin, Mark Schwartz, and Samuel Wagner (1981), "Imitation Costs and Patents: An Empirical Study," *Economic Journal*, Vol. 91(364), pp. 907-223.

Marshall, Alfred (1920), *Principles of Economics*, 8th Ed., New York: MacMillan & Co.

Martin, William, and Devanish Mitra (2001), "Productivity Growth and Convergence in Agriculture and Manufacturing," *Economic Development and Cultural Change*, Vol. 49(2), pp. 403-422.

Mataloni, Raymond J., Jr. (2000), "U.S. Multinational Companies, Operations in 1998," *Survey of Current Business*, July, pp. 26-45.

Mayer, Jörg (2001), "Technology Diffusion, Human Capital and Economic Growth in Developing Countries," *United Nations Conference in Trade and Development Discussion Paper*, No. 154, June.

Mazumdar, Joy (1996), "Do Static Gains from Trade Lead to Medium-Run Growth?" *Journal of Political Economy*, Vol. 104(6), pp. 1328-1337.

Mbaku, John M. (1989), "Export Growth and Economic Performance in Developing Countries: Further Evidence from Africa," *Journal of Economic Development*, Vol. 14, pp. 127-142.

McCallum, John (1995), "National Borders Matter: Canada-U.S. Regional Trade Patterns," *American Economic Review*, Vol. 85, pp. 615-623.

McKinsey Global Institute (1993), *Manufacturing Productivity*, Washington, DC: McKinsey and Company, Inc.

McNab, Robert M., and Robert E. Moore (1998), "Trade Policy, Export Expansion, Human Capital and Growth," *Journal of International Trade and Economic Development*, Vol. 7, pp. 237-256.

Meier, Gerald M. (1988), *Asian Development*, Madison: University of Wisconsin Press.

Messerlin, Patrick A. (2001), *Measuring the Costs of Protection in Europe: European Commercial Policy in the 2000s*, Washington, DC: The Institute for International Economics.

Michaely, Michael (1977), "Exports and Growth: An Empirical Investigation," *Journal of Development Economics*, Vol. 4(1), pp. 49-53.

Michalopoulos, Constantine, and Keith Jay (1973), "Growth of Exports and Income in the Developing World: A Neoclassical View," AID Discussion Paper 28.

Mill, John Stuart (1848), *Principles of Political Economy*, London, U.K.: Longmans, Green.

Mishima, Kazuhiro (1999), "Learning by New Experiences: Revisiting the Flying Fortress Learning Curve," in Naomi R. Lamoreaux, Daniel M. G. Raff, Peter Temin, eds., *Learning by Doing in Markets, Firms, and Countries*, Chicago: University of Chicago Press, pp. 145-184.

Mokyr, Joel (1990), *The Lever of Riches*, New York: Oxford University Press.

Mokyr, Joel (2002), *The Gifts of Athena*, Princeton, NJ: Princeton University Press.

Moore, Robert E. (1992), "The Level of Development and GSP Treatment: An Empirical Investigation into the Differential Impacts of Export Expansion," *Journal of World Trade*, Vol. 26, pp. 19-30.

Moran, Theodore H. (1999), *Foreign Direct Investment*, Washington: D.C.: Institute for International Economics.

Morck, Randall, Daniel Wolfenzon, and Bernard Young (2004), "Corporate Governance, Economic Entrenchment and Growth," NBER Working Paper 10692, August.

Moschos, Demetrios (1989), "Export Expansion, Growth and the Level of Economic Development: An Empirical Analysis," *Journal of Development Economics*, Vol. 30, pp. 93-102.

Mundell, Robert A. (1957) "International Trade and Factor Mobility," *American Economic Review*, Vol. 47(3), pp. 321-335.

Myrdal, Gunnar (1956), *Economic Theory and the Underdeveloped Regions*, London: G. Duckworth & Co.

Navaretti, Giorgio Barba, and David Tarr (2000), "International Knowledge Flows and Economic Performance: A Review of the Evidence," *The World Bank Economic Review*, Vol. 14(1), pp. 1-15.

Nickell, S. J. (1996), "Competition and Corporate Performance," *Journal of Political Economy*, Vol. 104(4), pp. 724-746.

Nickell, S. J. , D. Nicolitsas, and N. Dryden (1997), "What Makes Firms Perform Well?" *European Economic Review*, Vol. 36, pp. 1055-1085.

Nordhaus, William D. (1969), *Invention, Growth and Welfare: A Theoretical Treatment of Technological Change*, Cambridge, MA: MIT Press.

North, Douglass C. (2005), *Understanding the Process of Economic Change*, Princeton, NJ: Princeton University Press.

OECD (1997), *Technology and Industrial Performance*, Paris: Organisation for Economic Cooperation and Development.

OECD (1998), *Human Capital Investment*, Paris: Centre for Educational Research and Innovation, OECD.

Otani, Ichiro, and Delano Villaneuva (1990), "Long-Term Growth in Developing Countries and Its Determinants: An Empirical Analysis," *World Development*, Vol. 18, 769-783.

Owen, Geoffrey (2001), "A Perfect Climate for International Success," *The Financial Times*, November 6.

Pack, Howard (2000), "Industrial Policy: Growth Elixer or Poison?" *The World Bank Research Observer*, Vol. 15(1), pp. 47-67.

Pack, Howard, and Kamal Saggi (1999), "Exporting Externalities, and Technology Transfer," World Bank Working Paper, February 23.

Papageorgiou, Demitris, Michael Michaely, and Armeane M. Choski, eds. (1991), *Liberalizing Foreign Trade*, Vols. 1-7, Oxford: Blackwell.

Parente, Stephen L., and Edward C. Prescott (2000), *Barriers to Riches*, Cambridge, MA: MIT Press.

Park, Jong H. and Penelope B. Prime (1997), "Export Performance and Growth in China: A Cross-Provincial Analysis," *Applied Economics*, Vol. 29, pp. 1353-1363.

Park, Jungsoo (2004), "International and Intersectoral R&D Spillovers in the OECD and East Asian Economies," *Economic Inquiry*, Vol. 42(4), pp. 739-757.

Park, Walter G. (1995), "International R&D Spillovers and OECD Economic Growth," *Economic Inquiry*, Vol. 23(4), pp. 571-591.

Petty, William (1682), "Another Essay in Political Arithmetic," in Charles Henry Hull, ed. (1899), *The Economic Writings of Sir William Petty*, Cambridge, U.K.: Cambridge University Press.

Plant, Arnold (1934), "The Economic Aspects of Copyright in Books," *Economica*, New Series, Vol. 1(2), pp. 167-195.

Polanyi, Michael (1958), *Personal Knowledge: Towards a Post Critical Philosophy*, London: Routledge.

Porter, Michael (1990), *The Competitive Advantage of Nations*, New York: Free Press and MacMillan.

Prebisch, Raúl (1950), *The Economic Development of Latin America and Its Principal Problems*, Lake Success, NY: United Nations Department of Social Affairs.

Prebisch, Raúl (1959), "Commercial Policy in the Underdeveloped Countries," *American Economic Review*, Papers and Proceedings, Vol. 49(2), pp. 251-273.

Pritchett, Lant (1997), "Divergence, Big Time," *Journal of Economic Perspectives*, Vol. 11(3), pp. 3-17.

Psacharopoulos, George (1994), "Returns to Investment in Education: A Global Update," *World Development*, Vol. 22(9), pp. 1325-1341.

Rajan, Raghuram G., and Luigi Zingales (2003), *Saving Capitalism from the Capitalists*, New York: Crown Publishing.

Ram, Rati (1985), "Exports and Economic Growth: Some Additional Evidence," *Economic Development and Cultural Change*, Vol. 33, pp. 415-425.

Ram, Rati (1987), "Exports and Economic Growth in Developing Countries: Evidence from Time-Series and Cross-Section Data," *Economic Development and Cultural Change*, Vol. 36(1), pp. 51-72.

Rana, Pradumna B. (1986), "Exports and Economic Growth: Further Evidence from Asian LDCs," *Pakistan Journal of Applied Economics*, Vol. 5, pp. 163-178.

Rana, Pradumna B. (1988), "Exports, Policy Changes, and Economic Growth in Developing Countries After the 1973 Oil Shock," *Journal of Development Economics*, Vol. 28, pp. 261-264.

Rapping, Leonard (1965), "Learning and World War II Production Functions," *Review of Economics and Statistics*, Vol. 47, pp. 81-86.

Rashid, Aneesa I. (1995), "Trade, Growth, and Liberalization: The Indian Experience, 1977-1989," *Journal of Developing Areas*, Vol. 29, pp. 355-370.

Rebelo, Sergio (1991), "Long-Run Policy Analysis and Long-Run Growth," *Journal of Political Economy*, Vol. 99, pp. 500-521.

Rhee, Yung, Bruce Ross-Larson, and Gary Purcell (1984), *Korea's Competitive Edge: Managing Entry into the World Market*, Washington, DC: World Bank.

Ridley, Matt (1996), *The Origins of Virtue*, New York: Penguin Books.

Rigobon, Roberto, and Dani Rodrik (2004), "Rule of Law, Democracy, Openness, and Income: Estimating the Interrelationships," NBER Working Paper 10750, September.

Rivera-Batiz, Luis A., and Paul M. Romer (1991), "Economic Integration and Endogenous Growth," *Quarterly Journal of Economics*, Vol. 56, pp. 531-555.

Robertson, D.H. (1938), "The Future of International Trade," *The Economic Journal*, Vol. 48(189), pp. 1-14.

Rodrigo, G. Chris (2000), "East Asia's Growth: Technology or Accumulation?" *Contemporary Economic Policy*, Vol. 18(2), pp. 215-227.

Rodriguez, Francisco, and Dani Rodrik (1999), "Trade Policy and Economic Growth: A Skeptics Guide to the Cross-National Evidence," NBER Revised Working Paper, No. 7081.

Rodriguez, Francisco, and Dani Rodrik (2001), "Trade Policy and Economic Growth: A Skeptics Guide to the Cross-National Evidence," in Ben Bernanke and Kenneth S. Rogoff, eds., *NBER Macroeconomics Annual 2000*, Cambridge, MA: MIT Press.

Rodrik, Dani (1992), "Closing the Productivity Gap: Does Trade Liberalization Help?" in G.K. Helleiner, ed., *Trade Policy, Industrialization, and Development: New Perspectives*, WIDER Studies in Development Economics, Oxford: Clarendon Press, pp. 155-175.

Rodrik, Dani (1997), "Discussion of Baldwin, Francois, and Portes' 'The Costs and Benefits of Eastern Enlargement: The Impact on the EU and Central Europe,'" *Economic Policy*, April, pp. 170-173.

Rodrik, Dani, Arvind Subramanian, and Francesco Trebbi (2002), "Institutions Rule: The Primacy of Institutions over Geography and Integration in Economic Development," *NBER Working Paper*, No. w9305, November.

Romer, Paul M. (1986), "Increasing Returns and Long-Run Growth," *Journal of Political Economy,* Vol. 94(5), pp. 1002-1037.

Romer, Paul M. (1990), "Endogenous Technological Change," *Journal of Political Economy*, Vol. 95, pp. S71-S102.

Romer, Paul M. (1993), "Idea Gaps and Object Gaps in Economic Development," *Journal of Monetary Economics*, Vol. 32, pp. 543-573.

Romer, Paul M. (1994a), "New Goods, Old Theory, and the Welfare Cost of Trade Restrictions," *Journal of Development Economics*, Vol. 43(1), pp. 5-38.

Romer, Paul M. (1994b), "The Origins of Endogenous Growth," *Journal of Economic Perspectives*, Vol. 8(1), pp. 3-22.

Romer, Paul M. (1998), "Economic Growth," in David R. Henderson, ed., *The Fortune Encyclopedia of Economics*, New York: Warner Books.

Romer, Paul M. (2001), "Comment on 'It's Not Factor Accumulation: Stylized Facts and Growth Models,'" *The World Bank Economic Review*, Vol. 15(2), pp. 225-227.

Rosenberg, Nathan (1972), "Factors Affecting the Diffusion of Technology," *Explorations in Economic History*, Vol. 0(1), pp. 3-33.

Rosenberg, Nathan (1976), "On Technological Expectations," *Economic Journal*, Vol. 86, pp. 523-535.

Rosenberg, Nathan (1994), *Exploring the Black Box, Technology, Economics, and History*, Cambridge, U.K.: Cambridge University Press.

Rothbard, Murray (1995), *Economic Thought Before Adam Smith: An Austrian Perspective on the History of Economic Thought*, Vol. 1, Hants, U.K.: Edward Elgar.

Ruttan, Vernon W. (2001), *Technology, Growth, and Development*, New York: Oxford University Press.

Ryan, B., and N. C. Gross (1943), "The Diffusion of Hybrid Seed Corn in Two Iowa Communities," *Rural Sociology*, Vol. 8(1), pp. 14-24.

Sachs, Jeffrey D., and Andrew Warner (1995), "Economic Reforms and the Process of Global Integration," *Brookings Papers on Economic Activity*, No. 1, pp. 1-118.

Saggi, Kamal (2000), "Trade, Foreign Direct Investment, and International Technology Transfer: A Survey," *World Bank Working Paper*.

Sakellaris, Plutarchis, and Daniel J. Wilson (2001), "Quantifying Embodied Technological Change," Federal Reserve Bank of San Francisco Working Paper 2001-16, October.

Sala-i-Martin, Xavier (1997), "I Just Ran Two Million Regressions," *American Economic Review*, Vol. 87(2), pp. 178-183.

Salvatore, Dominick (1983), "A Simultaneous Equations Model of Trade and Development with Dynamic Policy Simulations," *Kyklos*, Vol. 36, pp. 66-90.

Salvatore, Dominick, and Thomas Hatcher (1991), "Inward Oriented and Outward Oriented Trade Strategies," *The Journal of Development Studies*, Vol. 28(4), pp. 7-25.

Samuelson, Paul A. (2004), "Where Ricardo and Mill Rebut and Confirm Arguments of Mainstream Economists Supporting Globalization," *Journal of Economic Perspectives*, Vol. 18(3), pp. 135-146.

Sarkar, Jayati (1998), "Technological Diffusion: Alternative Theories and Historical Evidence," *Journal of Economic Surveys*, Vol. 12(2), pp. 131-176; and Chapter 5 in Vernon W. Ruttan (2001), *Technology, Growth, and Development*, New York: Oxford University Press.

Sazanami, Yoku, Urata Shujiro, and Kawai Hiroki (1995), *Measuring the Costs of Protection in Japan*, Washington, DC: Institute for International Economics.

Schap, David (1985), "X-Inefficiency in a Rent-Seeking Society: A Graphical Analysis," *Quarterly Journal of Economics and Business*, Vol. 25(1), pp. 19-25.

Scheve, Kenneth F., and Matthew J. Slaughter (2001), *Globalization and the Perceptions of American Workers*, Washington DC: Institute for International Economics.

Schiff, Maurice, and Yanling Wang (2003), "Regional Integration and Technology Diffusion: The Case of the North American Free Trade Agreement," World Bank Policy Research Working Paper WPS3132, Sept. 30.

Schiff, Maurice, Yanling Wang, and Marcelo Olarreaga (2002), "Trade-Related Technology Diffusion and the Dynamics of North-South and South-South Integration," World Bank Policy Research Working Paper 2861, June.

Schmookler, Jacob (1966), *Invention and Economic Growth*, Cambridge, MA: Harvard University Press.

Schumpeter, Joseph (1912), *Theorie der Wirtschaftliche Entwicklung*, Leipzig: Duncker & Humbolt.

Schumpeter, Joseph (1934), *The Theory of Economic Development*, Cambridge, MA: Harvard University Press.

Schumpeter, Joseph (1947), *Capitalism, Socialism, and Democracy*, 2nd edition, New York: Harper and Brothers.

Schumpeter, Joseph (2005), "Development," *Journal of Economic Literature*, Vol. 43(1), pp. 108-120.

Seabright, Paul (2004), *The Company of Strangers: A Natural History of Economic Life*, Princeton, NJ: Princeton University Press.

Segerstrom, Paul S. (1998), "Endogenous Growth Without Scale Effects," *American Economic Review*, Vol. 88, pp. 1290-1310.

Semenick Alam, Ila M., and Andrew R. Morrison (2000), "Trade Reform Dynamics and Technical Efficiency: The Peruvian Experience," *World Bank Economic Review*, Vol. 14(2), pp. 309-330.

Sengupta, Jati K. (1993), "Growth in NICs in Asia: Some Tests of New Growth Theory," *Journal of Development Studies*, Vol. 29(2), pp. 342-357.

Sengupta, Jati K., and Juan R. Espana (1994), "Exports and Economic Growth in Asian NICs: An Econometric Analysis for Korea," *Applied Economics*, Vol. 26, pp. 45-51.

Serletis, A. (1992), "Export Growth and Canadian Economic Development," *Journal of Development Economics*, Vol. 38, pp. 133-145.

Shan, Jordan, and Fiona Sun (1998), "On the Export-Led Growth Hypothesis for the Little Dragons: An Empirical Reinvestigation," *Atlantic Economic Journal*, Vol. 26(4), pp. 353-371.

Shatz, Howard J., and Anthony J. Venables (2000), "The Geography of International Investment," in G. L. Clark, M. Feldmand, and M.S. Gertler, eds., *The Oxford Handbook of Economic Geography*, Oxford: Oxford University Press.

Sheehey, Edmund J. (1990), "Exports and Growth: A Flawed Framework," *Journal of Development Studies*, Vol. 27, pp. 111-116.

Sheehey, Edmund J. (1992), "Exports and Growth: Additional Evidence," *Journal of Development Studies*, Vol. 28, pp. 730-734.

Sjöholm, Fredrik (1996), "International Transfer of Knowledge: The Role of International Trade and Geographic Proximity," *Weltwirtschaftliches Archiv*, Vol. 132, pp. 97-115.

Skinner, Jonathan, and Douglas Staiger (2005), "Technology Adoption from Hybrid Corn to Beta Blockers," NBER Working Paper 11251.

Smith, Adam (1776 [1976]), *An Inquiry into the Nature and Causes of the Wealth of Nations*, Chicago: University of Chicago Press.

Solow, Robert M. (1956), "A Contribution to the Theory of Economic Growth," *Quarterly Journal of Economics*, Vol. 70(1), pp. 65-94.

Solow, Robert M. (1957), "Technical Change and the Aggregate Production Function," *Review of Economics and Statistics*, Vol. 39, pp. 312-320.

Solow, Robert M. (1960), "Investment and Technological Progress," in Kenneth Arrow, Samuel Karlin, and Patrick Suppes, eds., *Mathematical Models in the Social Sciences*, Stanford, CA: Stanford University Press.

Song, L., and T. Chen (1995), "On Exports and Economic Growth: Further Evidence," *Pacific Economic Papers*, Vol. 242, pp. 1-23.

Spolaore, Alesina, and Romain Wacziarg (2000), "Economic Integration and Political Disintegration," *American Economic Review*, Vol. 90(5), pp. 1276-1296.

Sprout, Ronald V.A., and James H. Weaver (1993), "Exports and Economic Growth in a Simultaneous Equations Model," *Journal of Developing Areas*, Vol. 28(4), pp. 289-306.

Srinivasan, T. N. (1997), "As the Century Turns: Analytics, Empirics, and Politics of Development," Working Paper, Economic Growth Center, Yale University, December.

Summers, Robert, and Alan Heston (1991), "The Penn World Table (Mark 5): An Expanded Set of International Comparisons, 1950-1988," *Quarterly Journal of Economics*, Vol. 106(9), pp. 272-368.

Sun, Haishun, and Ashok Parikh (2001), "Exports, Inward Foreign Direct Investment (FDI) and Regional Economic Growth in China," *Regional Studies*, Vol. 35(3), pp. 187-196.

Sung-Shen, N., Basudeb Biswas, and Gopal Tribedy (1990), "Causality Between Exports and Economic Growth: An Empirical Study," *Journal of Economic Development*, Vol. 15(1), pp. 47-61.

Supo Alege, P. (1993), "Export and Growth in the Nigerian Economy: A Causality Test," *Indian Journal of Economics*, Vol. 73, pp. 397-416.

Svensson, Peter (1998), "Strategic Trade Policy and Endogenous R&D-Subsidies: An Empirical Study," *Kyklos*, Vol. 51(2), pp. 259-275.

Syron, Richard F., and Brendan M. Walsh (1968), "The Relation of Exports and Economic Growth," *Kyklos*, Vol. 21, pp. 541-545.

Tan, Kim-Seng, and Sock-Yong Phang (2005), "From Efficiency-Driven to Innovation-Driven Economic Growth: Perspectives from Singapore," World Bank Policy Research Working Paper 3569.

Teece, David J. (1977), "Technology Transfer by Multinational Firms: The Resource Cost of Transferring Technological Know-How," *Economic Journal*, Vol. 77(1), pp. 49-77.

Teresi, Dick (2002), *Lost Discoveries*, New York: Simon and Schuster.

Thompson, Peter (2001), "How Much Did the Liberty Shipbuilders Learn? New Evidence for an Old Case Study," *Journal of Political Economy*, Vol. 109(1), pp. 103-137.

Tinbergen, Jan (1962), *Shaping the World Economy*, New York: Twentieth Century Fund.

Tullock, Gordon (1967), "The Welfare Costs of Tariffs, Monopolies, and Theft," *Western Economic Journal*, Vol. 5(3), pp. 224-232.

Tullock, Gordon (1993), *Rent Seeking*, Brookfield, VT: Edward Elgar.

Tyler, William G. (1981), "Growth and Export Expansion in Developing Countries: Some Empirical Evidence," *Journal of Development Economics*, Vol. 9, pp. 121-130.

Ulku, Hulya (2004), "R&D, Innovation, and Economic Growth: An Empirical Analysis," IMF Working Paper WP/04/185, September, 2004.

Vamvakidis, Athanasios (1998), "Regional Integration and Economic Growth," *The World Bank Economic Review*, Vol. 12(2), pp. 251-270.

Van Biesebroeck, Johannes (2003), "Exporting Raises Productivity in Sub-Saharan African Manufacturing Plants," NBER Working Paper w10020, October.

Van den Berg, Hendrik (1996a), "Trade as the Engine of Growth in Asia: What the Econometric Evidence Reveals," *Journal of Economic Integration*, Vol. 11, pp. 510-538.

Van den Berg, Hendrik (1996b), "Libre comercio y crecimiento: la evidence econometrica para America Latina," *Comercio Exterior*, Vol. 46, pp. 364-373.

Van den Berg, Hendrik (1997), "The Relationship Between International Trade and Economic Growth in Mexico," *North American Journal of Economics and Finance*, Vol. 8(1), pp. 1-21.

Van den Berg, Hendrik (2004), *International Economics*, New York: McGraw-Hill.

Van den Berg, Hendrik, and James R. Schmidt (1994), "Foreign Trade and Economic Growth: Time Series Evidence from Latin America," *The Journal of International Trade and Economic Development*, Vol. 27, pp. 249-268.

Venables, Anthony J. (2003), "Winners and Losers from Regional Integration Agreements," *Economic Journal*, Vol. 113, pp. 747-761.

Ventura, Jaume (1997), "Growth and Interdependence," *Quarterly Journal of Economics*, Vol. 107(2), pp. 57-84.

Vernon, Raymond (1966), "International Investment and International Trade in the Product Cycle," *Quarterly Journal of Economics*, Vol. 80(2), pp. 190-207.

Vohra, Rubina (2001), "Export and Economic Growth: Further Time Series Evidence from Less-Developed Countries," *International Advances in Economic Research*, Vol. 7, pp. 345-350.

von Hippel, Eric (1994), "Sticky Information and the Locus of Problem Solving: Implications for Innovation," *Management Science*, Vol. 40(4), pp. 429-439.

Wacziarg, Romain (2001), "Measuring the Dynamic Gains from Trade," *World Bank Economic Review*, Vol. 15(3), pp. 393-429.

Wacziarg, Romain, and Karen Horn Welch (2003), "Trade Liberalization and Growth: New Evidence," NBER Working Paper w10152, December.

Wall, Howard J. (2000), "Using the Gravity Model to Estimate the Costs of Protection," *St. Louis Federal Reserve Bank Review*, Vol. 81(1), pp. 33-40.

Weitzman, Martin L. (1996), "Hybridizing Growth Theory," *American Economic Review*, Vol. 86(2), pp. 207-212.

Weitzman, Martin L. (1998), "Recombinant Growth," *Quarterly Journal of Economics*, Vol. 113(2), pp. 331-360.

Whalley, John, and Colleen Hamilton (1996), *The Trading System After the Uruguay Round*, Washington, DC: Institute for International Economics.

World Bank (1987), *World Development Report 1987*, Washington, DC: World Bank.

World Bank (1992), *World Development Report 1992*, Washington, DC: World Bank.

World Bank (1993), *The East Asian Miracle*, New York: Oxford University Press.

World Bank (2001), *World Development Report 2000/2001*, Washington, DC: World Bank.

Xu, Bin, and Jianming Wang (1999), "Capital Goods Trade and R&D Spillovers in the OECD," *Canadian Journal of Economics*, Vol. 32(5), pp. 1258-1274.

Yaghmaian, Behzad (1994), "An Empirical Investigation of Exports, Development and Growth in Developing Countries: Challenging the Neo-Classical Theory of Export-Led Growth," *World Development*, Vol. 22(12), pp. 1977-1995.

Yaghmaian, Behzad, and Reza Ghorashi (1995), "Export Performance and Economic Development: An Empirical Analysis," *The American Economist*, Vol. 39, pp. 37-45.

Yarbrough, Beth V., and Robert M. Yarbrough (2000), *The World Economy*, 5th Ed., Fort Worth, TX: Harcourt.

Young, Alwyn (1991), "Learning-by Doing and the Dynamic Effects of International Trade," *Quarterly Journal of Economics*, Vol. 106(2), pp. 369-405.

Young, Alwyn (1992), "A Tale of Two Cities: Factor Accumulation and Technical Change in Hong Kong and Singapore," in Olivier Blanchard and Stanley Fisher, eds., *NBER Macroeconomics Annual 1992*, Cambridge, MA: MIT Press.

Young, Alwyn (1995), "The Tyranny of Numbers: Confronting the Statistical Realities of the East Asian Growth Experience," *Quarterly Journal of Economics*, Vol. 104, pp. 641-679.

Zachary, G. Pascal (1999), "An Era for Mice to Roar," *The Wall Street Journal*, Feburary 25, pp. B1, B8.

Zeile, William J. (1997), "U.S. Intrafirm Trade in Goods," *Survey of Current Business*, February.

Zhang, Shuguang, Yansheng Zhang, amnd Zhongxin Wan (1998), *Measuring the Costs of Protection in China*, Washington, DC: Institute for International Economics.

Zhu, Susan Chun (2005), "Can Product Cycles Explain Skill Upgrades?" *Journal of International Economics*, Vol. pp. 131-155.

Author Index

Subject Index

About the Authors

Joshua J. Lewer is associate professor of economics and associate director of economic graduate programs at West Texas A&M University. He received his B.A. degree from Augustana College in 1995, and his M.S. and Ph.D. from the University of Nebraska-Lincoln in 1999 and 2000. At Nebraska, Joshua's dissertation advisor was Hendrik Van den Berg. In his dissertation he examined how the composition of a country's international trade affects its growth performance. Outside of academics, he has worked as a registered representative with Prudential Investments. Today, Joshua's research interests are in the fields of international economics, international trade, and economic growth and development. He has published numerous articles in those areas. Recently, he has examined the causes and effects of immigration on economic growth and international trade flows. Since completing this book, *International Trade and Economic Growth*, Joshua has been working on a second manuscript, *Microeconomics for MBA's*, with his West Texas A&M colleague Neil Terry. He enjoys spending time with his family and is an avid, but bogey, golfer.

Hendrik Van den Berg is associate professor of economics at the University of Nebraska–Lincoln, where since 1989 he has taught economic growth and development, international economics, international finance, and international business. He received B.A. and M.A. degrees in economics from the State University of New York at Albany in 1971 and 1973, respectively, and M.S. and Ph.D. degrees in economics from the University of Wisconsin–Madison in 1987 and 1989. After graduating from SUNY at Albany, he was commercial attache at the United States Embassy in Managua, Nicaragua, and the United States Trade Center in São Paulo, Brazil. In 1979, Hendrik left the Foreign Service to take the position of planning manager at Singer do Brasil, the Brazilian subsidiary of the U.S. based Singer Company. In 1985, he decided to return to his first love, economics, and he enrolled in the PhD program at the University of Wisconsin. Hendrik has published numerous articles on exchange rates, international trade, alternative estimates of economic growth, and the empirical relationship between international trade and economic growth. He has written two textbooks, *Economic Growth and Development* (2001) and *International Economics* (2004), both published by McGraw-Hill.